Global Justice in East Asia

As a fascinating study of global justice in Asia, this book presents a series of contributions reflecting upon the conditions of a greater involvement of East Asian traditions of thought in the debate on global justice.

Including chapters on diverse issues such as global social inequalities, human rights practice, and the functioning of international institutions, this book examines the political cultures of East Asia in order to help political theorists better appraise the distinctiveness of non-Western ideas of justice. Confirming the persistence of a strong social ethos, the contributions also demonstrate the long-lasting influence of Buddhism, Taoism, and Confucianism in shaping East Asian public conceptions of justice.

Bringing much needed non-Western voices to the global justice debate, this book will appeal to students and scholars of politics, law, and philosophy, as well as activists involved in the global justice movement.

Hugo El Kholi is a Research Fellow in the Department of Philosophy (Zhuhai) at Sun Yat-sen University, China. His current research interests are global justice, Enlightenment philosophy, and contemporary Chinese political thought.

Jun-Hyeok Kwak is Professor of the Department of Philosophy (Zhuhai) at Sun Yat-sen University, China. His main research interests lie at the crossroads of political philosophy from Socrates to Machiavelli, contemporary political theory, and comparative political philosophy.

Political Theories in East Asian Context

Series Editor: Jun-Hyeok Kwak

Political Theories in East Asian Context aims to shed light on the essential theoretical issues spanning East Asia by situating them within cross-cultural frameworks that attend both to the particularity of East Asia as well as the potentially universal patterns arising from East Asia's current issues that can be studied for global prosperity. It reconsiders issues like historical reconciliation, nationalism, multicultural coexistence, political leadership, republicanism, and regional integration, with a view to opening the discourse of particular issues to a wider theoretical horizon. Including intellectuals in the fields of political science, history, ethnic studies, sociology, and regional studies, this interdisciplinary endeavor is a deliberative forum in which we can reflect on ethical problems facing East Asia in the global era.

1 **Inherited Responsibility and Historical Reconciliation in East Asia**
Edited by Jun-Hyeok Kwak and Melissa Nobles

2 **Patriotism in East Asia**
Edited by Jun-Hyeok Kwak and Koichiro Matsuda

3 **Worlding Multiculturalisms**
The Politics of Inter-Asian Dwelling
Edited by Daniel P. S. Goh

4 **Republicanism in Northeast Asia**
Edited by Jun-Hyeok Kwak and Leigh Jenco

5 **Religion and Nationalism in Asia**
Edited by Giorgio Shani and Takashi Kibe

6 **Leo Strauss in Northeast Asia**
Edited by Jun-Hyeok Kwak and Sungwoo Park

7 **Global Justice in East Asia**
Edited by Hugo El Kholi and Jun-Hyeok Kwak

For more information about this series, please visit: https://www.routledge.com

Global Justice in East Asia

Edited by
Hugo El Kholi and Jun-Hyeok Kwak

Routledge
Taylor & Francis Group
LONDON AND NEW YORK

First published 2020
by Routledge
2 Park Square, Milton Park, Abingdon, Oxon OX14 4RN

and by Routledge
52 Vanderbilt Avenue, New York, NY 10017

Routledge is an imprint of the Taylor & Francis Group, an informa business

British Library Cataloguing-in-Publication Data
A catalogue record for this book is available from the British Library

Library of Congress Cataloging-in-Publication Data
A catalog record has been requested for this book

ISBN: 978-0-367-28098-7 (hbk)
ISBN: 978-0-429-31704-0 (ebk)

Typeset in Times New Roman
by codeMantra

Contents

Contributors

Julian CULP is an Assistant Professor of Philosophy at the American University of Paris, France. He works in political philosophy and philosophy of education, with a focus on problems of democracy and justice in a globalized world. He received his Habilitation and PhD in Philosophy from the Goethe-Universität in Frankfurt am Main, Germany. His publications include *Global Justice and Development* (2014) and *Democratic Education in a Globalized World* (Routledge, 2019).

Hugo EL KHOLI is a Research Fellow at Sun Yat-sen University (Zhuhai Campus, China). He holds a doctorate in Political Science from the Paris Institute of Political Studies. Before joining the Department of Philosophy (Zhuhai), he received doctoral research fellowships from the universities of Oxford and Princeton as well as a post-doctoral fellowship from Sciences Po's Center for International Studies and Research (CERI). He has taught Philosophy, Politics, International Relations, and History at several higher education institutions in France, including Sciences Po and the French Naval Academy. His current research focus is on theories of global justice, Kantian practical philosophy, and contemporary Chinese political thought.

Jun-Hyeok KWAK is 100 Talented Professor of Philosophy at Sun Yat-sen University (Zhuhai Campus, China). He received his PhD from the University of Chicago in 2002. Before joining Sun Yat-sen University in 2016, he taught at various universities including Korea University, Kyungpook National University, University of Bologna, and the University of Chicago. His research interests lie at the crossroads of political philosophy from Socrates to Machiavelli and contemporary sociopolitical theories. He has published numerous articles on Machiavelli, republicanism, patriotism, comparative philosophy, and global justice in various languages, including "Republican Patriotism and Machiavelli's Patriotism" (*Australian Journal of Political Science*, 2017). He is currently serving as the General Editor of the Routledge Series "Political Theories in East Asian Context."

LI Shaomeng is an Associate Professor in the School of Philosophy, Beijing Normal University. His research centers on Western political philosophy and

Chinese political thought. His recent publication is *John Rawls's Theory of Institutionalism: The Historical Movement toward Liberal Democracy* (2009).

TAN Ankui is Professor and Dean of the School of Government at Sun Yat-sen University (Guangzhou Campus). He received his PhD in Philosophy from Peking University and was a visiting scholar at the University of Chicago from 2009 to 2010 and Harvard-Yenching from 2014 to 2015. His research focuses on several topics in political philosophy, including political neutrality, public reason, deliberative democracy, and human rights.

Kok-Chor TAN is a Professor of Philosophy at the University of Pennsylvania. He works mainly in political and moral philosophy. Recent works include *Justice, Institutions and Luck* (2012) and *What Is This Thing Called Global Justice?* (Routledge, 2017). Current projects include papers on personal responsibility in context of institutional injustice and global justice under non-ideal conditions. He holds a PhD in Philosophy from the University of Toronto.

George TSAI is an Associate Professor of Philosophy at the University of Hawaii. He received his BA (Economics and Moral & Political Thought, double major) from Amherst College and his PhD in Philosophy from the University of California, Berkeley. His research interests are in moral and political philosophy, broadly understood to encompass contemporary and comparative perspectives on these subjects, as well as such related areas as moral psychology and philosophy of law. He has published many articles in leading journals including *Philosophy & Public Affairs* and *Journal of Political Philosophy*.

UMEMORI Naoyuki is Professor of Political Science at Waseda University (Tokyo, Japan). He received his PhD from the University of Chicago and specializes in the History of Modern Japanese Political Thought. His research interests include nationalism, colonialism, Asianism, socialism, and anarchism. In addition to numerous articles for Japanese journals, he has contributed chapters to several academic volumes published by Taylor & Francis.

WANG Binfan is a PhD student in the Department of Political Science, University of Toronto. His research centers on the comparison between ancient Chinese thought and contemporary Western political theory, especially on global justice, meritocracy, and nationalism. His recent publication includes "Meritocracy as a political system: a commentary on Bell's The China Model" in *Philosophy East and West*.

YU Yih-Soong is a Research Associate in Philosophy at Sun Yat-sen University (Zhuhai Campus, China). He holds a PhD in Chinese Philosophy from Sun Yat-sen University (Guangzhou Campus, China). His current research interest lies in Confucianism and Chinese political thought. His publications include "Wang Fuzhi's thought of virtue cultivation" (*Journal of Sun-Yat-Sen University*, 2019) and "The analysis of Mencius' heart of shame and disdain" (*Confucius Studies*, 2019).

Introduction

Hugo El Kholi and Jun-Hyeok Kwak

During the last thirty years, the academic debate on global justice, which initially focused on the question of material inequalities, has progressively broadened its scope to encompass other issues just as relevant to the reality of global injustice. Discussions about the theory and practice of human rights, the functioning of international institutions, and the moral significance of global climate change have thus become an integral part of the debate (for an overview, see Tan 2017 or Brock 2017). This change in focus has strongly modified the sociology of the field. Critical theorists, republican scholars, and postcolonial thinkers have joined an original nucleus of liberal thinkers chiefly interested in the distributive aspects of justice. Their respective inputs, sometimes expressed in the form of radical critiques, have greatly contributed to improving our understanding of the complex reality falling under the concept of global justice.

The latest and maybe most striking of these critiques came from postcolonial thinkers, who blame the global justice literature for remaining essentially Western-centric and for ignoring non-Western philosophical traditions. In its most radical formulation, this critique goes as far as assimilating the global justice literature to a neocolonial enterprise aiming to impose Western moral and epistemic values on non-Western populations. Without necessarily accepting the full force of this critique, Western political theorists responded positively to its underlying concern by adopting a more critical attitude toward their own normative practices. Not all of them, of course, are willing to trade their deep-rooted belief in the existence of a universal ideal of justice for the postcolonial belief in the incommensurable diversity of moral standpoints. But virtually all of them are now disposed to establish a dialogue with non-Western philosophical traditions.

This change in attitude has fostered refreshing contributions from regions of the world that had so far remained silent, such as Africa (Masolo 2014; Metz 2014; Chimakonam 2017; Okeja 2017) or the Indian subcontinent (Rathore 2012; Kukathas 2013; Sen 2017). These contributions have helped political theorists to better appraise the distinctiveness of non-Western conceptions of justice as well as the necessity to think more deeply about the conditions of their accommodation by existing theories of global justice.

Unfortunately, not all regions of the world have so far responded to the call. Voices from East Asia, in particular, have been conspicuous by their absence. This is all the more surprising given that the region is called to play a greater part on the world stage as its relative weight in the global economy continues to grow and as the United States progressively relinquishes its global leadership role (Cha 2016; Clark and Ricketts 2017; Edwards 2018). East Asia, with China as its main driving force, is expected to assume increased responsibilities within international institutions and thereby also to more strongly influence global norm-making in the future (Kavalski 2013; Kristensen and Morgan 2018). This perspective can only incite global justice scholars to learn more about the political culture of the region and more specifically about the rich philosophical traditions and the distinctive social ethos that shape East Asian conceptions of justice.

This book takes a first step in that direction by presenting a series of contributions reflecting upon the conditions of a greater involvement of East Asian traditions of thought in the debate on global justice. It contains three chapters by Western political theorists who, confronted with growing accusations of parochialism and Western-centrism, engage in a critical reflection on their own normative practices and the conditions of an opening to non-Western traditions. The book also comprises several chapters written by East Asian scholars relying on their traditional conceptual resources to engage with Western theories of global justice. Their contributions confirm that the persistence of a strong social ethos and the long-lasting influence of the Three Teachings (Buddhism, Taoism, and Confucianism) have shaped in East Asia public conceptions of justice that are clearly distinct from their Western counterparts. It is time that these conceptions be not only represented, but actively reinvested in the global justice debate.

Critical reflections on Western parochialism

The accusations of "parochialism" and "Western-centrism" that have recently surfaced in the global justice literature attest to a widespread feeling of uneasiness with what is perceived as a form of academic domination exercised by Western scholars working in the liberal tradition (e.g., Maffettone and Rathore 2012; Flikschuh 2014, 2017; Metz 2014; Graness 2015; Williams and Death 2016; Chimakonam 2017; Masaka 2017; Shapcott 2017). These accusations are often more polemical than conceptually sophisticated, but two distinct lines of criticism can nevertheless be distinguished for the sake of analytical clarity.

The first is that Western scholars tend to base their theories of global justice exclusively on concepts integral to their own culture, with the assumption that their meaning is both immediately accessible to everyone around the world and relatively uncontroversial (Graness 2015, 127; Chimakonam 2017). This tendency constitutes a form of *value parochialism* because most of these concepts, such as the concepts of the citizen, the state, and political legitimacy, are "value-laden": they cannot be defined without resorting to values specific to Western political morality (Carter 2015).

The reliance of Western scholars on such concepts negatively affects the legitimacy of their normative claims. Their critics may argue that the conceptions of global justice they advocate are nothing but sophisticated elaborations of the culturally situated concepts on which they rely, so that their conceptions of global justice just are, *in fine*, globalized versions of Western liberalism. Hence the widespread conviction, which has come to be shared even by scholars firmly rooted in the liberal tradition, that "the global justice debate has in many ways often simply elevated a particular local philosophical perspective – broadly, the Rawlsian liberal egalitarian perspective, to the status of global if not universal validity" (Flikschuh 2017, 56–57).

Those who issue such accusations consider that the tendency of Western political theorists to rely on culturally situated concepts reflects both a lack of critical distance from their own moral beliefs and a lack of interest in what does not belong to (or at least is not congenial with) Western political morality – an attitude at odds with the sort of intellectual curiosity generally expected from philosophers. Based on this diagnosis, they conceive of their task as being to find a "corrective to our current state of ignorance regarding the thoughts or views of distant others in the context of global normative theorizing" (Flikschuh 2014, 1). This corrective consists, firstly, in encouraging "the incorporation of comparative political theory [...] into thinking about global justice" (Shapcott 2017, 1) and, secondly, in inciting Western political theorists to be both more critical of their own "prejudicial modes of thinking" and better disposed toward the views of their non-Western colleagues (Flikschuh 2014, 3; 2017, 5).

The second line of criticism emerging in the global justice literature is the charge of *epistemic parochialism*. This criticism aims at the pretension of Western global justice theorists to formulate universally valid prescriptions by relying on what they consider to be objective norms of practical reasoning. In contrast to value parochialism, epistemic parochialism targets not the specific concepts as being culturally or morally biased but the aspiration of contemporary normative philosophy to formulate universally valid principles by relying on its own epistemic norms of practical reasoning. For its detractors, this sort of parochialism reflects "a form of philosophical arrogance" inherited from the Enlightenment (Caney 2000, 60). They consider that, confident in the capacity of reason to be normative in and of itself, Western philosophers in general, and global justice theorists in particular, have developed a tendency to "mistak[e] unavoidable perspectivalism for an assuredly universal viewpoint" (Flikschuh 2017, 48).

In most cases, accusations of epistemic parochialism proceed from a post-modern feeling of disenchantment with the modern discourse of rational emancipation from local traditions, cultures, and religions. Those who harbor this feeling understand Western theories of global justice as proceeding from the same meta-narrative of rational emancipation, according to which "a statement with truth-value is deemed acceptable if it is cast in terms of a possible unanimity between rational minds" (Lyotard 1984, xxiii–xxiv). They criticize the resulting attitude of global justice theorists who, imbued with a feeling of self-aggrandizement, conceive of themselves as working for the good of everyone around the globe when in fact they practice a form of "epistemic imperialism" consisting in imposing their subjective norms of practical reasoning on others. In reaction to this form of "epistemic injustice," critics strive to show that it is through a series of contingent historical events rather than a sustained philosophical effort that the Western standard of practical reasoning, "which was not always self-evident to everyone, has been made to look obvious far beyond the ground where it originated" (Chakrabarty 2000, 43).

These accusations of parochialism, either in their axiological or their epistemic versions, pose a significant challenge to Western political theorists by forcing them to reconsider some of their deep-seated epistemological beliefs and methodological practices. The three contributions comprising the first part of this volume participate in this reflexive effort, each in its own way. In his chapter (Chapter 1), Kok-Chor Tan starts by addressing the concern, repeatedly voiced in the literature, that liberal internationalism is inherently interventionist. Liberal internationalism is the most commonly accepted standard of international legitimacy, which holds that all states have the responsibility to protect the basic human rights and fundamental freedoms of their citizens and that failure to do so makes them prone to military intervention by the international community (UN 1945: art. 1). This standard is used to identify the states that must be regarded as actors in good standing of the international community, but these are also the states that are potentially concerned with the normatively more demanding project of working toward a fairer world. If this standard itself is biased against non-liberal states, then the whole philosophical enterprise promoting global justice starts off on the wrong foot.

Tan denies, however, that liberal internationalism is particularly inclined to military intervention against non-liberal states simply in virtue of its commitment to basic human rights and freedoms. Those who make that claim fail to distinguish between the normative demands of liberal justice, as expressed by the liberal standard of international legitimacy, and the practical modalities of their enforcement by the international community. Yet this distinction is reflected in the UN procedure for military intervention, which counts two distinct stages: the *justification* of intervention and the *authorization* of the use of force. Thus, a case must first be made establishing that the situation under consideration truly violates the fundamentals of liberal justice. Only once this case is made – that is, once intervention has been justified – can the authorization to intervene militarily be granted through well-codified procedures, which include a vote of the UN Security Council. This authorization depends not on the moral considerations used to justify intervention but on a careful practical assessment of the situation. Typically, the authorization to use force is only granted as a last resort, when non-military alternatives have all been exhausted and military action remains the only conceivable way to stop ongoing violations. Another limiting condition is that the force employed must be strictly proportional to the resistance met. These two fundamental requirements – last resort and proportionality – are "normatively prior" to and therefore independent from the demands of liberal justice. In Tan's view, this shows that liberal internationalism is not especially interventionist. In fact, failing to meet the liberal standard of international legitimacy does not automatically make a state a target for military intervention.

Having allayed concerns about interventionism, Tan turns his attention to another set of accusations raised against his preferred conception of global justice, liberal cosmopolitanism. Because liberal cosmopolitanism extends the normative demands of liberal justice to non-Western states, it is sometimes viewed as a form of moral imperialism. Tan replies that, if we understand by moral imperialism the unjustified imposition of certain moral views on others, those who are prepared to engage in genuine moral deliberation instead of simply foisting their views on others cannot be blamed for it. Genuine deliberation not only involves a commitment to support one's views with reasons one genuinely thinks others can accept, but also the willingness to respond to rational challenges raised against those views and the willingness of potentially revising those views if it appears, in the course of the deliberation, that they are rationally flawed.

Tan concedes, however, that there is a thin line between dogmatism and the staunch advocacy of one's views, so that a willingness to engage in genuine deliberation with others may not be enough to guard against accusations of imperialism. Cosmopolitan liberals should therefore also adopt a "fallibilistic posture" going beyond the epistemic requirements of rational justification and deliberation. Such a posture implies in addition acknowledging that "one may have got the facts wrong and that getting another perspective on what the case is and being ready to adjust one's understanding of events is essential for genuine inter-moral deliberation" (Kok-Chor Tan in Chapter 1). Tan considers that taking a posture of moral fallibilism would contribute to bringing to the global justice debate the degree of openness to non-Western moral traditions that it currently lacks.

In an effort to exemplify this posture, Tan suggests in the last part of his chapter that liberal internationalists can learn from the *Zhuangzi*, one of the foundational texts of Daoism traditionally attributed to the Chinese Master Zhuang Zhou (c. 369 BC–286 BC). Drawing on a careful selection of passages, he interprets Master Zhuang as claiming that our moral views depend on our subjective experience and that we may simply be unable to comprehend the moral truth in its entirety from any particular viewpoint. This aspect of the Dao can be seen as an invitation to epistemic modesty in line with the fallibilist approach he advocates. Just like Master Zhuang, the liberal cosmopolitans adopting this approach must be fully committed to their moral views while remaining accessible to the thought that certain aspects of liberal political morality may be mistaken and may have to be revised.

In his chapter (Chapter 2), Julian Culp complements Tan's critical efforts by questioning his own democratic approach to global justice. This approach, inspired by the works of Iris Marion Young and Rainer Forst, shifts attention from the principles regulating the distribution of social goods to the decision-making procedures conditioning their adoption. The key idea behind this shift is that the purely distributive aspects on which liberal political theorists almost exclusively focus do not exhaust the normative content of the idea of justice. Justice also and more fundamentally demands equality of respect between persons. Before asking "who should receive what?", political theorists should therefore wonder "in what conditions" and "according to what procedures" we can decide "who receives what" if we are to respect this moral demand of equality of respect. Culp's answer to this subsidiary question is distinctively liberal and democratic. In his view, equality of respect can only be achieved through democratic political arrangements, insofar as those arrangements allow individuals to adjudicate their conflicting claims in a way acceptable to each and every person involved.

In the domestic context, this requirement is best fulfilled within Western liberal democracies, whose institutions and public political culture support the right type of decision-making practices. But if we want to respect the moral demand of equality at the global level as well, we must create a new institutional framework enabling people all over the world to engage at the transnational level in the same type of decision-making practices. Now these transnational practices, just as their domestic counterparts, carry with them distributive obligations insofar as certain basic socioeconomic conditions must be fulfilled for people to be able to fully participate in them. It is this distinctively democratic conception of global justice, which starts from a consideration of our fundamental commitment to equality of respect, that Culp intends to defend here against the accusations of parochialism and Western-centrism.

These accusations claim that the liberal-democratic standard of political justification on which the democratic conception of global justice relies is specifically Western, so that its application to non-Western contexts constitutes a form of postcolonialism. Culp replies that it is abusive to characterize liberal-democratic ideals as a specifically Western normative standard. Other standards exist in the West, and the democratic standard is also present in most non-Western political cultures, even if, for contingent historical reasons, it might not be as dominant today in those cultures as it is in the West. Relying on the writings of contemporary Confucian scholars, Culp thus argues that the Confucian tradition also incorporates a basic moral demand for equality of respect between persons, which makes it compatible with the democratic approach to justice.

Moving from the democratic to the political approach, Hugo El Kholi addresses in his chapter (Chapter 3) the claim that political conceptions of global justice, which are in principle devoid of any commitment to specific moral, religious, and metaphysical beliefs, are immune to accusations of parochialism and Western-centrism. To that end, he starts by assessing the most common interpretation of the political approach to justice, which takes the Rawlsian notion of "reasonableness" to be a freestanding epistemic standard allowing to reach a political consensus in the absence of deeper moral, religious, or metaphysical agreement. Reasonableness, in this interpretation, is a neutral notion transcending cultural specificities and thereby enabling the creation of an autonomous political sphere regulated by principles whose normative force does not depend on their being grounded in substantive moral values. Unfortunately, El Kholi argues that the normative potential of reasonableness depends, at a deeper level, on a commitment to a distinctively Kantian conception of autonomy making the acknowledgment of the normative nature of rationality the very criterion of morality. Despite their claim to cultural neutrality, political conceptions of global justice therefore remain ultimately dependent on Western meta-ethical beliefs. As such, they are just as exposed to the charge of epistemic parochialism as comprehensive conceptions.

El Kholi's argument may be better appreciated when considered within a historical framework. The Western political theorists working in the field of global justice practice a distinctive form of practical reasoning they call "normative theorizing." Normative theorizing is an activity based on a set of epistemic norms reflecting the belief that practical reason is capable of self-legislation (Sangiovanni 2008). This conviction, which has a long pedigree, can be traced back to the Enlightenment. According to the most commonly accepted narrative, one of the main features of the Enlightenment has been to call into question the epistemic framework which had guided philosophical inquiry throughout the middle Ages.[1] Whereas the scholastic tradition had relegated philosophy to an ancillary function by forcing it to conform to the epistemic standards of theology (Maritain 1955: 15), the Enlightenment allowed for its emancipation by restoring its status as an independent discipline operating on its own epistemic terms.

Central to this epistemic empowerment was the conviction that our norms of conduct must reflect the requirements of reason, not conventions inherited from the past or imposed by religious or political authorities. It is the redefinition of philosophical activity on this basis that made practical philosophy an essentially normative discipline. Instead of seeking to conform to a providential order displayed by nature or revealed by religion, the task of moral and political philosophers became to derive authoritative practical norms from the consideration of human rational nature. In an effort to characterize this major turning point in the history of Western philosophy, Alasdair MacIntyre, for example, explains that Enlightenment thinkers "share in the project of constructing [...] sound arguments [...] which [...] move from premises concerning human nature as they understand it to be to conclusions about the authority of moral rules and precepts" (MacIntyre 1981: 50).

It is generally considered that this project reached its full development with Kant, who made reason itself the foundation of practical knowledge through the "invention of autonomy" (Lindley 1986; Schneewind 1988). It is therefore not surprising that the political approach to justice, which is based on Rawls's interpretation of Kant's method in ethics, remains ultimately dependent on this fundamental meta-ethical belief in the normative dimension of reason.

Contextual appraisals

This volume also comprises contributions that reflect upon the conditions of a meaningful involvement of East Asian scholars in the global justice debate. George Tsai in his chapter (Chapter 4) strives to show that, contrary to what is commonly assumed, the philosophical roots of contemporary discussions on global justice extend far beyond the confines of the Western tradition. The question of the extent of our moral responsibilities to others, which underlies a large part of these discussions (e.g., Singer 1972; Miller 1988; Arneson 2003; Waldron 2003; Chatterjee 2004), was also central to the classical philosophical debate which opposed, at the dawn of the Warring states period (475 BC–221 BC), the disciples of Confucius (571 BC–479 BC) and the followers of Mozi (c. 470 BC–c. 371 BC). Whereas Confucians relied on the concept of "graded love" (*ai you chadeng* 愛有差等) to argue that our moral responsibilities to others depend on our relationships with them, Mohists maintained that human beings have a "natural disposition" (*xing* 性) for "impartial love" (*jian'ai* 兼愛) inclining them to care for everyone equally, irrespective of special relationships. Anyone familiar with the global justice debate can only be tempted to draw an analogy between the opposition of these two views and the opposition of "ethical universalism" and "ethical particularism," which played a structuring role in the early discussions on global justice (see Miller 2002). Tsai thus emphasizes the structural similarities between the Mohist doctrine and the consequentialist form of cosmopolitanism advocated most prominently by Peter Singer (1972).

But beyond these structural similarities, what Tsai wants to highlight is the proximity of basic moral intuitions between the participants in these two debates. This proximity appears clearly when considering the intuitions on which Rawls relies in his seminal work on distributive justice, which provided the background against which the global justice debate initially developed. First is Rawls's claim that the "basic structure" of society is the "primary subject of justice" (Rawls 1971, 7). Tsai suggests that this claim reflects the same basic moral intuition as the choice of the Confucians to make the family the primary subject of ethical life. Both Rawls and the Confucians consider that ethical thinking should start with a consideration of those central social structures that shape people's lives, namely those structures that have a deep and pervasive impact on their life prospects. Second is Rawls's claim that certain facts about the world, such as people's natural abilities or the social milieu in which they are born, are morally arbitrary and should therefore be neutralized when thinking about justice. Tsai argues that this idea, shared by the Mohists, is crucial to the development of global egalitarianism insofar as it allows realizing that certain global facts, such as one's nationality at birth, are just as morally arbitrary and consequential for one's life as domestic factors. Hence the need to extend the scope of egalitarianism to the world at large.

The sharing of these basic moral intuitions, which form the core of our moral sensibility, is arguably more significant than structural affinities between full-blown theories. It constitutes a deeper form of commonality and reveals that East Asian culture carries with it the type of moral sensibility necessary to identify the problem of global justice as morally significant. This realization contributes to playing down the accusations of parochialism by showing that, even if in its current form the global justice debate may be Western-centric, it is based on philosophical concerns that are shared by both traditions. This relieves Western scholars from the pressure of having to revise their views to make sure that they sufficiently accommodate non-Western traditions. And it also relieves non-Western scholars from having to ask for accommodation, thereby placing themselves in the subordinate position of a petitioner. Instead, Chinese scholars are encouraged to exercise their intellectual autonomy and to develop their own, self-standing views rooted in Chinese culture. Tsai's contribution is thus an effort to show Chinese scholars that they can appropriate the global justice debate for themselves, without having to situate themselves within the conceptual framework developed by Western academics over the last fifty years. Not only do they possess within their own philosophical tradition the conceptual resources necessary to address the problem of global justice, but the problem itself makes perfect sense within their own cultural context.

The contribution of Umemori Naoyuki (Chapter 10) attests to a similar effort of intellectual re-appropriation. Instead of discussing some aspect of the contemporary Western literature, Umemori strives to show that Japanese intellectual history has its own tradition of thought about global justice, which predates Western interest in the question by half a century. The leading figure of this tradition was Kōtoku Shūsui (1871–1911), a political activist and radical intellectual known in the West primarily for having introduced Anarcho-communism to Japan in the 1890s. Umemori points out that the introduction of those ideas stimulated reflections of Japanese scholars not only on domestic forms of injustice, such as social inequalities and political corruption, but also on the global forms of injustice falling under the label of "imperialism."

Although imperialism at the time was not yet conceptualized as the highest stage of capitalism (Lenin 2010 [1916]), it had already been clearly identified as an ideological product of capitalist society. Kōtoku, as for him, conceived of it as the aspiration of a country to build for itself a political and economic empire by conquering foreign territories and subduing their native populations. He understood this aspiration as developing at the juncture of patriotism, nationalism, and capitalism and was convinced that it could only lead to grave acts of injustice against foreign populations. In response to that threat, he called for a worldwide revolution aiming to free all the nations of the world from the domination of the army, the abuses of aristocratic rule, and the monopoly of the capitalist class on the means of production. He thought of this revolution as a worldwide movement reaching "beyond differences of race or nation" to form "a grand confederation under the banner of socialism" (Kōtoku quoted by Umemori, in Chapter 10). In this respect, Kōtoku's views are perfectly in line with the Marxist orthodoxy of the time, as advocated by the Second International. Where Kōtoku diverges from this orthodoxy is in the rationale leading him to reject imperialism and promote instead a form of political cosmopolitanism.

It was an integral part of the doctrine of the Second International that imperialism, because of its militarist dimension, could only increase domestic social injustices by imposing on the working class the additional burden of a war effort that did not correspond to its class interest (e.g., Luxemburg 1951 [1913]). In this view, imperialism had to be resisted out of concern for domestic justice and more broadly for the fate of the working class. But Kōtoku's rejection of imperialism and the philosophical roots of his cosmopolitanism are not to be found in this Marxist rationale. Umemori argues that they reside instead in his Confucian belief in the fundamental goodness of human beings. Kōtoku believed that human beings are naturally moved by selfless love, empathy, and charity, namely virtues which do not predispose them to discriminate between family members, political associates, and distant others when it comes to helping people in need.[2] In his view, any political ideology that goes against this fundamental ethical "predisposition" (*xing*), in the manner of patriotism or imperialism, is both misleading and dangerous.

In this interpretation, Kōtoku's views are therefore better described as an original form of syncretism between Confucian ethics and Marxism, an originality which attests to the relevance of East Asian traditions of thought to the problem of global justice. By shedding light on this singularity in Kōtoku's views, Umemori wants to encourage contemporary East Asian scholars to break free of the epistemic framework imposed by the Western literature and rely instead on their own philosophical traditions when approaching the global justice problem.

The following two chapters (Chapters 5 and 6) adopt a different approach. Instead of reflecting upon the conditions of a re-appropriation of the global justice debate by East Asian scholars, they use the sources and methods of Western political philosophy to try to express a viewpoint that remains distinctively East Asian. In his chapter (Chapter 5), Li Shaomeng thus adopts the comparative approach to evaluate the prospects for an intensification of the cooperation between China and the West on global governance and more specifically on global justice. In his view, the main determining factor of global politics is neither the distribution of power among states nor the normative framework formed by international institutions but the influence of domestic political cultures on state preferences and ultimately state behavior.

Equipped with this distinctively liberal assumption,[3] Li starts by analyzing Chinese political culture, which he characterizes as being essentially "authoritarian." He points out that, very early in the history of China, the authoritarian nature of political power facilitated the emergence of a strong state, with a centralized bureaucracy and the capacity to project its power efficiently over a large territory. The rise of such a state had a determining influence on the conceptualization of political legitimacy, which was made dependent upon the state's capacity to provide the population with the public goods necessary for the proper development of social, economic, and cultural life. This particular historical construction of the concept of political legitimacy differs significantly from what happened in the West, where different historical circumstances gave rise to a conception that rather makes political legitimacy dependent upon the state's capacity to justify the exercise of coercive power to each and every person subjected to it.

This difference explains why there is no equivalent, in the history of Chinese political thought, to the Western liberal developments emphasizing individual rights and liberties. Chinese political culture simply does not contain any theoretical elaboration of the necessity to protect those rights and liberties against the authoritarian tendency of political power. In the West, the Roman and early modern republican traditions contributed to inscribe in the public political culture the idea that, given the corrupting nature of power and the moral imperfection of human beings, the exercise of political authority must be framed both by institutional checks and balances and by the constant attention paid by citizens to the respect of their individual rights. In China, the dominant Confucian culture, with its core values of loyalty and respect for established hierarchies, rather encouraged an attitude of subjection to the sovereign and incited citizens to place their trust in the moral rectitude and benevolence (*ren* 仁) of power-holders. Li describes this attitude as an attitude of "passive obedience" inevitably leading to a form of "fatalist apathy" and to the resigned acceptance of worldly injustices.

Those differences in domestic political cultures run deep, but Li does not regard them as an insuperable obstacle to international cooperation. He shares with numerous other East Asian scholars the conviction that the economic and cultural exchanges taking place between China and the West in the age of globalization will push Chinese political culture to evolve toward less authoritarianism and more liberalism (for similar claims, see Moody 1984 or He 2006). Borrowing those concepts from Rawls, he argues, more specifically, that this evolution will eventually make the Chinese state "reasonable" or "decent," that is to say, accessible to the standard of political reasoning underpinning political liberalism. Such an evolution would enable cooperation between China and the West without requiring a perfect convergence of their respective political cultures. Li is thus confident that the global process of liberalization "will [eventually] lead to a certain overlapping consensus over a certain conception of global order and global justice".

This confidence is not shared by Tan Ankui, who relies in his chapter (Chapter 6) on a comparative analysis of the different forms of coercion to argue against global egalitarianism. In his view, the specificity of state coercion lies in the citizens' absence of concrete alternative to their condition as subjects. For if citizens can, in principle, renounce their citizenship and migrate to another state, it is only to be faced with the obligation to subject to the coercive power of this other state. It is the absence of alternative to this condition of subjection which grounds, according to Tan, our duties of justice. The situation is different for states, however, since they can choose to withdraw from the international community and live in a state of autarky. This shows that they are not subjected to the same kind of coercive power from international institutions as citizens from states, which explains the difficulties faced by Western scholars when trying to justify an extension of the concept of justice beyond national borders. In Tan's view, such an extension simply cannot be properly conceptualized within a Westphalian system reserving to nation-states the authority of coercing fully and unescapably.

Based on these observations, Tan critically assesses the works of Chinese philosopher Zhao Tingyang, who has been praised by many for introducing the traditional concept of "All-under-Heaven" (*tianxia* 天下) into the global justice debate (Zhao 2019 [2011]). The main interest of this concept, according to its promoters, is precisely that it contains the normative resources necessary to go beyond the Westphalian vision of a world fragmented into nation-states and think instead of the problem of global justice with "the oneness of the world" as starting point (Tan Ankui in Chapter 6). This conception, however, implies reforming the current system of international politics and transferring political sovereignty from nation-states to the world itself, conceived as "a political agent" in its own right (Tan Ankui in Chapter 6).

The problem, according to Tan, is that the notion of *tianxia* lacks the normative thickness necessary to serve as a basis of a fully fledged system. As of today, Zhao's theory, which remains admittedly a work in progress, is far from being sufficiently precise when it comes to describe the concrete institutional arrangements that could instantiate the *tianxia* ideal. This weakness has already been highlighted elsewhere (e.g., Callahan 2008; Chang 2011), but Tan Ankui goes one step further by suggesting that "the lack of explicit institutional construction is probably rooted in the nature of the '*tianxia* system' itself" (Tan Ankui in Chapter 6). In the same vein, he also points out that, despite Zhao's criticism of Rawls for his refusal to expand his theory of justice as fairness to the world at large, his own theory is devoid of any principled justification of global egalitarianism. In fact, as Tan recalls, the *tianxia* system developed historically as a very distinctive form of cosmopolitanism positing China at the center of the world. In this respect, the *tianxia* system may be seen as incorporating a covert form of Chinese nationalism (a point also made by Chang 2011 and Callahan 2007). With this specificity in mind, Tan concludes that, at this stage of their economic and political development, China and the other East Asian countries should not concern themselves with the problem of global justice. Instead, they should follow the order of priority integral to the *tianxia* ideal and focus on strengthening their domestic standards of political legitimacy and social justice.

East Asian insights into global justice

Republican theorists have recently suggested that states rather than individuals should be placed at the center of creating and reforming global justice.[4] This drift to a "state-based" rationale for global justice is not surprising in the sense that concerns over social justice within bounded societies or geopolitical territories lie at the center of republican thinking about civic responsibility and democratic rights. On the one hand, for "civic" republicans who overtly or emphatically reject cosmopolitan attempts to identify social justice with global justice, a set of transcendental principles across sociopolitical contexts cannot be applied in order to extend civic commonality toward compatriots to a moral commitment to humanity as a whole (Taylor 1996, 119–121; Sandel 1998, 338–349). On the other hand, for "democratic" republicans who put forward political participation as an imperative civic virtue, the cosmopolitan identification of universal rights as preconditions for republican citizenship cannot be employed as an appropriate strategy for enhancing the capacity of citizens for democratic deliberation (Honohan 2001; White 2003, 201–222; Schuppert 2014, 117–176).[5]

There is, however, a further concern in the recent shift to a state-based rationale for global justice in republicanism. That is the question of domination across borders. In particular, neo-Roman republicans, whose theoretical backdrop is consistently one of the Roman republican traditions, offer an incipient groundwork for a paradigm shift in the scholarly debate over global justice. Two theoretical contributions made by neo-Roman republicans are worthy of our attention with respect to domination across borders.[6] First, neo-Roman republicans provide better terms with the state as an appropriate actor for actualizing global justice in the international realm. Neo-Roman republicanism puts forward the role of the state in fostering non-domination against domination across borders (Pettit 1997, 31 & 129–170, 2010). At the same time, it maintains that individuals across borders can secure their non-dominated sociopolitical conditions when their states are effective against domination domestically and internationally (Laborde and Ronzoni 2016, 280–281). Second, the neo-Roman republican approach switches the question of global justice from "distribution" to "power." As Pettit points out (2016, 49), what freedom as non-domination requires in the international realm is not a contingent absence of subordination but a form of power to actualize non-domination. At this juncture, the central question raised by them is not "whether a distribution is correct" but "how that distribution is made and by whom."

It is undeniable that the turn led by the neo-Roman republicans is valuable. However, neo-Roman republicans still leave the problems with reciprocal non-domination between states unresolved, particularly in regard to the problem of the "Western" parochialism of the global justice debate, and with respect to the problem of realizing non-domination in the deliberative stance between states whose voices in the current global system are asymmetrical according to their military and economic power. Certainly, differing from those liberal theorists who attempt to extend liberal domestic principles to the global realm, the neo-Roman republicans do not impose any culturally embedded standard as the supreme value. Nevertheless, if they suggest non-domination as a regulative ideal or a "gateway" good that would guide deliberation between states about what global justice requires in particular cases, they should explain more clearly a feasible "non-dominating" way by which the discursive stance between states is built into the global system and thereby actualizes reciprocal non-domination between states. Otherwise, freedom as non-domination could become another normative value into which substantially "Western" cultural components are smuggled. In other words, as Jun-Hyeok Kwak in his chapter (Chapter 9) points out, the problem of asymmetrical justificatory power between states can hardly be resolved with an appeal to the general concern of avoiding domination, in that involuntary subjection to the arbitrary will of others cannot be welcome.

Chinese-style cosmopolitanism, which is elaborated with the reinterpretation of *tianxia* in the chapters by Tan Ankui (Chapter 6), Yu Yihsoong (Chapter 7), Wang Binfan (Chapter 8), and Jun-Hyeok Kwak (Chapter 9), evolves a non-Western account of global justice which takes seriously a "non-dominating" relationship between states. At first glance, it appears to be similar to the neo-Roman republican turn to "state-based" global justice. With practical concerns, the advocates of Chinese-style cosmopolitanism take the nation-state system for granted and thereby do not aim at a transnational community. And they pursue an anti-transcendental ideal that is capable of guiding all states without imposing a set of value-laden standards that they should meet in the first place. However, they differ from the neo-Roman republican theorists in the sense that they put forward moral duty or moral value in terms of the ideal harmony between all peoples. Unlike the neo-Roman republicans who associate the ideal of non-domination with the ubiquity of the tendency of peoples toward avoiding domination in the actual world (Pettit 2017, 333–339), they dream of a family-hood between states conceptualized through Confucian relational virtues with which each state is constructed and performed as a moral subject that seeks to realize the ideals of *tianxia* (Zhao 2009, 13 & 93–94; Gan 2012, 139–145; Wu 2013, 26–38).

At this juncture, the notion of *tianxia* in Chinese-style cosmopolitanism marks the convergence between deontological duty and virtue ethics. It is deontological, since one of their core commitments is to safeguard the moral autonomy of each state. But it is virtue-ethical as well in view of the fact that the cultivation of virtue which starts with an individual person and ends up with that of the world is the pivotal driver of realizing the ideals of *tianxia*. Wang in his chapter (Chapter 8) puts an emphasis on the virtue-ethical sources of Chinese-style cosmopolitanism. In particular, he claims that the notion of "benevolence" in Mencius, which brackets an exemplary virtuous person (*junzi*) and a good governance in the principle of the "kingly way" (*wangdao* 王道), will supplement the Rawlsian view of global justice which unduly limits the probability of justice to the realization of fair distribution. In contrast, Yu in his chapter (Chapter 7) emphasizes the deontological characteristics of Confucianism. The conjunction of Kang Youwei's renderings of the Western conception of "liberty" (*ziyou* 自由) with his analysis of Chinese-style Cosmopolitanism is designed to uncover the problems of the world order hinging on the notion of *tianxia*. Concomitantly, it is aimed at shedding light on the need to readdress the question of the autonomy of each state in the current debates on Chinese-style Cosmopolitanism.

Through the lens of the periphery surrounding China, the traditional notion of *tianxia* can be rendered as the justification of a hierarchical order, in which China was placed at the center of such a hierarchical order while the neighboring countries were nothing but tributary states. In this context, even if the ideal of *tianxia* is able to evoke the voluntary obligation by neighboring states to the most civilized state, its realization cannot be just without establishing a deliberative stance in which each state has equal access to justification for global justice. Jun-Hyeok Kwak in his chapter (Chapter 9) reads the world order conceptualized with the traditional Chinese notion of *tianxia* in this way. More specifically, explicating the alternative view of *tianxia* in which any centrism that placed one's country at the center was rejected, he argues that Chinese-style cosmopolitanism lacks feasibility not because it idealizes a goal that is not attainable in the actual world but because it does not provide us with a regulative principle that secures democratic deliberation in the global realm and subsequently helps better promote a cooperative relationship between states against domination. In similar vein, Umemori Naoyuki in his chapter (Chapter 10) explores the trajectory of sociopolitical and philosophical discussions on global justice in Japan which has been shaped through the idiosyncratic positionality that has led most Japanese to identify themselves with the center as well as the periphery. The conclusion of his chapter is that this sort of ambiguous positionality is no longer unique to Japanese people but universal in contemporary global society. Taking these two chapters together, we come to see that any discussion of global justice in the Northeast Asian context needs to supply a regulative principle that can help better establish a discursive stance between states without a central hegemon.

The main purpose of this volume, however, is not to formulate such a principle, which at this stage remains elusive, but only to offer a platform for Western and East Asian scholars to initiate a dialogue on an equal footing. Our main editorial concern has been to facilitate exchanges and mutual understanding between the contributors, leaving them entirely free to formulate their views without any constraints as to the approach they wanted to adopt. This volume will have achieved its goal if it simply succeeds in raising the readers' awareness of the distinctiveness of East Asian conceptions of justice and of the importance of reinvesting them in the global justice debate.

Notes

1 Describing the European Enlightenment as a unitary philosophical project is admittedly an oversimplification. The different traditions generally brought under this label, such as the French *Lumières*, the German *Aufklärung*, and the Scottish Enlightenment, differ in significant respects (Porter 1990, 10–11; Schneewind 1988, 8). What matters here, however, is not so much the authenticity of this unitary account of the Enlightenment (in the sense of its fitness to historical reality) as the intellectual linkage that contemporary moral and political philosophers are willing to acknowledge with it through the collective representation of this project. What matters, in other words, is the normative dimension of the Enlightenment narrative for the contemporary practice of practical philosophy.

2 Note, however, that Kōtoku's interpretation of the classical concept of *ren*仁 is in fact closer to the Mohist interpretation than to the traditional Confucian interpretation. For more details on these interpretations, see Tsai in this volume.

3 Li accounts for state preferences as being determined mainly by domestic public political cultures rather than by the interests of a certain subset of domestic societies, the degree of inclusion of domestic markets into the global economy, or the different types of domestic political system. In this respect, Li is at variance with the most influential liberal theories of international relations (for a typology of these theories, see Moravcsik 2008), but his approach remains characteristically liberal insofar as he takes seriously the determining influence of domestic preferences on state behavior.

4 One exception would be James Bohman whose argument for transnational democracy far exceeds the state-based rationale for global justice. Suggesting a "democratic minimum," defined by him as "the linchpin that makes it possible for the transformation of democracy itself to be the basis for more justice" (2005, 104), he maintains that the problem of domination across borders should be solved in the same way in which the democratic minimum is met to secure the capacity of citizens to initiate deliberation in a political community. Briefly, his republican idea does not reside in the state-based rationale for global justice but in a transnational democracy of peoples across borders (2007, 28–36).

5 Except for David Miller, the republican theorists exemplified in the latter category above differentiate themselves from participatory or communitarian republicans. However, they can be categorized at least as "democratic" republicans in the sense that they put forward democratic practice as the most imperative way of raising republican civility. In a vein similar to the latter sense, some non-republican theorists also find fault with "strong" cosmopolitanism in which specific values shaped through democratic practice in a political community and specific justifications for the state's domestic coercion and international action

in the sense of democratic accountability are largely neglected (Rawls 1999; Blake 2001; Nagel 2005; Sangiovanni 2007; Ypi 2008; Stilz 2009, 57–110, 2011).

6 The most up-to-date discussions of domination across borders in neo-Roman republicanism can be found in the book (2015) edited by Barbara Buckinx, Jonathan Trejo-Mathys, and Timothy Waligore. This book contains the most significant development of current republican ideas about global justice.

References

Arneson, Richard. 2003 "Consequentialism vs. Special-Ties Partiality." *The Monist* 86(3): 382–401.

Arneson, Richard. 2009. "What Do We Owe to Distant Needy Strangers?" In *Peter Singer Under Fire*, edited by Jeffrey Schaler. Chicago, IL: Open Court, 267–293.

Blake, Michael. 2001. "Distributive Justice, State Coercion, and Autonomy." *Philosophy & Public Affair* 30(3): 257–296.

Bohman, James. 2005. "The Democratic Minimum: Is Democracy a Means to Global Justice?" *Ethics & International Affairs* 19(1): 101–116.

Bohman, James. 2007. *Democracy across Borders: From Demos to Demoi*. Cambridge, MA: MIT Press.

Brock, Gillian. 2017. "Global Justice." In *The Stanford Encyclopedia of Philosophy*, edited by Edward N. Zalta. https://plato.stanford.edu/archives/spr2017/entries/justice-global/

Buckinx, Barbara, Jonathan Trejo-Mathys and Timothy Waligore. 2015. *Domination and Global Justice: Conceptual, Historical, and Institutional Perspectives*. New York: Routledge.

Callahan, William. 2007. "*Tianxia*, Empire and the World: Soft Power and China's Foreign Policy Discourse in the 21st Century." *BICC Working Paper Series* 1(1): 1–24.

Callahan, William. 2008. "Chinese Visions of World Order: Post-Hegemonic or a New Hegemony." *International Studies Review* 10: 749–761.

Carter, Ian, 2015. "Value-freeness and Value-neutrality in the Analysis of Political Concepts." In *Oxford Studies in Political Philosophy*, Vol. 1, edited by David Sobel, 279–306. Oxford: Oxford University Press.

Cha, Taesuh. 2016. "The Return of Jacksonianism: The International Implications of the Trump Phenomenon." *The Washington Quarterly* 39(4): 83–97.

Chakrabarty, Dipesh. 2000. *Provincializing Europe: Postcolonial Thought and Historical Difference*. Princeton, NJ: Princeton University Press.

Chang, Chishen. 2011. "*Tianxia* System on a Snail's Horns." *Inter-Asia Cultural Studies* 12(1): 28–42.

Chatterjee, Deen (ed.). 2004. *The Ethics of Assistance: Morality and the Distant Needy*. Cambridge: Cambridge University Press.

Chimakonam, Jonathan. 2017. "African Philosophy and Global Epistemic Injustice." *Journal of Global Ethics* 13(2): 120–137.

Clarke, Michael and Anthony Ricketts. 2017. "Donald Trump and American Foreign Policy: The Return of the Jacksonian Tradition." *Comparative Strategy* 36(4): 366–379.

Edwards, Jason. 2018. "Make America Great Again: Donald Trump and Redefining the U.S. Role in the World." *Communication Quarterly* 66(2): 176–195.

Flikschuh, Katrin. 2014. "The Idea of Philosophical Fieldwork: Global Justice, Moral Ignorance, and Intellectual Attitudes." *The Journal of Political Philosophy* 22(1): 1–26.

Flikschuh, Katrin. 2017. "Should African Thinkers Engage in the Global Justice Debate?" *Philosophical Papers* 46(1): 33–58.

Gan, Chunsong [干春松]. 2012. 『重回王道—儒家与世界秩序』. 上海: 华东师范大学出版社.

Graness, Anke. 2015. "Is the Debate on 'Global Justice' a Global One? Some Considerations in View of Modern Philosophy in Africa." *Journal of Global Ethics* 11(1): 126–140.

He, Li. 2006. "Returned Students and Political Change in China." *Asian Perspective* 30(2): 5–29.

Honohan, Iseult. 2001. "Friends, Strangers or Countrymen? The Ties between Citizens as Colleagues." *Political Studies* 49: 51–69.

Kavalski, Emilian. 2013. "The Struggle for Recognition of Normative Powers: Normative Power Europe and Normative Power China in Context." *Cooperation and Conflict* 48(2): 247–267.

Kristensen, Peter Marcus and Pippa Morgan. 2018. "Leadership with Chinese Characteristics." *Chinese Political Science Review* 3(1): 1–9.

Kukathas, Chandan. 2013. "On Sen on Comparative Justice." *Critical Review of International Social and Political Philosophy* 16(2): 196–204.

Laborde, Cécile and Miriam Ronzoni. 2016. "What Is a Free State? Republican Internationalism and Globalisation." *Political Studies* 64(2): 292–296.

Lenin, Vladimir. 2010 [1916]. *Imperialism, the Highest Stage of Capitalism*. London: Penguin Classics.

Lindley, Richard. 1986. *Autonomy*. Atlantic Highlands, NJ: Humanities Press International.

Luxemburg, Rosa. 1951 [1913]. *Accumulation of Capital*. London: Routledge.

Lyotard, Jean-Francois. 1984 [1979]. *The Postmodern Condition: A Report on Knowledge*. Minneapolis: University of Minnesota Press.

MacIntyre, Alasdair. 1981. *After Virtue: A Study in Moral Theory*. Notre Dame, Indiana: University of Notre Dame Press.

Maritain, Jacques. 1955. *An Essay on Christian Philosophy*. New York: Philosophical Library.

Masaka, Dennis. 2017. "'Global Justice' and the Suppressed Epistemologies of the Indigenous People of Africa." *Philosophical Papers* 46(1): 59–84.

Masolo, Dismas. 2014. "Re-Charting Global Ethics." *Journal of Global Ethics* 10(1): 38–44.

Metz, Thaddeus. 2014. "Harmonizing Global Ethics in the Future: A Proposal to Add South and East to West." *Journal of Global Ethics* 10(2): 146–155.

Miller, David. 1998. "The Ethical Significance of Nationality." *Ethics* 98: 647–662.

Miller, David. 2002. "Two Ways to Think about Justice." *Politics, Philosophy & Economics* 1(1): 5–28.

Moody, Peter Jr. 1984. "Political Liberalization in China: A Struggle between Two Lines." *Pacific Affairs* 57(1): 26–44.

Moravcsik, Andrew. 2008. "The New Liberalism." In *The Oxford Handbook of International Relations*, edited by Christian Reus-Smit and Duncan Snidal, 235–254. Oxford: Oxford University Press.

Nagel, Thomas. 2005. "The Problem of Global Justice." *Philosophy & Public Affairs* 33(2): 113–147.

Okeja, Uchenna (ed.). 2017. *African Philosophy and Global Justice. Philosophical Essays*. London: Routledge.

Pettit, Philip. 1997. *Republicanism*. New York: Oxford University Press.

Pettit, Philip. 2010. "A Republican Law of Peoples." *European Journal of Political Theory* 9(1): 70–94.

Pettit, Philip. 2016. "The Globalized Republican Ideal." *Global Justice: Theory Practice Rhetoric* 9(1): 48–68.

Pettit, Philip. 2017. "Political Realism Meets Civic Republicanism." *Critical Review of International Social and Political Philosophy* 20(3): 331–347.

Porter, Roy. 1990. *The Enlightenment*. London: Macmillan.

Porter, Thomas. 2012. "Rawls, Reasonableness, and International Toleration." *Politics, Philosophy & Economics* 11(4): 382–414.

Rathore, Aakash Singh. 2012. "The Romance of Global Justice? Sen's Deparochialization and the Quandary of Dalit Marxism." In *Global Justice: Critical Perspective*, edited by Sebastiano Maffettone and Aakash Singh Rathore. London: Routledge: 163–175.

Rawls, John. 1971. *A Theory of Justice*. Cambridge, MA: Harvard University Press.

Rawls, John. 1999. *The Law of Peoples*. Cambridge, MA: Harvard University Press.

Sandel, Michael. 1998. *Democracy's Discontent, America in Search of a Public Philosophy*. Cambridge, MA: Harvard University Press.

Sangiovanni, Andrea. 2007. "Global Justice, Reciprocity, and the State." *Philosophy & Public Affairs* 35(1): 3–39.

Sangiovanni, Andrea. 2008. "Normative Political Theory: A Flight from Reality?" In *Political Thought and International Relations: Variations on a Realist Theme*, edited by Duncan Bell, 219–239. Oxford: Oxford University Press.

Schneewind, Jerome B. 1998. *The Invention of Autonomy*. Cambridge: Cambridge University Press.

Schuppert, Fabian. 2014. *Freedom, Recognition and Non-domination, A Republican Theory of (Global) Justice*. New York: Springer.

Sen, Amartya. 2017. "Ethics and the Foundation of Global Justice." *Ethics & International Affairs* 31(3): 261–270.

Shapcott, Richard. 2017. "Global Justice: Shaped Rather than Found." *International Relations* 32(1): 104–123.

Singer, Peter. 1972. "Famine, Affluence, and Morality." *Philosophy and Public Affairs* 1(3): 229–243.

Stilz, Anna. 2009. *Liberal Loyalty*. Princeton, NJ: Princeton University Press.

Stilz, Anna. 2011. "Nations, States, and Territory." *Ethics* 121(3): 572–601.

Tan, Kok-Chor. 2017. *What Is This Thing Called Global Justice?* London: Routledge.

Taylor, Charles. 1996. "Why Democracy Needs Patriotism," In *For Love of Country?* edited by Joshua Cohen, 119–121. Boston, MA: Beacon Press.

Waldron, Jeremy. 2003. "Who Is My Neighbor? Humanity and Proximity." *The Monist* 86(3): 333–354.

White, Suart. 2003. *The Civic Minimum*. New York: Oxford University.

Williams, Huw and Carl Death. 2016. *Global Justice: The Basics*. London: Routledge.

Wu, Jiaxiang [吴稼祥]. 2013. 『公天下: 多中心治理与双主体法权』. 桂林: 广西师范大学出版社.

Ypi, Lea L. 2008. "Statist Patriotism." *The Journal of Political Philosophy* 16(1): 48–71.

Zhao, Tingyang [赵汀阳]. 2009. 『坏世界研究: 作为第一哲学的政治哲学』. 北京: 中国人民大学出版社.

Zhao, Tingyang. 2019. *Redefining A Philosophy for World Governance*, translated by Liqing Tao. Singapore: Springer.

Part 1

Critical reflections on parochialism and Western-centrism

1 Liberal internationalism, intervention, and moral imperialism[1]

Kok-Chor Tan

Introduction

Some observers worry that liberal internationalism greases the path for military international intervention. These critics need not affirm the extreme position that no intervention is ever permissible. They can allow, for instance, that international intervention to counter a clear case of genocide is permissible if not even mandatory in some respect. Their worry is that liberal internationalism's commitment to universal individual rights and freedom sets a standard for state legitimacy that many states in the world today fail to meet. Accordingly, liberal internationalism makes the just cause for intervention a condition that is very easy to meet. At least, so a critic might warn against.[2]

Liberal internationalism itself is a complex position that admits of variations within it. One extreme version can be called "liberal cosmopolitanism" which requires that all countries internally meet the basic liberal standards of rights and freedoms if they are to be in good standing in the international order. Liberal cosmopolitanism, thus, takes individuals in the world as such to be the basic unit of liberal justice regardless of their citizenship. States are legitimate or not depending on how successfully they meet the liberal rights and liberties of their own citizens.[3] Another version that lies toward the other end of the liberal internationalist spectrum is what we can call "liberal statism." Unlike liberal cosmopolitanism, liberal statism takes the fundamental liberal principles to apply among states rather than directly to individuals in the world at large. In this respect, states are the basic moral actors, and liberal principles regulate their conduct toward other states as well as the background international institutions against which they interact with each other. But even the statist version of liberal internationalism is committed to the protection of basic human rights and holds that state sovereignty is contingent on states providing for the conditions of the realization of basic rights, such as the right to security and subsistence (Shue 1990).

Thus, while liberal cosmopolitanism seems *especially* vulnerable to the charge of interventionalism, liberal internationalism as a general position faces this objection. For the purpose of this chapter, the internal contest between cosmopolitanism and statism need not detain us. Quite independently of the kind of moral political commitments that liberal *cosmopolitanism* or liberal *statism* affirms, the basic theme of this discussion is that there is a space between a state's legitimacy, on the one side, and the permissibility of external actors to intervene in that state, on the other. That is, liberalism does not entail some form of liberal interventionism.

Before proceeding, I clarify that the aim of this chapter is not to provide a defense of military intervention. I take it for granted that there are conditions under which military intervention is permissible (and even obligatory in extreme cases). My aim is to assuage concerns that liberal internationalism (or liberal cosmopolitanism) is interventionistic. Military intervention is hardly the standard way by which values are to be promoted or even enforced internationally, and there are moral conditions on when going to war is permissible that apply independently of *any particular* theory of international justice. It is also worth noting that discussions on the *moral conditions of permissible intervention* do not show that interventions will be effectively carried out in all cases where they are permissible. Nor does the discussion of the ethics of intervention imply that the necessary global institutional arrangements or global power relations required for the consistent and impartial performance of intervention are already present. That these moral standards are at present poorly enforced, unevenly applied, or without institutional backup does not mean that there are no such standards.[4]

The limits of intervention[5]

In *The Law of Peoples*, John Rawls asks if there are conditions under which military intervention to protect individuals against the tyranny of their own state is permitted. He writes, "Is there ever a time when forceful intervention might be called for?" (Rawls 1999, 94 n 6). Rawls's own response is that if "the offenses against human rights are *egregious* and the society does not respond to the imposition of sanctions, such intervention in the defense of human rights would be acceptable and would be called for" (94, my italics).[6] In such cases, a "people's right to independence and self-determination is no shield from that condemnation, nor even from coercive intervention by other people in *grave cases*" (38, my italics). Thus it is not just human rights violations that will trigger the consideration for intervention. Only "egregious" or "grave" cases of violations provide a just cause for war. Moreover, the presence of a just cause (though necessary) is not a sufficient condition for a justified intervention/war for Rawls, as is the case for most just war theorists. Other conditions will have to be met, such as the lack of responsiveness to non-military measures (what is often loosely labeled the "last resort" condition), to note the additional requirement that Rawls himself identifies in the above quotation. But my main point for now is that, for a liberal internationalist like Rawls, violations of human rights as such do not present a just cause for intervention; only "egregious", "grave" violations count as such a cause. Human rights violations are not as such triggers for intervention; only extreme cases of human rights violation provide a probable cause.

So, even on Rawls's brand of liberal internationalism, where basic human rights set the standards of state legitimacy – in the sense that states that violate basic human rights are regarded as "outlaw states" and without good standing in the Society of Peoples – violations of basic rights per se do not raise the case for intervention or other military actions such as blockades (in the form of encompassing economic sanctions). A society that fails to protect basic human rights forfeits its status as a member in good standing in the Society of Peoples, but what the appropriate response is on the part of the international society is a separate matter. As Rawls puts it: "What to do on these questions is, however, essentially a matter of political judgment and depends upon a political assessment of the likely consequences of various policies" (93). The fact that a basic principle of international justice – that of not violating basic human rights – has been offended against by a state is no reason for taking a particular kind of enforcement action against that state. We have to evaluate the seriousness of the violation, the urgency of the situation, the available range of responses, and their respective potential consequences to determine the right and effective course of action, and here the exercise of good judgment is indispensable.

In sum, just because liberal internationalism regards the respect and protection of human rights as a minimum condition of legitimacy, it does not follow that any systemic violation of basic human rights by a state justifies outside intervention against it. While respect for human rights sets the benchmark for legitimacy, only egregious or grave violations of human rights count as a just cause for intervention. Failure of legitimacy does not mean permission to intervene. Furthermore, if limiting the just cause for military action to "grave" violations is not already stringent enough, other moral requirements must be met under most just war theories for the use of force to be fully justified. Some of the conditions commonly proposed include requirements such as last resort (as noted by Rawls), proportionality, and reasonable success. What is worth noting is that the common moral conditions for justified intervention and war do not derive specifically from liberal morality. Instead they derive from more general ethical theories and moral theories of war.[7] As long as one accepts some notion of basic individual entitlement (on whatever philosophical grounding) to life, security of persons, bodily integrity, there can be convergence on some conception of just cause along the lines of Rawls. And the appropriateness of using military force to defend basic human rights from egregious violation (Have we met the proportionality requirement? Is this a reasonable last resort?) is assessed by reference to general moral ideas and just war theories, not the principles of liberal morality as such. A liberal internationalist is not any more interventionist than other conceptions of global morality that affirm some idea of the inviolability of persons and the moral necessity of war in extreme situations. Liberal internationalism, at least in the version offered by Rawls, does not open the floodgates to intervention but is in fact in line with common morality on this matter.[8] To put the essential point in a different way, while liberal internationalism defines the standards of international justice and legitimacy, how these standards ought to be *enforced* is defined by more general just war theories. With regard to justice, liberals and nonliberals will definitively disagree; with regard to when it is morally acceptable to wage war to defend one's ideal of justice, liberals and nonliberals need not disagree.

Now some may note that unlike the liberal internationalism of the sort Rawls advances, liberal cosmopolitanism is more demanding and therefore more prone to intervene. As noted, liberal cosmopolitanism defends a form of liberal internationalism that takes liberal principles to have global validity and application for all societies. But this worry is misplaced. As modest versions of liberal internationalism are subject to and limited by the general conditions of justified war (limiting conditions that are themselves not specifically liberal) in terms of how liberal values are to be protected and when intervention is permitted, so cosmopolitan versions of liberal internationalism are similarly morally constrained. A liberal cosmopolitan may have a more exacting requirement for state legitimacy, requiring that all states protect and respect certain individual liberal rights and freedoms. But this does not mean that any state that fails to reach this liberal standard of legitimacy is straightaway a fair target for intervention. The limiting conditions for going to war apply to the liberal cosmopolitan position as well. These are basic moral conditions that precede and are normatively prior to liberal cosmopolitan principles. Indeed, it will be hard to defend an intervention for the purpose of, say, defending the liberal freedom of expression. Leaving aside the fact that even liberal morality allows for different interpretation of the scope of this freedom, military intervention solely to protect such a liberal right will not by any stretch of the imagination meet the last resort and proportionality conditions for just military action. Liberal cosmopolitanism may be more critical of nonliberal societies than liberal statism, but it is not therefore more interventionistic.

But there is, however, a different kind of worry that liberal cosmopolitanism seems more vulnerable to than liberal statism. This is the concern that it might be morally interventionistic or, to put it in another way, more morally imperialistic. That is, its demands that states respect and protect the liberal rights of their own citizens can come across as an external moral imposition, indeed an imposition of a political morality that is typically associated with the West. This is a worry that should give liberal cosmopolitans some pause given the history of Western colonialism and imperialism. I will turn to this concern with moral imperialism next.

Moral imperialism

Liberal internationalism, especially its cosmopolitan version, has a universalistic moral stance. It affirms and promotes a rather substantial morality, a morality that is typically said to be Western or at least Western in origin, in a world order that is culturally pluralistic and diverse. Does this amount to a kind of "moral imperialism"? I will attempt to assuage these concerns with the following observations.[9]

First, liberal internationalism (including liberal cosmopolitanism) does not *just* attempt to impose a particular conception of justice globally, but it attempts to extend that conception *based on moral reasons* that it believes to have broad appeal and that all can potentially come to share. It is the case that liberal cosmopolitanism requires a critical stance and response toward nonliberal states and will advocate for a conception of global justice that declares in principle that nonliberal states are unjust. In this sense, it exerts significant institutional pressures on nonliberal states to reform. But moral criticism and urging reform by appeal to justice per se is not disrespectful if the critic is prepared to give reasons for her stance. To put it curtly, moral imperialism implies an unreasoned imposition of a moral position. Liberal internationalism does not simply impose but argues for its morality.

Thus, if what is objectionable about moral imperialism is that it involves the imposition of a particular moral view on others *without giving them reasons* they can potentially come to accept, cosmopolitanism is not objectionably imperialistic. What cosmopolitanism advocates is the more modest stance that it can be part of an acceptable liberal foreign policy to *critically engage* decent societies over matters of domestic political organization and to use measures like trade incentives to motivate reform. But critical engagement is a two-way street, and liberals have the responsibility to attend to and respond to arguments from the other side. Accordingly, liberals will occasionally have to revise their original evaluations if critical dialogue reveals that the critics have failed to properly appreciate the facts. More significantly, it means that liberals will have to continually work on their defense of individual equality, to come up with new and better arguments in light of new challenges and counterresponses. If moral imperialism is the smug imposition of a moral view on others without listening to what they have to say, cosmopolitanism need not be a form of moral imperialism.

Responsiveness to the counterarguments from the other side implies also that liberal states have to accept criticisms of their own particular domestic practices and either provide reasoned arguments for these or revise or eliminate these practices. The cosmopolitan ideal, even though it is a globalized account of liberal justice, does not presume that all liberal states are, in practice, fully just and beyond rebuke. Problems of racism, economic inequality, overexploitation of the environment are some examples of failings within many liberal states that are subject to both internal and external criticisms. And allowing for outside criticisms can sometimes help identify problems that internal critics for reasons of cultural proximity are not sensitive to.

Indeed, for this reason, both sides to the dispute benefit from the critical engagement that cosmopolitan toleration calls for. Of course from the liberal perspective, it will be hoped that the ideas of decent societies will be revised based on its collision with liberalism, while liberalism itself is understood anew due to this confrontation. But this presumption of the truth of one's own view is not necessarily parochial – we must access the moral world from a particular point of view (and within the liberal point of view is a universalizing tendency). What is required is that cosmopolitan liberals be ready to offer reasons for their convictions, reasons that they can reasonably believe that others can accept, and be prepared to receive and respond to criticisms in turn. And as also noted, the result is not presumed to be always one-sided: critical engagement with other societies may expose actual flaws within liberal societies in need of correction.

In short, the cosmopolitan ideal can be seen as grounded on the moral belief that all persons are entitled to protection of their autonomy. Its account of toleration is motivated by the need to respond to situations in which persons are denied this protection by their own states. In this respect, it is not a refutation of the cosmopolitan ideal that it has a universalist agenda for this is precisely and explicitly its purpose. Concerns about the cosmopolitan ideal's potential dogmatism can be assuaged if the cosmopolitan project is presented with reasons and is responsive to counterarguments.

Cautioning the liberal internationalist against moral dogmatism is *not* a call against taking a stance. Obviously the liberal internationalism proposed here stakes a normative position and will challenge (and presumptively reject) moral commitments that contradict liberal values. No doubt there will be extremist views that will oppose fundamental liberal values, and possibly no further dialogue will successfully achieve at some mutually acceptable outcome. With regard to these, the liberal internationalist will obviously remain firmly opposed. But again how this opposition is to be enforced or acted on is a separate question to be answered taking various contingencies into account along with sound judgment. Nor do I presume that once liberalism adopts a more fallibilistic posture, all nonliberal views can come to join a consensus around liberalism.

Adopting a fallibilistic posture will also require acknowledgment of one's own mistakes and failures, in the past or ongoing. With respect to ongoing failures, liberal internationalists have to acknowledge the global inequality and power imbalance that are pressing issues of global justice but less often attended to. This makes the liberal internationalists' typical focus on matters of international political justice – civil and political rights – selective and therefore seemingly self-serving. And uneven enforcement or defense of liberal rights in cases where it involves "allies" of the liberal internationalists casts doubt on the sincerity of their commitments to liberal justice.

Moral fallibilism requires the readiness to accept that one may have got the facts wrong, and that getting another perspective on what is the case and being ready to adjust one's understanding of events is essential for genuine intermoral deliberation. And sometimes, reflection and deliberation can even require revisions to one's principles and value commitments. All of this is to suggest that there is nothing inherently morally imperialistic about defending liberal internationalism, if by moral imperialism we mean the rigid and unbending imposition of a moral view point without any regard for what the other side has to say. But it is important to note, as stressed above, that this moral modesty is not the same as moral capitulation.

Lessons from the *Zhuangzi*

Regarding moral modesty and fallibilism, there are lessons that the liberal internationalists can learn from other traditions. Thus, in keeping with the spirit of cross-cultural engagement as is the theme of this volume, I hazard a brief digression to point out some lessons that liberal internationalist can take away from the *Zhuangzi*, the eponymous collection of writings attributed to the ancient Chinese philosopher Zhuangzi.[10]

Zhuangzi is commonly interpreted as a skeptic regarding universal knowledge and specifically the universality of moral standards. For instance, the *Zhuangzi* notes:

> Once you and I start arguing, if you win and I lose, then are you really right and am I really wrong? If I win and you lose, then am I really right and you are really wrong? ... Whom shall we get to set us straight.
>
> (Zhuangzi 2005, 223)

This skepticism that there are no external standards that the parties to a deep philosophical disagreement can agree on and appeal to "to set them straight," is sometimes read as a reason for embracing relativism, including ethical relativism. If we can't know the whole truth, then let us not pretend to have universal knowledge of right and wrong. Right and wrong at best then can only be relative to our relevant experiences. As another passage has it: "What is this is also that, and what is that is also this. This is both right and wrong" (217).

But we can also interpret the *Zhuangzi* as a defense of another way of understanding morality. Rather than as an endorsement of relativism, we can also see the *Zhuangzi* to be as a call for a kind of "moral perspectivalism". Moral perspectivalism, as I regard it here, is the idea that our moral understanding is limited to what we can know and experience and that our moral knowledge is thus only limited to a particular perspective or point of view. There is no universal point of view, let alone a view from nowhere, from which we grasp the whole of morality. What we have is necessarily only one dimension or facet of the whole picture. Our moral world view, our moral perception and the moral judgments we form based on this perspective, is in this way special and limited to us. The *Zhuangzi* says: "Life is bounded. Knowledge is unbounded. Using the bounded to follow the unbounded is dangerous" (224). That is, to claim from our bounded, limited experience that we have true and complete knowledge risks error and is hubristic. Since our knowledge is limited to our socially confined and subjective experiences, we should keep an open mind. We have to acknowledge the presence of other points of view, other moral perspectives that we could be blind to.

Consider this well-known passage:

> So we have the rights and wrongs of the Confucians and the Mohists. Each calls right what the other calls wrong, and each calls wrong what the other calls right. But if you want to right their wrongs and wrong their rights, it's better to throw them open to the light.
>
> (217)

This rich passage has been interpreted in different ways, from a defense of moral skepticism to a defense of moral relativism. But it has also been read, a reading that I prefer, as a position on epistemic and moral modesty. What the passage tells us, as I draw from it, is that if we, actors in moral disagreement, want to have a better understanding of each other and our respective positions, including our own, and to be more self-aware of their limitations, we should "throw them open to the light." Here, Zhuangzi, as I am taking this passage, does not say we immediately accept our opponent to be right and that we are also right (relativism) or renounce the truth or rightness of our own view or any view for that matter (skepticism).

So what are we to do? One option, perhaps that Zhuangzi himself intends, is that we retain a non-judgmental attitude and not try to fit things as they appear to us into our preconceived categories and definitions. But there is another possibility, a further step, on what to do next, admittedly perhaps not one required by *Zhuangzi* but nonetheless consistent with and inspired by it. This is that we take on the additional task of subjecting our own views to critical reflection and analysis. That is, the epistemic modesty and perspectivalism that Zhuangzi urges, I am suggesting, can compel us to become more aware of the necessity of subjecting our own commitments and arguments to further critical reflection. That we likely only have part of the whole truth in all matters – the lesson Zhuangzi teaches – should move us to consider that our pronouncements and arguments are based on incomplete facts and necessarily limited understanding. We thus remain on guard for epistemic failures on our own part. Whereas Zhuangzi is sometimes interpreted to be suggesting that moral disagreements aren't resolvable, I am suggesting that critical self-reflection can be a tool toward a complete understanding of the nature of a moral disagreement and to find a way forward.

The famous passage in the *Zhuangzi*, where Zhuangzi says he does not know whether he dreamt he was a butterfly the previous night, or whether the self-conscious being is in fact a butterfly dreaming now that it is Zhuangzi, will remind Western readers of Descartes' dream hypothesis. Given the skeptical program in the Zhuangzi, this is a reasonable conclusion to make. But as commentators have pointed out, this passage is in service of a different point – that of the fundamental unity of all beings. The idea here is something like this. There is a fundamental sameness and oneness in nature, but each is realized as a conscious subject in different forms and with distinct perspectives. The point I would like to draw from this is the perspectivalist ideal that there are different perspectives, different points of view that are not obvious to us given our limited condition and particular angle and consciousness through which we view the world.

In short, as I understand it, one lesson we may draw and generalize from the *Zhuangzi* is not that we should renounce our moral commitments out of skepticism or that we concede to moral relativism and therefore eschew from international and other forms of cross-cultural moral engagement and judgment.[11] The lesson, most relevant to this chapter, is that we accept a certain moral modesty (as opposed to certainty) that we each adopt a more fallibilistic stance toward our own commitments. We don't surrender our moral commitments, but we engage the other side with an open mind, with the presumption that there are points of view that we are not privileged to, that our moral understanding and vision may be that of a limited perspective, that the whole truth is perhaps our different perspectives put together.

This, again, does not mean the end of criticism and debate. We should continue to argue for our position but with the presumption in the background that we might find, at the end of the day, that our principles and judgments are mistaken. This allows for rigorous, even heated, arguments, but it also makes the critical dialogue sincere and well intentioned.

One might say then, inspired by the perspectivalism of the *Zhuangzi*, that the problem of international moral imperialism lies not in the commitment to state-transcending universal principles as such but in the lack of reflectiveness and lack of ethical modesty. To be committed to certain universal ideals and principles is one thing; to stand by them with the clarity and zealousness of a fanatic is another. The problem in short is not with liberal internationalism or even liberal cosmopolitanism but a kind of moral fanaticism that is not necessary to, nor exclusive to, liberal internationalism. Indeed, in the present world, where the dangers we face are not the consequence of the lack of commitments and beliefs in moral rightness and righteousness, but that of extremism of beliefs and commitments, the recommendation of Zhuangzi (at least as I am drawing from the tradition) that we adopt a more reflective and modest stance toward our own commitments is one we will all do well to heed. Liberal internationalists must stand up for their principles of international political morality. But they should also realize that the moral categories they draw on, the moral judgments they pass, are necessarily from a limited perspective.

Conclusion

The distinction between the principles of liberal internationalism and military intervention as a method of enforcing these principles is especially salient if we accept that the moral judgments we pass are necessarily from a particular perspective. This does not mean, to reiterate, that liberal internationalism has to surrender its universalizing outlook. But with a morally modest attitude, the liberal internationalist will take special care in how she can go about arguing for and defending these values. And this does not mean that there can't be occasions when intervention is morally warranted, as in extreme cases where time is of the essence and the moral violation severe. But given that there is always some uncertainty in our own understanding and many competing points of view that may be outside our perspectival grasp, intervention is not something to be undertaken lightly. When it is justified and called for, we must recognize it for the moral tragedy that it is, a morally unavoidable act that comes with significant moral costs.

Notes

1 I am extremely grateful to Hugo El Kholi for his astute and detailed comments on an earlier draft and to Yu Yih- Soong for comments on Zhuangzi and epistemic modesty.
2 "Intervention," henceforth, is taken to mean military intervention. There are of course other forms of interferences short of military intervention that are also coercive in effect. But my special concern here is with military intervention since some commentators take it that human rights violation – which is a failure of a basic condition for state legitimacy – suffices as a justification for military intervention. See John Tasioulas (2009). Some read the function of human rights in John Rawls's *The Law of Peoples* (Rawls 1999), in this way, including Jeremy Waldron, who calls this "the Armed Intervention" account of human rights (Waldron 2018). But one of the claims of this chapter – to be elaborated on below – is that Rawls does not tie human rights to armed intervention in this immediate sense. Although Rawls takes respect for human rights to be a necessary condition for state legitimacy (or more precisely for a state to be in "good standing"), it is only special cases of rights violation that potentially justify military intervention.
3 For one study of cosmopolitan justice, see Brock (2009).
4 Recent discussions on intervention have moved on to discussions on the duty to intervene and not just the permissibility thereof. I discuss this question in Tan (2005, 2015). In international discourse, this shift in thinking about intervention is reflected in the adoption of "The Responsibility to Protect" doctrine. But the right of intervention must be presumed for there to be a responsibility to intervene, and the issue in this chapter is just that human rights violations, much less violations of liberal rights, do not per se provide a permissibility condition under standard just war theories.
5 This section draws on Tan (2010).
6 See also the following remark: "An outlaw state that violates these rights is to be condemned and in grave cases may be subjected to forceful sanctions and even to intervention" (Rawls 1999, 81).
7 See Boyle (2004) and Nardin (2002).
8 Michael Blake identifies the various prudential and moral reasons that on balance can count against intervention in spite of a just cause (Blake 2013).
9 I will recall some arguments made previously in Tan (2011).
10 *Zhuangzi* (2005). The *Zhuangzi* is a cryptic text that is the subject of a millennial of competing commentaries. I am not attempting a novel interpretation or a new systematic scholarly reading of the text. I am simply turning to it as a source of inspiration and to point out how this complex work can instigate further

thoughts that are germane to the present discussion. The only requirement is that I do not draw lessons from the *Zhuangzi* that are plainly contradictory to its main theses or its intention (and I hope my extrapolation is within reason in this respect).

11 If one were to emphasize Zhuangzi as a thoroughgoing moral relativist, then liberal internationalism itself (since it is not relativistic) let alone any form of external criticism (much less military intervention) would be ruled out. As mentioned in the endnote above, it will be beyond the scope and interest of this chapter to attempt a holistic interpretation of the *Zhuangzi*. My goal again is to emphasize the perspectivalism (not relativism) of Zhuangzi as an idea that liberal internationalists can take guidance from.

References

Blake, Michael. 2013. *Justice and Foreign Policy*. Oxford: Oxford University Press.

Brock, Gillian. 2009. *Global Justice: A Cosmopolitan Account*. Oxford: Oxford University Press.

Boyle, Joseph. 2004. "Traditional Just War Theory and Humanitarian Intervention." In Nardin and Williams, 31–57.

Nardin, Terry. 2002. "The Moral Basis of Humanitarian Intervention." *Ethics and International Affairs* 16(1): 57–71.

Rawls, John. 1999. *The Law of Peoples*. Cambridge, MA: Harvard University Press.

Shue, Henry. 1990 (2nd Edition). *Basic Rights*. Princeton, NJ: Princeton University Press.

Tan, Kok-Chor. 2015. "Humanitarian Intervention as a Duty." *Global Responsibility to Protect* 7(2): 121–141.

Tan, Kok-Chor. 2011. "Two Conceptions of Liberal Global Toleration." *Monist* 94(4): 489–505.

Tan, Kok-Chor. 2010. "Enforcing Cosmopolitan Justice: the problem of Intervention." In Pierik and Werner, 155–178.

Tan, Kok-Chor. 2005. "The Duty to Protect." In Nardin and Williams, 84–116.

Tasioulas, John. 2009. "Are Human Rights Essentially Triggers for Intervention?" *Philosophy Compass* 4(6): 938–950.

Waldron, Jeremy. 2018. "Human Rights: A Critique of the Rawls/Raz Approach." In *Human Rights: Moral or Political*, edited by Adam Etinson, 117–138. Oxford: Oxford University Press.

Zhuangzi. 2005. *Zhuangzi*. Translated by Paul Kjellberg. In *Readings in Classical Chinese Philosophy*, edited by Philip J. Ivanhoe and Bryan W. Van Norden, 207–254. Indianapolis: Hackett Publishing.

2 On the compatibility of global democratic justice and Confucianism

Julian Culp

Introduction

The aim of this chapter is to defend a distinctively democratic conception of global distributive justice against the criticism that it is parochial or Western-centric. Subsequently I will refer to this criticism as "postcolonial critique," because many postcolonial scholars are concerned about the Western bias that philosophers display in their conceptualizations of normative concepts such as democracy, justice, or development (cf., e.g., Escobar 2012). So the question whether a democratic way of understanding global distributive justice suffers from such a bias is the subject matter of this chapter. In response to this question, I will draw on Confucian political thought and argue that because basic democratic ideas can also be found in the East Asian context, a democratic conception of global distributive justice is not necessarily parochial.

But what exactly is the basic idea of a democratic conception of global distributive justice? A democratic conception maintains that the question "What is a just global distribution of resources?" should be answered indirectly by responding first to the question "Who decides what counts as a just global distribution of resources?" In that way, the central upshot of my democratic conception is that reducing global distributive injustice requires us to remove the economic obstacles that block an effective participation in the political deliberation about how to conceive distributive justice at a global level.

The general importance of defending this democratic conception of global distributive justice against the charge of parochialism or Western-centrism seems at first hand rather obvious, a conception of *global* distributive justice that claims *universal* validity would fail on its own terms if it turned out that the principles that it defends are parochial or Western-centric. If that were the case, then these principles could not be plausibly applicable to non-Western contexts such as the East Asian one. And thereby to vindicate the validity of the democratic conception of global distributive justice against the charge of parochialism is a mandatory part of an adequate justification of such a conception of global justice.[1]

There is, however, yet another and more determinate reason why it is necessary to defend this democratic conception of global distributive justice against such a postcolonial critique. This reason is connected to the claim of the democratic conception that it is able to offer a solution to the problem of disagreement regarding how to conceive and achieve distributive justice. This problem of disagreement exists, because there are many, apparently reasonable, conceptions of distributive justice available. Therefore how does one make a decision between these conceptions? The solution that the democratic conception provides is to abstain from philosophically determining which principles of ideal distributive justice are fully justified. Instead, it contends that such principles can and should be justified through a democratic discourse. It limits itself to justifying only those – merely basic but not perfectly ideal – distributive principles that would have to be realized for such democratic conditions to come about. So according to the democratic conception of justice, the economic conditions necessary for being able to participate in democratic decision-making become the justified claims of (basic) distributive justice even though there might be further ideal principles of distributive justice that are justifiable through a democratic discourse.

But from the postcolonial perspective, the idea of justifying a conception of distributive justice in this manner might be regarded as deeply problematic. A postcolonial theorist might say that defending the moral importance of distributive principles by showing their relevance for democratic discourse is parochial or Western-centric (cf. Mignolo and Escobar 2010; Andreotti and de Souza 2012). Yet if that were the case, then the democratic conception itself encountered the problem of disagreement.

Thus in this chapter, I will focus on the kind of disagreement that concerns the democratic conception's reliance on democratic ideas which postulate that all human beings must be effectively recognized as equal normative authorities within democratic discourse. More specifically, I will examine whether or not there are compelling reasons to believe that especially those who endorse an East Asian and Confucian normative perspective can – at least in principle – share this democratic perspective. Thereby I aim to show that the democratic conception of global justice is not parochial or Western-centric and that it therefore does not fall prey to what we can dub as the postcolonial critique.

This chapter unfolds in Section 1 by sketching out the democratic conception of global distributive justice by situating it within the ongoing normative-theoretical debate about global distributive justice. Section 2 articulates in greater detail the possible critique that this democratic conception is parochial or Western-centric and specifies furthermore the way in which this critique can be understood as a postcolonial one. Section 3 responds to the postcolonial critique that my democratic conception of global justice is parochial. It has a particular focus on the East Asian context and relies on several "democratic" interpretations of Confucian political philosophy.

These are interpretations on whose accuracy I rely without further arguing that it is plausible to regard democratic arrangements as compatible, at least in principle, with Confucian political culture and thought. So because of the possibility of a Confucian form of democratic thinking and practice, I argue that it is inadequate to regard a democratic conception of justice as Western-centric. And therefore my conclusion is that the parochialism critique of the democratic conception of global distributive justice fails in the East Asian context.

The "Western" debate about global distributive justice and its universalizability

About a decade ago, a stalemate between the so-called globalist theorists on the one hand and the statist theorists on the other hand characterized the academic debate about global distributive justice. The core of the dispute between these two camps of theorists turned the question as to whether or not some egalitarian principles of distributive justice apply globally among all individuals or only among the co-citizens within a state. Within the context of this debate, the globalists affirm a principle of global interpersonal distributive equality. The statists, however, recognize solely a principle of domestic interpersonal distributive equality. And additionally they either claim that the principles of justice do not at all apply beyond the state or hold that only some sufficientarian principles can be recognized as globally valid. For example, some statists hold that the satisfaction of the basic needs of all individuals globally is a mandatory requirement of global distributive justice.

The globalist theorists include scholars such as Charles Beitz (1999a), Thomas Pogge (1989), Darrel Moellendorf (2002), and Kok-Chor Tan (2004). These scholars are Rawlsians insofar that all of them argue that John Rawls' difference principle should be recognized as globally valid. The global difference principle that the globalist theorists defend says that the distribution of justice-relevant goods such as income and wealth, for example, should be to the maximum benefit of the members of the least-well-off group globally. But the statist scholars, however, hold that only state coercion grounds requirements of egalitarian distributive justice. Therefore they restrict the validity of egalitarian distributive principles like Rawls's difference principle to the boundaries of the nation-state model. Such statist scholars include Michael Blake (2001) and Thomas Nagel (2005). Other scholars who are statists by virtue of the fact that they limit distributive egalitarian principles to the state are Samuel Freeman (2007) and Andrea Sangiovanni (2007). These other scholars, however, do so on the ground that a reciprocal form of cooperation presently exists solely at the level of the nation-state.

Charles Beitz (1999b) labeled the two camps of theorists within this debate the "cosmopolitan liberals" and the "social liberals," respectively. By now the terms statism and globalism are more common and also seem to be more adequate. This is because the social liberals, to which the statist scholars belong, recognize certain minimal or sufficientarian concerns of justice or humanity beyond the state. Therefore they may also be viewed as being cosmopolitans of a certain kind, which is why it seems inappropriate to frame the debate as if it occurred between cosmopolitans and non-cosmopolitans.[2]

Beitz was able to characterize the academic debate about global distributive justice as a liberal debate, thereby, as a controversy between two strands of liberal political philosophy. It shows that non-liberal perspectives have been of (much) lesser, if any, importance in the framing of this particular debate. It is therefore indeed relevant and fitting to consider to what extent this liberal framing has resulted in forming conceptions of global distributive justice that are parochial or Western-centric.

This statement must be qualified, however, because one of the major concerns of John Rawls's work on global justice, *The Law of Peoples* (1999), was to determine the principles which should regulate the interactions between liberal societies and non-liberal societies. Thereby Rawls was acutely aware of the fact that whichever principles he used to justify as principles of global justice, he could not simply argue from a liberal point of view and expect that this point of view actually was, or could be, universally shared. Indeed, Rawls states in the *Preface* of his work that he sets himself the task of articulating principles of "liberal foreign policy" (1999, 10). But in *The Law of Peoples*, he nevertheless also considers non-liberal points of view and ends up envisioning a just global order which consists of both liberal and non-liberal – yet decent – societies.

Moreover, cosmopolitan normative theorists such as Simon Caney (2005, ch. 1) have also paid considerable attention to the question of whether the "cosmopolitan liberal" kind of conception of global distributive justice can be made universally valid. Thus, considering the parochialism or Western-centrism objection to a particular conception of global distributive justice is by no means a particularly novel approach. Yet in the last few years, there has been a heightened awareness and concern regarding the potential cogency of this objection (cf. Flikschuh 2014; Williams and Warren 2014; Okeja 2017). This may be due in part, at least, to the fact that some cosmopolitan theorists do not seem to have taken this objection seriously enough.

A case in point might be Pogge (1989, 271) who has argued that if an intercultural, global dialogue about principles of global distributive justice were to take place, the resulting consensus would consist precisely of the egalitarian ideal that the theorists have already envisioned. Others, like Moellendorf (2002, 24), has merely postulated that the moral conception of the person that grounds the globally valid egalitarian distributive principles is universal in kind and hence cannot be reasonably rejected.

But the problem shared by these ways of dealing with the parochialism objection is that they attempt to ground the validity of global egalitarian principles of distributive justice without addressing the core of that objection. For the core of this objection is that although certain normative principles might be applicable in the particular context of the West, they cannot be plausibly applied to other contexts such as the global or the East Asian one, because they are relevantly different. Hence the objection says, in effect, that the distributive principles like a global version of the Rawlsian difference principle are insufficiently context-sensitive.

The problem of the way in which Pogge and Moellendorf respond to this objection is that they do not actually present any argument as to why the global difference principle is sufficiently context-sensitive and can be suitably applied to contexts such as the East Asian one. Instead, they beg the question: either they merely postulate that a global, intercultural dialogue would lead to a consensus in favor of their distributive norms or they suggest that a supposedly universal moral concept alone, such as that of a moral person, would lead directly to substantive distributive ideals of global justice.[3] These are unsatisfactory answers, which is why it should be of little surprise that more recent thinkers such as Melissa Williams and Mark Warren (2014), Katrin Flikschuh (2014), and Uchenna Okeja (2017) urge us to reconsider the universalizability of the arguments that contemporary philosophers employ when theorizing global justice.

A democratic conception of global distributive justice

This chapter focuses on the question of the universalizability of a distinctively democratic conception of global distributive justice. It abstains from the globalist or liberal cosmopolitan claim that egalitarian principles of distributive justice should be recognized globally. The democratic conception of distributive justice will instead make the more modest, but still extremely demanding, claim that those economic conditions must be in place that are necessary for enabling political actors to participate in democratic decision-making. But before addressing the question of the universalizability of this conception in the next section, let us further characterize in greater detail an understanding and rationale for this democratic conception of global justice.

My democratic conception of global justice has been deeply influenced by Young's article "Displacing the Distributive Paradigm" (1990, ch. 1), in which she sets out a fundamental challenge for theories of distributive justice that are primarily distribution-oriented. In that article, she especially criticizes the emphasis that several political philosophers place on discussing the question as to what should be considered as the appropriate metric relative to which one should make distributive assessments. Within the so-called "Equality of What?" debate, several philosophers have agreed that distributive justice requires an equal distribution of justice-relevant goods, but they disagree relative to which specific goods the distribution should be equalized. Some argue, for example, that all-purpose resources should count as the "currency" of egalitarian justice (Dworkin 2000). Similarly, Rawls (2001, 57–60, 168–175) and Pogge (2010) defend the relevance of so-called primary goods, which also include monetary resources like income and wealth. Sen, by contrast, makes the claim that capabilities, that is, effective freedoms to do certain things or enjoy certain states of affairs, should be recognized as the currency of egalitarian distributive justice (Sen 1997).

Young's critique of this debate is not, however, that distributive questions of justice do not matter at all. Rather, her critique is meant to show that it is necessary, as she (1990, 37) puts it, to displace "the distributive paradigm in favor of a wider, process-oriented understanding of society, which focuses on [...] decision-making structures." Hence she suggests modifying the terms of reference of a theory of justice from a predominantly distribution-oriented and thus goods-centered perspective to an analysis of the decision-making structures that entail that certain distributions of goods come about. Moreover, focusing on such structures is also of great importance, because they determine the economic system of producing goods, as well as who decides who receives and contributes what.

Similarly, Rainer Forst (2014, ch. 1) defends the philosophical relevance of refraining from a purely distributive "picture" of justice and highlights the centrality of a political "picture" of justice which concentrates on questions of public decision-making. He (2007a, 300) aptly labels this necessary transition the "political turn" in the debate about how to theorize justice. Forst's (2007b, 260) account implies that those who participate in a social and political order should not be viewed solely as the recipients of goods. Rather, they must also be recognized as political agents who call for justifications of the social order in which they participate. In that manner, Forst insists, justice primarily centers not so much on "what you have" but rather on "how you are treated" as a political subject.

Without any further argument, we will now assume that the insights that Young and Forst provide in their works are correct in so far that it is implausible to assume that the core meaning of justice refers solely to the distributive or substantive issues. Theories of justice should also focus on the political or procedural aspect of the concept of justice. My understanding of a democratic conception of global justice adopts this insight and transfers it to the global level.

Similarly to the globalist theorists of global justice mentioned above, I also criticize those theories of justice as being incoherent when they focus exclusively on domestic or national issues (Culp 2014, ch. 3). Processes of globalization will render it inadequate to limit the *scope* of the conceptions of justice to the boundaries of the nation-state. On the one hand, it is not only the case that due to globalization it is no longer plausible to believe that certain demands of justice that reach beyond the boundaries of the nation-state are unfeasible. And on the other hand, the conditions that I believe to justify certain demands of justice, namely the existence of social relationships with pervasive impact, which give rise to questions about their justifiability, now exist globally and no longer only domestically (cf. Beitz 1983, 111; Abizadeh 2007).

Thus I (2014, ch. 5) adopt in an internationalist manner the political turn that I identified in the works of Young and Forst when theorizing global justice (cf. Christiano 2010; Pettit 2010). This means that I defend a democratic conception of global justice that consists of specific requirements at the international as well as at the domestic level. The requirements at the *inter*national level are those that represent internally and sufficiently just states that ought to have sufficient justificatory power in the international processes of opinion and will formation. These international processes of opinion and will formation represent "international political discourses" in which the official or formally recognized political agents, such as representatives of states, exchange reasons about their views as to what is empirically the case and what ought to be done, by whom and how.

At this point, the question may arise as to how one ought to consider, in more concrete terms, the key features and institutions of such international discourses. In my view, the representatives of internally sufficiently just states must be able to construct democratically the internationally valid and substantive principles of justice, upon which the specific shape of a just international order is to be erected and based. A fundamental requirement of properly arranged and reasonably democratic international political discourses is the establishment of the basic structures of justification which enable their members, as Forst (2011, 9) puts it, "to demand and provide justifications and to challenge false legitimations." While on the domestic level this substantive, fundamental requirement can be institutionally realized by a certain form of deliberative democracy, it is far less clear as to how this fundamental requirement can be met internationally in the absence of a world state and a well-informed and connected global civil society.

Arguably, the most central aspect of properly arranged international discourses is that state representatives ought to have sufficient justificatory power in international processes of opinion and will formation. State representatives should be able to participate in discursively constructing the substantive principles based upon which the international order and its central institutions are organized.[4] Such international processes would have to mediate the views of the state members via their government officials. But additionally there should also exist further *transnational* processes of opinion and will formation among citizens from various states, often times organized in transnational social and political movements, which should enable citizens to co-determine international decision-making.

In addition, since the justifications for any kind of international order must be ultimately justifiable to the states' citizens, the internationalist conception also calls for basic structures of justification at the *intra*national level. Domestically, structures of justification must enable citizens to demand and provide justifications and to challenge false legitimations for the particular shape of their domestic social and political orders. As long as this domestic requirement remains unmet, the international practices of justification lack the normative quality necessary to reasonably presume the moral acceptability of the agreements reached in international processes of opinion and will formation. And this is because, without the effective political opportunity to question the opinions expressed and the decisions taken by the representatives of states, the citizens are not sufficiently taken into account when the states' international priorities are being determined.

In a nutshell, hence, my internationalist conception of global democratic justice consists of a two-pronged approach. Its realization requires the establishment of basic structures of justification on both the inter- and intranational levels, which presuppose domestic, inter- and transnational justificatory discourses to construct the principles that determine the fundamental shape of the domestic and international political orders. Although my conception is anchored in the fundamental importance of democratic decision-making, it also has nevertheless very significant consequences for conceiving the global distributive justice. The procedures for the institutionalization of certain political decision-making have several distributive aspects. Certain economic relations must be realized in order to facilitate a more democratic decision-making. The political agents, for example, need health care in order to be able to make good use of their cognitive and communicative abilities. They also require a certain degree of material security in order to avoid being forced to consent to the view of the more powerful agents. In these ways, a primarily political conception of democratic justice must also pay careful attention to distributive considerations and condemn, for example, democracy-undermining economic inequalities (cf. Forst 2012, 5–7).

After having clarified in some detail the way in which global distributive justice has been conceived democratically and internationally, I will now turn to the question as to what extent, if at all, the postcolonial critique of parochialism or Western-centrism applies to this particular conception of global justice. I begin, however, by looking at the origins and meaning of postcolonial theory so as to further specify the distinct character of what is meant by the postcolonial critique.

Analyzing the postcolonial critique of global democratic justice[5]

The beginnings of postcolonial theory were located in literary studies where it emerged through a critique of the nearly exclusive focus on European writers, especially the British ones, within the curricula of English Departments in formerly colonized societies (cf. Thiong'o 1995). The theorists referred to as "postcolonial theorists" criticized this focus, because it prevented the members of the colonized societies from reflecting critically upon their lifeworlds through literature (cf. Thiong'o 1995, 441). But now postcolonial theory has become also an important part of disciplines such as anthropology, history, political science, and philosophy.

As in the case of other theoretical paradigms such as liberalism, Marxism, or feminism, however, scholars tend to disagree on how to define postcolonial theory. The relatively broad, albeit unspecific, definition of this subject matter is the critical analysis of the enduring effects of colonialism. These effects are comprised of the contemporary social relations within both the formerly colonized and the formerly colonizing societies, as well as the current relations between and across these societies (cf. Kerner 2012).

It is a basic assumption of postcolonial theorists that there presently exist "neo-colonial" practices which characterize these relations and reproduce injustices, although these practices have a different appearance than the previous colonial ones which they have replaced. Therefore, following this definition, the prefix "post" in postcolonial theory is not meant to suggest that ever since the formal end of colonialism the sociopolitical injustices that had emerged within, across, and between formerly colonized and formerly colonizing societies have disappeared. To the contrary, postcolonial theory assumes that these injustices have enduring effects that persist even once that colonialism has officially been terminated. Thereby postcolonial theory has as its subject matter the study of enduring injustice within, between, and across formerly colonized and formerly colonizing societies.

Again, the basic idea behind the Western parochialism objection to my conception of global democratic justice is that it involves an arbitrary extrapolation of normative standards from one social context to another. It postulates that even if democratic principles might be an appropriate normative standard for assessing political orders in Western societies, they are an inadequate standard for non-Western ones. The presumption of the universality of such principles is flawed, because due to non-Western societies' distinct features, a different standard is needed in this case. Thereby my democratic conception of global justice follows the normative logic of colonial practices, which consisted of an analogous arbitrary extrapolation. And in that sense, it is apt to speak of the parochialism objection as a postcolonial critique.

By way of further illustration of the way in which the parochialism objection is postcolonial, consider how postcolonial scholars have analyzed the way in which, in the case of colonial India, "the 'universal' discourse of English literature [...] was consciously adopted as the vehicle for educating the Indian élites in tenets of civilized morality" (Ashcroft, Griffiths and Tiffin 1995a, 55). Their analysis shows that the colonial policies relied on the idea of the universal validity of Western education in order to justify its use within non-Western contexts. The allegedly universal character of Western education isolated the colonial educational practice from critique, since it supposedly did not pursue any particularistic agenda. By contrast, the non-Western education was regarded as particularistic and could not therefore meet the "universal" standards of Western education. Thereby the use of Western education in non-Western societies implies a "fixing" or "positioning" of the non-Western societies into an inferior position.

As Edward Said points out in his seminal study of the Western construction of "the Orient," the West has achieved what he describes as "flexible *positional* superiority, which puts the Westerner in a whole series of possible relationships with the Orient without ever losing the relative upper hand" (Said 1995, 90). Along similar lines, Helen Tiffin argues with regard to the colonial educational practices,

> [T]he very texts which facilitated such material and psychic capture were those which the imposed European education systems foisted on the colonized as the 'great' literature which dealt with 'universals'; ones whose culturally specific imperial terms were to be accepted as axiomatic at the colonial margins.[6]

The flipside of the alleged universality and superiority of English and Western education was the downgrading of the non-Western literary works and scholarly productions (cf. Tiffin 1995, 97).[7] And this, in turn, implied regarding the non-Western cultures and its members as inferior, since they have not been able to produce comparable works that would be worthwhile to learn and teach. As John Docker (1995, 443) argues, "[t]he white colonizing society removes the indigenous culture to an inferior level by virtue of the superiority of the metropolitan culture it is establishing."

Accordingly, from a postcolonial perspective, the underlying problem of the democratic conception of global distributive justice might be that such a conception reflects neocolonial academic practices that prevent political philosophers like myself to recognize the inappropriateness of applying Western normative standards of justice to the world at large. Therefore it is crucial to consider the Western parochialism objection to my democratic conception of global justice and to revise this conception in ways which render it better justified overall.

This way of using postcolonial theory is in itself an exercise in postcolonial theory, since that theory is not necessarily aporetic or simply negative. Rather, many postcolonial theorists recognize the possibility of emancipation and liberation and do in fact appeal to universal standards themselves when vindicating the need for such emancipation and liberation. Anthony Kwame Appiah, for example, distinguishes postcolonial from postmodern theory:

> Postcoloniality, [...] and its *post*, like postmodernism's, is also a post that challenges earlier legitimating narratives. And it challenges them in the name of the suffering victims. [...] But it challenges them in the name of the ethical universal; in the name of humanism, 'la gloire pour l'homme.' And on that ground it is not an ally for Western postmodernism but an agonist.
>
> (1995, 123)

The major point of this chapter is not that of rejecting the postcolonial critique of my democratic conception of global distributive justice but rather to further develop this conception in light of the insights that can be gained from a critical analysis of this critique. Following this brief contextualization of the Western parochialism objection within postcolonial theory, I will now lay out several reasons as to why I have found that whichever value it may still have, this objection ultimately fails to undermine my democratic conception of global justice.

My first response to the Western parochialism objection is that the mere fact that the principles of global democratic justice which emerged in Western contexts does not render them inapplicable within non-Western contexts. This is because the principles that have emerged in the West should not be regarded as principles that are constitutive of the (entire) West, since they are contested within the West itself. Therefore it is inadequate to hold that they should not apply to non-Western contexts simply because they represent principles with a Western origin.

One way in which to view more clearly this characterization of so-called Western principles is to observe that, even within the West, democratic principles do not emerge all of a sudden and are then generally recognized by all within the West. Instead, democratic principles arise within particular social constellations of the West before they then eventually "travel" throughout the West and find some adherents. But even if the normative principles of democratic justice eventually found the support of a considerably large share of the Western population, they would still continue to be contested by a good number of those who belong to the West themselves.

This indicates that it is inadequate to believe that the principles of my conception of democratic justice represent the empirically valid normative principles of justice in the West. A contrary point of view implies endorsing an excessively simplistic picture of Western culture and perhaps even of culture in general, according to which all members of a culture endorsed the same normative beliefs.[8] So it is too simple to regard principles of democratic justice as principles that effectively govern Western societies and which therefore must not be applied to non-Western contexts.

My second response argues that it is questionable on empirical grounds that the basic ideas of democratic justice pertain exclusively to the West. Hence it is a problematic stance to infer that democratic standards would be foreign or misplaced whenever they are applied outside the West. But it is true, nevertheless, that particularly in the East Asian context, it seems rather difficult to identify ideas of democratic justice within the political culture. Instead, it has become widely believed that Confucianism puts special emphasis on hierarchy and collective order rather than equal participation in decision-making. Samuel Huntington (1996, 238), for one, argues that the "Confucian heritage, with its emphasis on authority, order, hierarchy, and supremacy of the collectivity over the individual, creates obstacles to democratization." As A. T. Nuyen explains in a further manner, the incompatibility between Confucianism and democracy seems to be founded on ideas such as that "Confucian society is like a family and there is no place for [democratic] rights in a family" and that "Confucian values of unity and harmony conflict with the democratic values of plurality and choice" (2000, 135, 136).

There are several scholars, however, who believe that Huntington's analysis is exaggerated. Fukuyama, for example, maintains that Huntington's points "overstate the obstacles that Confucianism poses to the spread of a political system that is recognizably democratic in a Western sense" (1995, 25). Fukuyama argues instead that "Chinese Confucianism [...] does not legitimate deference to the authority of an all-powerful state that leaves no scope for the development of an independent civil society" (1995, 28).

There are scholars of Chinese political culture such as Keqian Xu who furthermore suggest that even "Confucian principles [...] are not only compatible with the value and idea of modern democracy, providing certain foundations for it, but will also possibly support the construction of a modern democratic system with Chinese features" (2006, 137). In addition, Xu asserts in his analysis of *Mencius*, one of the pre-Qin Confucian classics, that according to this writing, the source of political authority is claimed to be located in the people themselves. In a dialogue between Mencius and his student Wan Zhang, the question then arises as to how the Emperors Yao and Shun could have transmitted political authority. Xu points out that Mencius claims that the "Emperor cannot give the Empire to another by his own will, only Heaven and the people can give it to someone" (2006, 138). In his further elaboration of this case, Mencius (*Mencius*, 5A, 5) goes on to say that "Heaven sees with the eyes of its people; Heaven hears with the ears of its people."

Xu also highlights moreover another passage in which Mencius (7B, 14) places the people over the "*she ji*," which is a term which stands for the state, "The people are of supreme importance; the '*she ji*' come next; last comes the ruler" (2006, 139). Based on such reasoning, Xu maintains that "according to Mencius, the people are the ultimate origin of political power. Only the political power that has accountably come from the people may be considered legitimate" (2006, 139–140).

Nuyen also emphasizes in a similar manner that "there are passages in the *Mencius* in which it is stated that the people are important and the ruler is unimportant" (2000, 141). He buttresses this point by mentioning another important passage in which Mencius (5B, 9) addresses the question of civil disobedience: "if the ruler made serious mistakes, they would remonstrate with him, but if repeated remonstration fell on deaf ears, they would depose him." Daniel Bell also makes a similar claim when he argues that, in Imperial China, Confucianism was known for "encouraging disobedience and fostering a critical perspective vis-à-vis the state. Far from justifying blind adherence to the political status quo, Confucian values often provided the intellectual resources for social critics" (1999, 463).

In light of these democratic ideas within Confucian political thought, it should not come as a surprise that a number of scholars (cf. Hall and Ames 1999; Tan 2004; Ackerly 2005) have already explored in considerable length the possibility of developing a Confucian-style democracy. So East Asian political thought has become familiar with the idea of solving disagreements democratically. Hence it is inadequate to maintain that defending democratic ideas and building a theory of global distributive justice on their basis would be necessarily Western-centric and parochial. And so the basic idea of my democratic conception of global justice, which is that disagreements regarding the determination of the type of conception of global distributive justice which is the most just should be solved democratically, nevertheless requires a substantive defense by philosophical argument. But that is the case in the Western context just as much as it is the case in non-Western contexts like the East Asian one.

To conclude my analysis of the Western parochialism objection, let us consider yet another way of replying to the postcolonial critique, which consists of pointing toward the theory of multiple modernities. According to this theory, the social, economic, and political conditions found in non-Western societies are *not* fundamentally different from those found in Western societies (cf. Chakrabarty 2000; Eisenstadt 2000; Taylor 2002). In fact it is a central insight of the theory of multiple modernities that the idea of a uniform type of modernity that would characterize all societies throughout the world is flawed. So at first sight, one might think that the theory of multiple modernities could be employed in order to mount a critique of the idea of a universal conception of democratic justice. Such a critique would postulate that, since there are *multiple* processes of modernization, it is inadequate to assume that just one single conception of democratic justice is valid within all societies. And since the modernization processes in Western countries differ markedly from those in non-Western countries, it is especially misguided to employ a "Western" conception of democratic justice in non-Western societies (cf., e.g., Pollock et al. 2000).

The theory of multiple modernities itself is founded, however, on the notion that there are certain *core processes of modernization* which are shared throughout all societies, even though these processes unfold along different lines. The theory of multiple modernities remains a theory of modernization and does not give up the idea that there are certain patterns of social transformation that are shared across all societies which justify believing that the defining characteristics of contemporary societies can be properly deemed "modern" although they are modern in many different ways.

And perhaps most importantly, nearly the entire territory of the earth is spanned by states, which implies a distinctive way of organizing their social relations. These states rely on the monopoly of the use of coercion within a specifically demarcated territory, ascribe subjective legal rights to their citizens, and they use independent courts to guarantee – or, rather, to attempt to guarantee – the realization of these rights. Another key aspect of these modern core processes is the intensification of the pluralism of ways of life through the processes of globalization. Of course these processes are not recent phenomena that are causally responsible for the breaking up of homogeneous cultures and ways of life. Culturally homogeneous ways of life have in fact never existed, at least not for long stretches of time (cf. Waldron 2003). What processes of globalization supplement is the acceleration and deepening of the social pluralism (cf. Rosa 2013). This is because transnationalization or globalization deepens and multiplies exchanges across cultures and contributes thereby to their diversification. And so to the extent that there are these shared features across all societies around the globe, it need not therefore be implausible to maintain that there is a single standard of democratic justice applying to all of them.

This is especially the case given that this standard of democratic justice is highly flexible. This is because this conception allows and permits a lasting disagreement about what distributive justice requires and argues on this basis that democratic decision-making processes need to be available to facilitate the context-specific justification and implementation of public policies. My conception of democratic justice is therefore compatible with the idea that different public policies have to be pursued in the Western and the non-Western contexts. Thus even if modernity takes on very different shapes within different parts of the world, it does not imply that my conception of democratic justice is necessarily inadequate within the non-Western contexts.

Conclusion

This chapter has undertaken the task of examining a postcolonial critique of a distinctively democratic conception of global distributive justice by considering whether this conception is parochial or Western-centric. It started out by situating this democratic conception of global distributive justice within the current debate between the statist and globalist theorists about global justice, as well as by explaining the basic, political ideas of such a democratic conception. Following this, I have argued that the criticism of Western parochialism that tried to juxtapose itself against my global conception of democratic justice is in fact ill-founded. That criticism does not take into account that it does not hold true that democratic ideas can only be found in the history and present of Western political thought. As I explained in the previous section, there is a substantial amount of scholarship on East Asian philosophers that has already uncovered the existence of democratic ideas within the Confucian political context. Additionally I have maintained that it is problematic to regard democratic ideas as being exclusively Western, because these ideas are not shared equally among all those who belong to the West. In light of this fact, it is merely too simple to regard them as pertaining exclusively to the Western domain. Finally I concluded my discussion of the parochialism objection by referring to the theory of multiple modernities. Thereby I supported the idea that it is not altogether implausible to put forward a universal conception of democratic justice in a world that is shaped by certain core processes of modernization. To that effect, I also highlighted the context-sensitivity of my democratic conception of distributive justice, which not only permits but requires that, in differing social contexts, political actors justify different kinds of distributive principles.[9]

Notes

1 Here I am relying implicitly on a method of justification that is congenial to that which Rawls has dubbed a "wide" understanding of the method of reflective equilibrium. Wide reflective equilibrium requires more than just identifying a conception of justice that coheres with one's pre-theoretical and well-considered judgments about its practical implications and its underlying rationale. A wide reflective equilibrium requires us to expose the basic normative ideas of a conception of justice to the opposing ideas and arguments of alternative conceptions of justice (Rawls 1971, §9; 2001, §10.3).
2 Cf. also Mathias Risse, who states that '[w]e live on a "cosmopolitan plateau"' (2012, 10).
3 Moellendorf (2009, ch. 3) has recently taken up a noticeably more context-sensitive position. He argues now that in light of the type of association for which principles of justice are sought, subject-specific contents of justice have to be justified in conjunction with a context-insensitive, egalitarian distributive presumption.
4 Cf. Habermas (2008, 334) for his proposal for a transnational negotiation system among states.
5 The first half of this section is adapted from Culp (2019, ch. 7, sections 1–3).
6 More specifically, by reference to the work of *Robinson Crusoe*, Tiffin (1995, 98) argues that the study of "a canonical text at the colonial periphery also becomes an important part of material imperial practice, in that, through educational [...] institutions, it continually displays and repeats for the colonized subject [...] the processes of its annihilation, marginalization, or naturalization as if this were axiomatic, culturally ungrounded, 'universal', natural."
7 In a similar vein, Achebe (1995, 59) argues as follows, "In the nature of things the work of a Western writer is automatically informed by universality. It is only others who must strain to achieve it. As though universality were some distant bend in the road which you may take if you travel out far enough in the direction of Europe or America, if you put adequate distance between yourself and your home."
8 Adopting Michael Walzer's reconstructive interpretive method to educational philosophy, Amy Gutmann (1987) regards democratic education as constitutive of the US-American self-understanding. However, it is certainly not implausible to argue that economic efficiency is the distinctive normative ideal of the US-American society, which is an example that shows that normative educational principles are contested within the West itself.
9 Earlier versions of this chapter were presented at international conferences at the Justus-Liebig-Universität in Gießen, Germany, and the Sun Yat-sen University, China. I would like to thank the hosts of these events, Regina Kreide and Jeanette Ehrmann as well as Hugo El Kholi and Jun-Hyeok Kwak, respectively, for their hospitality and their acute comments. In Gießen, I also benefitted from the incisive comments of Katharina Kaufmann.

References

Abizadeh, Arash. 2007. "Cooperation, Pervasive Impact, and Coercion, On the Scope (Not Site) of Distributive Justice." *Philosophy & Public Affairs* 35 (4), 318–358.

Achebe, Chinua. 1995. "Colonialist Criticism." In Ashcroft, Bill, Gareth Griffiths and Helen Tiffin (eds.), *The Post-Colonial Reader*. London: Routledge, 57–61.

Ackerly, Brooke. 2005. "Is Liberalism the Only Way toward Democracy? Confucianism and Democracy." *Political Theory* 33 (4), 547–576.

Andreotti, Vanessa de Sousa and Lynn Mario de Souza (eds.) *Postcolonial Perspectives on Global Citizenship Education*. London: Routledge.

Appiah, Kwame Anthony. 1995. "The Postcolonial and the Postmodern." In Ashcroft, Bill, Gareth Griffiths and Helen Tiffin (eds.), *The Post-Colonial Studies Reader*. London: Routledge, 119–124.

Ashcroft, Bill, Gareth Griffiths and Helen Tiffin. 1995a. "Part II, Universality and Difference. Introduction." In *The Post-Colonial Studies Reader*. London: Routledge, 55–56.

Beitz, Charles. 1983. "Cosmopolitan Ideals and National Sentiment." *The Journal of Philosophy* 80, 591–600.

Beitz, Charles. 1999a [1979]. *Political Theory and International Relations*. 2nd ed. Princeton, NJ: Princeton University Press.

Beitz, Charles. 1999b. Social and Cosmopolitan Liberalism. *International Affairs* 75 (3), 515–529.

Bell, Daniel. 1999. "Democracy with Chinese Characteristics, A Political Proposal for the Post-Communist Era." *Philosophy East and West* 49, 451–491.

Blake, Michael. 2001. "Distributive Justice, State Coercion, and Autonomy." *Philosophy & Public Affairs* 30 (3), 257–296.

Caney, Simon. 2005. *Justice Beyond Borders*. Oxford: Oxford University Press.

Chakrabarty, Dipesh. 2000. *Provincializing Europe, Postcolonial Thought and Historical Difference*. Princeton, NJ: Princeton University Press.

Christiano, Thomas. 2010. "Democratic Legitimacy and International Institutions." In Besson, Samantha and John Tasioulas (eds.), *The Philosophy of International Law*. Oxford: Oxford University Press, 119–137.

Culp, Julian. 2014. *Global Justice and Development*. Basingstoke: Palgrave Macmillan.

Culp, Julian. 2019. *Democratic Education in a Globalized World*. London: Routledge.

Docker, John. 1995. "The Neocolonial Assumption in University Teaching of English." In Ashcroft, Bill, Gareth Griffiths and Helen Tiffin (eds.), *The Post-Colonial Studies Reader*. London: Routledge, 443–446.

Dworkin, Ronald. 2000. *Sovereign Virtue*. Cambridge, MA: Harvard University Press.

Eisenstadt, Shmuel N. 2000. "Multiple Modernities." *Daedalus* 129 (1), 1–29.

Escobar, Arturo. 2012. *Encountering Development*. Princeton, NJ: Princeton University Press.

Flikschuh, Katrin. 2014. "The Idea of Philosophical Fieldwork, Global Justice, Moral Ignorance and Intellectual Attitudes." *The Journal of Political Philosophy* 22 (1), 1–26.

Forst, Rainer. 2007a. "First Things First – Redistribution, Recognition and Justification." *European Journal of Political Theory* 6 (3), 291–304.

Forst, Rainer. 2007b. "Radical Justice – On Iris Young's Critique of the Distributive Paradigm." *Constellations* 14 (2), 260–265.

Forst, Rainer. 2011. "Transnational Justice and Democracy." *The Formation of Normative Orders Working Papers* 4, 1–18.

Forst, Rainer. 2012. *The Right to Justification – Elements of a Constructivist Theory of Justice.* New York: Columbia University Press.

Forst, Rainer. 2014. *Justification and Critique.* Cambridge: Polity Press.

Freeman, Samuel. 2007. "The *Law of Peoples*, Social Cooperation, Human Rights and Distributive Justice." In *Essays in Rawlsian Political Philosophy.* New York: Oxford University Press, 259–295.

Fukuyama, Francis. 1995. "Confucianism and Democracy." *Journal of Democracy* 6, 20–33.

Gutmann, Amy. 1987. *Democratic Education.* Princeton, NJ: Princeton University Press.

Habermas, Jürgen. 2008. "Secularism's Crisis of Faith: Notes on a Post-Secular Society." *New Perspectives Quarterly* 25 (4), 17–29.

Hall, David and Roger Ames. 1999. *The Democracy of the Dead, Dewey, Confucius, and the Hope for Democracy in China.* Chicago, IL: Open Court.

Huntington, Samuel. 1996. *The Clash of Civilizations and the Remaking of World Order.* New York: Simon & Schuster.

Kerner, Ina. 2012. *Postkoloniale Theorie zur Einführung.* Hamburg: Junius.

Mencius. 2003. *Mencius.* Translated by D.C. Lau. Hong Kong: The Chinese University Press.

Mignolo, Walter and Arturo Escobar. 2010. *Globalization and the Decolonial Option.* London: Routledge.

Moellendorf, Darrel. 2002. *Cosmopolitan Justice.* Boulder, CO: Westview Press.

Moellendorf, Darrel. 2009. *Global Inequality Matters.* Basingstoke and New York: Palgrave Macmillan.

Nagel, Thomas. 2005. "The Problem of Global Justice." *Philosophy & Public Affairs* 33 (2), 113–147.

Nuyen, A.T. 2000. "Confucianism, the Idea of *Min-pen*, and Democracy," *Copenhagen Journal of Asian Studies* 14, 130–151.

Okeja, Uchenna. 2017. "Introduction, Globalizing or Transcending Global Justice." *Philosophical Papers* 46 (1), 1–11.

Pettit, Philip. 2010. "A Republican Law of Peoples." *European Journal of Political Theory* 9, 70–94.

Pogge, Thomas. 1989. *Realizing Rawls.* Ithaca, NY: Cornell University Press.

Pogge, Thomas. 2010. "A Critique of the Capability Approach." In, Brighouse, Harry and Ingrid Robeyns (eds.), *Measuring Justice.* Cambridge: Cambridge University Press, 17–60.

Pollock, Sheldon, Homi Bhabha, Carol Breckenridge, and Dipesh Chakrabarty. 2000. "Cosmopolitanisms." *Public Culture* 12(3), 577–589.

Rawls, John. 1971. *A Theory of Justice.* Cambridge, MA: Harvard University Press.

Rawls, John. 2001. *Justice as Fairness.* Ed. Erin Parish. Cambridge, MA: Harvard University Press.

Risse, Mathias. 2012. *On Global Justice.* Princeton, NJ: Princeton University Press.

Rosa, Hartmut. 2013. *Social Acceleration.* New York: Columbia University Press.

Said, Edward. "Orientalism." In Ashcroft, Bill, Gareth Griffiths and Helen Tiffin (eds.), *The Post-Colonial Studies Reader.* London: Routledge, 87–91.

Sangiovanni, Andrea. 2007. "Global Justice, Reciprocity, and the State." *Philosophy & Public Affairs* 35 (1), 3–39.

Sen, Amartya. 1997 [1980]. *Choice, Welfare and Measurement*. Cambridge, MA: Harvard University Press, 353–372.

Tan, Sor-hoon. 2004. *Confucian Democracy, A Deweyan Reconstruction*. Albany: State University of New York Press.

Tan, Kok-Chor. 2004. *Justice Without Borders. Cosmopolitanism, Nationalism and Patriotism*. Cambridge: Cambridge University Press.

Taylor, Charles. 2002. "Modern Social Imaginaries." *Public Culture* 14 (1), 91–124.

Thiong'o, Ngugi wa. 1995. "On the Abolition of the English Department." In Ashcroft, Bill, Gareth Griffiths and Helen Tiffin (eds.), *The Post-Colonial Studies Reader*. London: Routledge, 438–442.

Tiffin, Helen. 1995. "Post-Colonial Literatures and Counter-Discourse." In Ashcroft, Bill, Gareth Griffiths and Helen Tiffin (eds.), *The Post-Colonial Studies Reader*. London: Routledge, 95–98.

Waldron, Jeremy. 2003. "Teaching Cosmopolitan Right." In Feinberg, Walter and Kevin McDonough (eds.), *Citizenship and Education in Liberal-Democratic Societies. Teaching for Cosmopolitan Values and Collective Identities*. Oxford: Oxford University Press, 23–55.

Williams, Melissa and Mark Warren. 2014. "A Democratic Case for Comparative Political Theory." *Political Theory* 42 (1), 26–57.

Xu, Keqian. 2006. "Early Confucian Principles, the Potential Theoretic Foundation of Democracy in Modern China." *Asian Philosophy* 16 (2), 135–148.

Young, Iris. 1990. *Justice and the Politics of Difference*. Princeton, NJ: Princeton University Press.

3 Are political conceptions of global justice parochial?

Hugo El Kholi

Introduction

Accusations of "parochialism" and "Western-centrism" have recently surfaced in the global justice debate (e.g., Maffettone and Rathore 2012; Metz 2014; Graness 2015; Williams and Death 2016; Chimakonam 2017; Flikschuh 2017, 2018; Masaka 2017; Shapcott 2017). For those who have followed the debate since its inception, these accusations are reminiscent of the criticisms formulated in the 1990s against early forms of cosmopolitan liberalism. The main grievance at the time was that the liberal tradition, being essentially Western, could not realize its cosmopolitan ambition without encroaching upon the fundamental rights of non-liberal societies to be "true to their traditions" and to "preserve their ways of life" (Parekh 1992, 170).

For long, the liberal reply only consisted in pointing out that, from a purely theoretical standpoint, there is no incompatibility between the cultural and historical origins of liberalism and its claim to universal validity (e.g., Tan 2000, 194–202). As Charles Beitz, the forefather of contemporary cosmopolitan liberalism, had pointed out in anticipation of potential criticisms, it is in fact one of the main specificities of liberalism to be internally geared toward universal expansion. Liberal political theorists are simply "compelled to take a global view in matters of social justice by features internal to [their] conceptions of moral personality, however parochial it may be" (Beitz 1983, 596).

This reply has been perceived by the critics of cosmopolitan liberalism as a form of self-justification rather than a genuine effort to address their concerns. As such, it could only reinforce their impression that, despite its emphasis on the notion of toleration, cosmopolitan liberalism remains a Western-centric approach insensitive to the diversity of worldviews. Unfortunately, the dialogue between Western liberal thinkers and their critics did not go beyond this initial exchange. Throughout the 2000s, the liberal view continued to dominate, unchallenged, the academic debate on global justice and to guide its development toward congenial themes, such as the much-discussed opposition, internal to the liberal tradition, between cosmopolitanism and statism. It is only in the last decade, with the contribution of postcolonial thinkers, that the concern which underpinned the early criticism of cosmopolitanism re-emerged in a slightly different and more virulent form. Through their work, which analyzes the domination mechanisms at work during the colonial period, those thinkers attracted the attention of the participants in the debate on the political implications of epistemic forms of domination comparable to what a global expansion of cosmopolitan liberalism would entail (e.g., Rao 2012; Kohn 2013; Bell 2019).

It is well known that, during the colonial period, the universalizing dimension of Western culture and philosophy was presented as a sign of intellectual superiority justifying colonialism (cf. Culp in Chapter 2). Somewhat less appreciated is the key role that the celebration of Western universalism played in delegitimizing local forms of discourse and, thereby, in establishing a form of epistemic domination which prevented the emergence of political dissent within colonized societies. In the light of this historical precedent, one better understands why theories such as cosmopolitan liberalism, which openly states its ambition to universalize an essentially Western tradition of thought, arouses the suspicion of decolonized peoples and more broadly of all those who have a sensitive understanding of colonial history. The failure of liberal political thinkers to appreciate this phenomenon explains why a genuinely global debate about global justice has never really been initiated and why the very concept of global justice has come to be seen by many non-Western scholars as a "metaphor for European superiority and power" (Kohn 2013, 187).

This situation is all the more unfortunate in that the liberal tradition has more to offer than the cosmopolitan theories developed by the first generation of global Rawlsian constructivists (Beitz 1979, 1983; Pogge 1989, 1992; Moellendorf 1996, 2002; Barry 1998). As early as the 1990s, Rawls's "political turn" provided liberal political theorists with new conceptual tools enabling them to address the problem of global justice from a non-cosmopolitan perspective. The exact nature and various implications of that turn have been studied extensively and are well known from students of political theory (e.g., Freeman 2007; Weithman 2010). For our purpose, it is sufficient to recall that Rawls's political turn, which is usually presented as an attempt to ensure the stability of his conception of justice, is underpinned by an epistemic turn in his approach to political justification. Setting aside his original conception of political objectivity in terms of rational truth, Rawls develops in *Political Liberalism* a distinctively practical account in which objectivity no longer sanctions the truth of a specific conception but is understood, rather, for its capacity to gain support from reasonable agents holding diverging comprehensive doctrines (*PL*, 44).[1] Objectivity, in this account, denotes the quality of a principle supported by an "overlapping consensus" of comprehensive doctrines about a certain conception of justice recognized by all as reasonable. The notion of truth is thus set aside in favor of the notion of "reasonableness," which becomes the only suitable criterion for fixing the objectivity of political principles (*PL*, 89–125; *CP*, 356). From that perspective, "to say that a political conviction is objective is to say that there are reasons, specified by a reasonable and mutually recognizable political conception [...], sufficient to convince all reasonable persons that it is reasonable" (*PL*, 119).

This epistemic turn has deep consequences for the nature and scope of political justification. The idea of reasonableness, as opposed to the concept of truth, does not provide an epistemic basis on which to build a theory of justice that could claim universal validity. It only provides a public foundation for the justification of political principles in the context of Western liberal-democratic societies. The substitution of truth by reasonableness implies, in other words, that instead of thinking of the principles of justice as "true," we conceive of them as "the principles most reasonable for us, given our conception of persons as free and equal, and full cooperating members of a democratic society" (*CP*, 340). Political principles are no longer objective in the sense of holding absolutely, irrespective of circumstances; their scope is limited to people holding the same epistemic standard of reasoning and the same basic conceptions of the person and society.

It is this specifically "political" approach that Rawls applied to the problem of global justice in *The Law of Peoples*. As many have noted, his intention in this short treatise was not to develop a cosmopolitan conception of justice that could potentially be shared by everyone around the world, but only to formulate the most appropriate principles to guide "the foreign policy of a reasonably just liberal people" (*LP*, 10 and 83). The Law of Peoples, which comprises these principles, is thus heavily dependent, both in its scope and its content, upon the distinctive epistemic commitment underpinning the political approach. Rawls's rejection of global egalitarianism, in particular, which initially created confusion among his most dedicated supporters, has been shown to result from his commitment to a practical conception of objectivity (Freeman 2006; Martin and Reidy 2006; Wenar 2016). These clarifications on the epistemic underpinnings of *The Law of Peoples* opened a new, more positive phase in the reception of Rawls's work. Even if they do not necessarily share all of his substantive conclusions, several leading liberal thinkers are now firmly convinced of the justificatory virtues of the political approach to justice. They consider that relying on a principle of public justification, such as "reasonableness" or "decency," is the most suitable approach to the problem of global justice and, more specifically, to the problem posed by global pluralism to political justification (e.g., James 2012; Porter 2012; Kaufman 2013; Nussbaum 2015; Wenar 2016). Even those who take accusations of parochialism and Western-centrism seriously, such as Katrin Flikschuh, concede that the political reformulation of liberalism is "the historically most reflective theoretical statement of liberal political morality currently available to us" and "our best available candidate for action-guiding liberal theorizing" (Flikschuh 2018, 10).

The great appeal that the political approach holds for liberal political theorists lies in the protection that a practical conception of objectivity provides against accusations of parochialism and Western-centrism. In contrast with their comprehensive counterparts, political conceptions of global justice cannot be blamed for aspiring to formulate universally valid principles of justice. Their purpose, as Rawls himself made clear, is only to identify principles that can be upheld in common by persons sharing the same epistemic standard of reasoning and the same basic conceptions of the person and society. This specificity explains why Rawls's approach is also very influential among East Asian political theorists, who see it as a more acceptable version of Western liberalism, less evidently tainted by imperialist tendencies. In a laudable effort to engage with this approach, several of them are thus currently occupied with assessing whether *The Law of Peoples* is compatible with the Three Teachings and whether some form of cross-fertilization is desirable (e.g., Bai 2015; Huang 2016; Tong 2017; or Wang in Chapter 8).

One can only welcome this collective effort, but it is surprising that none of the scholars in question has taken the time, before engaging in this work, to wonder whether there are good epistemic reasons for non-Western political actors to endorse a political conception of justice in the first place. As political theorists, they have an obvious academic interest in critically engaging with what their Western colleagues present as the most suitable approach to the problem of global justice. But what could possibly motivate non-academic actors who do not share in Western liberal political culture to uphold a distinctively political conception of global justice? The question here is not so much whether they can be convinced to endorse such a conception but rather whether the reasons they might do so are fully intelligible in the light of their own epistemic and metaphysical beliefs. The question, in other words, is whether they can become rationally motivated to uphold a political conception of justice without having to convert, in the process, to exogenous epistemic and metaphysical beliefs. For such is the true criterion of parochialism, if we understand parochialism as denoting the pretention of certain theories of global justice to universalize a culturally and historically situated worldview and impose it on others without consideration for their traditional systems of beliefs.

This chapter addresses this neglected question by taking a closer look at the account of motivation underpinning the political approach to justice, as originally formulated by Rawls. In the section "Political liberalism and the motivational basis of reasonable action," I start by critically reviewing the conventional Kantian interpretations of the Rawlsian notion of reasonableness and their implications for the question of motivation. In the section "Rawls and Kant on the motivational structure of practical agency," I go beyond these interpretations by resituating the question of motivation within the broader framework of Rawls's theory of political agency and by evaluating its degree of dependence on Kant's theory of moral agency. I conclude that political conceptions of justice are epistemically parochial because endorsing them implies subscribing to certain meta-ethical beliefs that are distinctively Kantian. This claim must be distinguished from the view, already expressed in the literature, that political conceptions of justice are parochial because those who endorse them must share certain historically and culturally situated conceptions of the person and society (e.g., O'Neill 1997). In my view, what makes a political conception parochial is not so much this substantive requirement as the epistemic requirement to share the meta-ethical beliefs necessary to a typically Kantian form of morality.

Political liberalism and the motivational basis of reasonable action

The literature contains a long series of criticisms questioning whether Rawls's practical recasting of political objectivity, independently from the notion of moral truth, is epistemically consistent. Perhaps the most influential among these were the respective criticisms of Joseph Raz and Jürgen Habermas, who both question the rationale behind an approach that seems to elevate the practical concern for political stability above the traditional epistemic requirement of giving our understanding of justice a deep moral foundation (Raz 1990, 8; Habermas 1995, 128). In what follows, I take a different and largely unexplored critical route by focusing instead on the theory of practical agency underpinning political liberalism. My intention is to question, more specifically, Rawls's account of the type of motivation that reasonable citizens must have to uphold a political conception of justice.

Let me take as a starting point for this questioning a marginal remark made by Bernard Williams in his celebrated essay on political realism (2005). In the introduction of this short piece, Williams briefly reflects upon Rawls's claim that political liberalism is not supported by a mere *modus vivendi* but rather by an "overlapping consensus" achieved among reasonable persons endowed with a sense of justice enabling them to submit the pursuit of their own conception of the good to the limits fixed by a shared conception of justice. This sense of justice is defined by Rawls as a "basic moral power" enabling persons not only to "understand" and "apply" the principles of justice, but also (and perhaps more importantly) to "act from" them (*PL*, 104–105). Based on this definition, clearly reminiscent of the Kantian distinction between acting "in conformity with duty [*pflichtmäßig*]" and acting "from duty [*aus Pflicht*]" (*G*, IV: 397–398; *KpV*, V: 81), Williams understands that the capacity of the Rawlsian person for a "sense of justice" involves a moral desire to "act from" the principles of justice in the same way as the accessibility of the Kantian subject to a "moral sense [*moralisches Gefühl*]" (*MS*, VI: 387) involves a certain responsiveness to the purely rational incentive to "act from" the moral law (*G*, IV: 406).[2] If that is correct, then it seems that political liberalism, which depends entirely on the possibility of an appeal to the sense of justice in question, features "the continuation of a (Kantian) morality as the framework of the system" (Williams 2005, 2).

In what follows, I critically assess this reading, which has the disturbing consequence of calling into question the aspiration of political liberalism to establish the autonomy of the political sphere. Remember that, in order to ensure the freestanding nature of his conception of justice, Rawls introduces a distinction between moral and political autonomy. In contrast to moral autonomy, which is a comprehensive notion covering all aspects of practical life, he defines political autonomy as the capacity of citizens to freely determine their public conduct based on certain principles that they give to themselves through a procedure of ideal reflection. Rawls is perfectly aware that, for this distinction to be philosophically meaningful, the "full autonomy of political life must be distinguished from the ethical values of autonomy and individuality [...] as expressed by the comprehensive liberalisms of Kant and Mill" (*PL*, 78). This implies supplementing political liberalism with a thoroughgoing theory of political agency capable of accounting for the motivation of reasonable citizens to uphold a political conception of justice independently from any reference to the notion of moral autonomy. In the absence of such an account, the concept of a strictly political conception of justice remains a pure chimera.

To prove the existence of a capacity for political autonomy in reasonable citizens, Rawls must explain why citizens acknowledge the obligation to comply with the principles of justice they give to themselves by following the procedure of ideal reflection – namely, the original position. But it is difficult to see how this can be done within a constructivist framework without at some point in the explanation entering metaphysical territory and conceding that the concept of autonomy expresses a form of "absolute spontaneity" akin to Kant's concept of "transcendental freedom" (*KrV*, A533/B561). Kant himself was perfectly aware of the difficulty in accounting for the motivation of free agents in general to comply with the demands of morality. While accounting for moral obligation requires positing that reason can be immediately practical (and thereby legitimating a practical use of the idea of freedom), accounting for moral motivation further entails getting to the bottom of the idea of freedom and proving its reality as an essential quality of human rational will. However, Kant himself doubts whether it lies within the power of human reason to take this latter step and explain how pure reason can be practical in and of itself, that is, how the categorical imperative (or any other procedure of ideal reflection for that matter) can yield a purely moral incentive capable of motivating human action. Kant describes the search for this explanation as the quest for "the philosopher's stone" (*LE*, XXVII: 1428), and it is precisely to avoid embroiling himself in that endless quest that Rawls endeavored to make justice as fairness freestanding.

In the light of these preliminary remarks, it seems obvious that the question of the motivation of actors will constitute a major difficulty for the cogency of Rawls's political approach to justice. Surprisingly, however, the question of the motivational basis of reasonable action is rarely discussed for itself in the Rawlsian literature. The few mentions that can be found emerge as a by-product of discussions primarily focused on the epistemic status of reasonableness. To better grasp how such discussions can move from epistemic considerations to the motivational question, let us consider a typical exchange between Gerald Gaus and Enzo Rossi, two of the leading scholars on "public reason liberalism."[3]

Shortly after the publication of *Political Liberalism*, Gaus argued that, contrary to Rawls's claim, reasonable citizens, insofar as they are rational, remain "committed to evaluating the rationality of the beliefs of others when these beliefs are appealed to in public justifications" (Gaus 1995, 257). They simply cannot bracket off their epistemic beliefs during public deliberation, because commitment to these beliefs is what makes them rational in the first place. They cannot function as rational actors engaged in deliberation about matters of justice independently of their rational epistemic beliefs. This is a problem, because through their reliance on these beliefs "controversial epistemological evaluations [...] re-enter public justification, and in so doing undermine the justificatory project of political liberalism" (Gaus 1995, 257). Hence Gaus's claim that political liberalism takes an epistemically self-defeating stance: by asking citizens to prioritize something they do not necessarily consider true over what they do take to be true, it violates the most basic epistemic requirement of rationality. Calling attention to this violation amounts to calling into question the possibility of creating an independent standard of justification by dissociating the reasonable from the rational.

Rossi replied that Gaus's criticism fails to recognize the distinct, non-epistemic motivational force encapsulated in the ideal of reasonableness. In Rossi's interpretation, this ideal does not require that reasonable citizens engage in an epistemic assessment of the truth value of publicly stated reasons, but only that they establish a hierarchy between the normative commitments derived from their comprehensive doctrines and the "substantive liberal normative commitments [...] embedded in the idea of reasonableness" (Rossi 2014, 15). Reasonable citizens, in other words, are "expected to have a (moral) motivation to forsake their preferred political framework in favor of one which others can also reasonably be expected to endorse in virtue of their commitment to a shared ideal of reasonableness" (Rossi 2014, 15).

In trying to save political liberalism from the internal contradiction pointed out by Gaus, Rossi thus displaces the problem from the epistemic domain to the question of motivation. This rhetorical move may do more harm than good, however, by putting the onus on the advocates of political liberalism to account for the motivation that reasonable citizens may have to prefer a publicly justified conception of justice to a conception more congenial to their comprehensive views. Rossi's own attempt to meet this challenge, which may be seen as an indirect response to William's remark, is worth quoting at length:

> the Rawlsian conception of public justification just demands that (reasonable) citizens form or possess a higher order—as it were—moral *belief* that, at least when deliberating about the basic structure of society,

> seeking fair terms of cooperation should take priority over pursuing the political arrangements that, *were they not committed to the ideals expressed by Rawlsian reasonableness*, it would be most rational for them to pursue in light of their comprehensive conception of the good. To use a familiar Kantian distinction, political liberalism's citizens are not required to act *from* the publicly justified reasons, but only *in accordance* with them; but they are required to act from the liberal commitment to seeking fair terms of cooperation. So in this sense the Rawlsian conception of public justification [...] just requires them to hold a belief according to which they will prioritise the pursuit of fair terms of cooperation over the pursuit of their own conception of the good.
>
> (Rossi 2014, 16, emphasis original)

The appeal to Kant in this passage is confusing for various reasons. Recall that, in Kant's theory of practical agency, agents do not act on "beliefs" or "reasons" but on maxims, which are subjective principles of action combining formal and material aspects. Whether a particular action is moral or not depends on which of the formal or material aspect of the subject's maxim serves as the determining ground of the will. When the subject is determined to act on accounts of the matter of his maxim (i.e., in consideration of the specific end pursued through it), he acts heteronomously, and his actions have no moral worth. In contrast, when the subject is determined to act on accounts of the form of his maxim (i.e., in consideration of the possibility that it becomes a universal law), he acts autonomously, and his actions are genuinely moral. The Kantian distinction on which Rossi relies in the above passage, between acting *from* duty and acting *in accordance* with duty, refers to the same fundamental distinction as to the determining ground of the will: acting from duty implies making duty itself the determining ground of the will, whereas acting in accordance with duty means that the will is determined by something other than duty itself, even if the action in question happens to be in line with what duty requires (*G*, III: 397). So when Rossi claims that reasonable citizens "are required to act *from* the liberal commitment to seeking fair terms of cooperation," what he means is that they act out of consideration for the liberal duty to seek fair terms of cooperation and not because they pursue the material ends of establishing a society functioning as a fair system of cooperation among equals.

The problem with that claim is that it commits the advocates of political liberalism to account for the incentive that citizens may have to comply with the liberal duty in question. It makes it incumbent upon political liberals to explain why citizens would be motivated by the mere thought of seeking fair terms of cooperation, independently of the consideration of any material end. Rossi seems to hold that the reasonable citizen's belief that he ought to do something is enough to motivate him to act on this belief. But Kant himself does not endorse such a strong form of moral internalism, according to which moral beliefs themselves motivate without the need for an accompanying desire. In his view, a belief must always be paired with an *incentive* if it is to produce an action (this aspect of Kant's doctrine is discussed at length in McCarty 1994 and Americks 2006, 89–107). Thus, in the case of a moral action, the principle that makes an action a duty by representing it as objectively necessary does not in itself motivate the subject to act. It is just a "theoretical cognition of a possible determination to act" (*MS*, VI: 218). The subject must also have an incentive connecting the theoretical cognition of his duty to a determining ground of the will. This incentive can be described in metaphysical terms either as the "fact of reason" (*KpV*, V: 47) or as the "feeling of respect for the law" (*KpV*, V: 76).

So what, in the end, are we to make of Rossi's attempt to interpret the Rawlsian notion of reasonableness in Kantian terms? Instead of clarifying the question of motivation (that he himself planted), his interpretation brings us back to the fundamental difficulty of accounting in non-metaphysical terms for the incentive behind reasonable behavior. Rossi may seek to avoid the charge by specifying that the duty to seek fair terms of cooperation (or the duty of civility) should be conceived as a legal duty rather than an ethical duty. After all, Kant himself distinguishes between wide (or perfect) ethical duties, which command the subject to achieve something, and narrow (or imperfect) legal duties, which command the subject to make something his end without necessarily having to achieve it (*MS*, VI: 391). The duty to seek (but not necessarily to attain) fair terms of cooperation among equals may be conceived along these lines as a narrow duty of Right toward others.

This line of defense does not work, however, insofar as the only reason Rossi's reasonable citizen is willing to act according to publicly justified reasons is that he acknowledges the duty to seek fair terms of cooperation as immediately authoritative. The citizen, in other words, does not simply bring his actions into conformity with publicly justified reasons in recognition of a legal obligation but makes respect for public justification the incentive for his actions. There is indeed a major difference between the mere conformity of one's actions with publicly justified reasons and the conformity of one's maxims of actions with the requirements of public justification. By bringing his maxims in line with the requirements of public justification, the reasonable citizen makes respect for the right of other citizens the motive of his actions and thereby widens his concept of duty beyond the concept of what is legally required. His willingness to comply with the requirements of public justification, to which Rossi appeals in the above passage, is thus a clear instance of what Kant calls "the universal ethical command [...] to act in conformity with duty *from* duty" (*MS,* VI: 391).

In the final analysis, the Kantian interpretation of the normative requirements associated with Rawlsian reasonableness raises more questions than it answers. Its shortcomings leave us with the impression that political liberalism lacks a coherent theory of practical agency capable of accounting for the motivational basis of reasonable action. In the next section, I evaluate the validity of this impression by determining the extent to which Rawls's theory of rational agency depends on Kant's theory of moral agency. My aim is to determine, more particularly, whether Rawls's theory successfully emancipates itself from the Kantian notion of moral autonomy and its transcendental component.

Rawls and Kant on the motivational structure of practical agency

Central to political liberalism is the commitment to remain neutral with respect to the various metaphysical beliefs that reasonable citizens may hold. The two basic conceptions of the person and society on which the constructivist procedure relies are thus said to be drawn from the public political culture of Western democratic societies rather than from a determinate metaphysical doctrine. Several critics have objected, however, that the conception of the person integral to political liberalism incorporates a Kantian-inspired moral psychology that seems to be metaphysically loaded (Wenar 1995; Tiffany 2006). Leif Wenar argues along these lines that Rawls's account of human motivation, which ascribes "conception-dependent desires" to individuals, contradicts the freestanding nature of political liberalism and thereby also the possibility of an overlapping consensus supported by the greatest possible number of comprehensive doctrines (Wenar 1995, 48–51). As defined by Rawls, conception-dependent desires are desires to act on principles that contribute to the achievement of a certain reasonable ideal of life. Admitting such desires is ascribing to the person a particular motivational structure in which "the principles we desire to act from are seen as belonging to, and as helping to articulate, a certain rational or reasonable conception, or a political ideal" (*PL*, 83–84; see also *LHMP*, 47, n.3). This structure is distinctively teleological insofar as conception-dependent desires account for our desire to act on certain principles in terms of a second-order desire derived from (and triggered by) the first-order desire to bring about a certain reasonable ideal. Not all philosophical accounts of human motivation admit of such desires. Followers of Bentham, Hume, or Hobbes do not make conception-dependent desires an integral part of the structure of human motivation and, as Wenar rightly pointed out, would therefore reject political liberalism.

Wenar's objection has the merit of highlighting a feature of Rawls's theory rarely commented upon, namely its reliance on "the conception-dependent desire to act in ways worthy of a reasonable and equal citizen" (*PL*, 85, n.33).[4] A first reason to admit to this desire is the crucial role it plays in allowing for the transition from a mere *modus vivendi* to an overlapping consensus (Wenar 1995, 51). Political liberalism would indeed remain purely utopian if it were not supported by a convincing account of the "psychological forces" capable of bringing about an overlapping consensus and sustaining it in the long run (*PL*, 158). The conception-dependent desire in question contributes to both aspects, by accounting not only for citizens' endorsements of this political ideal, but also for their desire to work toward its achievement, that is, for their desire to act on principles identified as contributing to its realization. The latter aspect is all the more crucial because nothing in the political conception of the person ensures that, besides their formal capacity for justice, citizens are also motivated to act on just principles. Remember that, on that conception, citizens are endowed with two basic moral powers: a capacity for the good and a sense of justice. But if there is no difficulty in associating their capacity for the good with a corresponding desire to pursue the particular system of ends deemed valuable by their comprehensive view, we should refrain from associating their sense of justice with a first-order desire to act from the principles of justice. This would amount to denying the strictly political nature of political liberalism by incorporating into the conception of the citizen a substantive end resting on a metaphysical belief in the value of justice. The desire to comply with the principles of justice can only be gained indirectly, through the conception-dependent desire to achieve a certain ideal of reasonableness. This conception-dependent desire – the desire to act and be recognized as a reasonable person within society conceived as a system of fair cooperation among equals – triggers the further desire to act from the principles of justice, recognized as the principles best suiting this purpose. Since citizens, as part of their being rational, have a fundamental desire to achieve this reasonable ideal, they are prepared to act on the principles most appropriate to this end. A second-order desire to comply with the principles of justice (what Rawls calls a "principle-dependent desire") is thus ascribed to citizens in an indirect, *teleological* fashion, through a consideration of the first-order desire to fulfill a certain reasonable conception of the person or, more precisely, the particular political ideal corresponding to this conception of the person.

To further elucidate the teleological dimension of conception-dependent desires, let me emphasize that, even if the fundamental aspiration of reasonable citizens is not, properly speaking, to realize justice as fairness, but rather to live in accordance with their own nature as reasonable and free persons, it is nevertheless part of this fundamental aspiration that they desire to become active members of a society conceived as a system of fair cooperation among free and equal persons, simply because society so conceived is the political ideal correlative to their reasonable nature (*PL*, 94). Realizing this ideal implies conforming to certain principles specifying the terms of fair cooperation, principles that can only be formulated through a procedure of ideal reflection simulating an agreement between reasonable citizens under conditions of fairness. In Rawls's account, reasonable and free citizens fairly situated in the original position thus naturally select the two principles of justice as fairness as the most appropriate principles to regulate the social and political institutions under which they are to live with each other. These principles are, in Rawls's own words, "the principles most appropriate to specify the fair terms of social cooperation between citizens regarded as free and equal" (*JF*, 79 and 39).

It is crucial here that conception-dependent desires as conceived by Rawls refer not to whatever conception one might hold but only to a reasonable conception of the person and, by extension, to a reasonable ideal of society as a fair system of cooperation among equals. It is to this ideal, and this ideal only, that Rawls refers when explaining that conception-dependent desires are desires to act from principles articulating "a certain rational conception, or a political ideal." This ideal is not the representation of an independent moral good that should be made an object of desire. It is a reasonable ideal of life – the ideal of living up to the standard of reasonableness – that translates into a political project, namely, the project of a society organized as a fair system of cooperation among free and equal persons. The reference to teleology in my account of the citizen's desire to conform to the principles of justice therefore does not conflict with the deontological nature of Rawls's theory. When I say that a desire to act from the principles of justice is gained from a teleological consideration of a certain political ideal, I do not mean that Rawls starts from a conception of the good that would be given independently of the right – citizens remain free to endorse whatever conception of the good their comprehensive doctrine prescribes. What I mean is that Rawls starts from a reasonable conception of the person allowing him to specify, through the original position, the principles of justice which, in turn, allow for discriminating between permissible and impermissible conceptions of the good.

To get a better sense of the role played by teleology within deontology, consider the limits of the standard account of the distinction between teleological and deontological theories. It is usually explained that, in contrast to teleological theories, which define the good prior to and independently of the right, deontological theories consider that the right, prescribed purely *a priori* by reason through our experience of duty, is to frame the good.[5] This priority granted to the right does not mean, however, that the good has no function in deontological theories. The right only draws the limits within which a person is free to pursue his own conception of the good. A conception of the good remains crucially needed to define the purpose of action. As Rawls summarizes nicely, "the right draws the limit; the good shows the point" (*LHMP*, 231). What this standard account neglects, however, by focusing exclusively on the relation of the right to the good, is that deontological theories must also ascertain the possibility of an *a priori* determination of the right by reason alone. The right itself must indeed come from somewhere, so that the fundamental question deontological theories have to address is actually whether the right can have its origin purely *a priori* in reason. This crucial point is best appreciated by briefly coming back to Kant and by examining the way in which his endorsement of deontology is supported by an account, most often overlooked, of the possibility of an *a priori* determination of the right by a rational will defined as good in itself.

The question central to the second *Critique* is the question of whether the will can be sufficiently determined by principles prescribed purely *a priori* by reason. In the (Analytic of Pure Practical Reason), Kant famously warns his readers against the paradox of adopting a method that answers this question by anticipation (*KpV*, V: 62–63). Suppose one starts by conceiving of the moral good as an object of desire. This amounts to placing the criterion of the good in the capacity of an object to trigger pleasure through sensibility. The possibility of a determination of the will purely *a priori* by reason would therefore be excluded from the start, even before one begins analyzing practical reason, for the capacity of an object to produce a feeling of pleasure can only be known by experience and by no means *a priori*. The only way to avoid this paradox is to reverse the methodological order. Instead of starting from the consideration of the moral good as a desirable object and then deducing the determining principles of the will, one should bring to light the rational principles that determine the will *a priori* and then seek to identify an object for that will in conformity with these principles. Hence the deontological claim integral to Kantian constructivism that "the concept of good and evil must not be determined before the moral law [...] but only [...] after it and by means of it" (*KpV*, V: 63). The often overlooked point that I would like to highlight is that this claim remains dependent upon the prior acknowledgment that something internal to the concept of pure rational will constitute the source of the *a priori* determining principles – namely, the source of the moral law. I contend that this something integral to pure rational will itself is expressed by the idea, with which Kant quite appropriately chooses to open the *Groundwork*, that pure rational will is good in itself.

What does it mean for a will to be good in itself? Kant explains that a good will is not regarded as good with respect to the things that it brings about or with respect to its efficacy in bringing about these things. A good will is good independently of its fruitfulness and its efficacy; it is good absolutely, through its willing only. This idea of an absolute worth that can be assessed with regard to nothing else but itself, however, runs the risk of making good will an empty concept, a chimera "grounded merely in a high-flown fantasy" (*G*, IV: 394). As Kant himself admits, there is "something [...] strange in this idea of the absolute worth of a will" that can only be clarified by considering the concept of a good will in relation to reason (*G*, IV: 395–396). For the fact that reason naturally governs the will makes the concept of a good will a rational concept with a substantive content. As a concept essentially governed by reason, the good will expresses in its willing a certain purposiveness congenial to rational nature itself. By thus making the purposiveness of rational nature "the matter of every good will" (*G*, IV: 437; see also IV: 429), Kant signifies that pure rational willing, though by definition insensitive to empirical ends, carries with it a certain *a priori* end that holds equally for all rational beings, simply in virtue of their being rational. This end is not a determinate end that would be made an object of the will but rather a general indeterminate end that expresses a certain purposiveness inherent in human actions. It can be described as the willingness to act always in accordance with what rational nature recommends, whatever the determinate end under consideration. When taking political ends in view, for example, this general purposiveness implies acting toward the political ideal correlative to a certain reasonable conception of the person, that is, the ideal of a society conceived as a fair system of cooperation among equals. And insofar as this ideal is regarded as a valid objective end, whatever contributes to its fostering also constitutes a legitimate end for the pure rational will.

What the idea of a will that is good in itself tells us is, therefore, that the *a priori* principles of right, which are to determine the will prior to the good, have their source in the will itself insofar as it is governed by reason. *Such is the idea that Rawls makes his own through the idea of conception-dependent desire.* To say that individuals have a basic desire to act from principles articulating a certain rational conception of the person, or a certain political ideal correlative to this conception, is similar to saying that they are endowed with a good will. In both cases, the person recognizes rationality itself to be the source of the *a priori* principles of right. The consciousness of this rational origin gives rise to a desire to act in conformity with a certain conception of reasonableness that can be specified either, with Kant, in terms of a capacity for moral autonomy or, with Rawls, in terms of a capacity for justice. Here is how Rawls interprets Kant's teaching on this point:

> Kant does not mean to teach us what is right and wrong [...] but to make us aware of the moral law as rooted in our free reason. A full awareness of this, he believes, arouses a strong desire to act from that law. This desire is a conception-dependent desire: it is a desire, belonging to us as reasonable persons, to act from an ideal expressible in terms of a conception of ourselves as autonomous in virtue of our free reason, both theoretical and practical.
>
> (*LHMP*, 148; see also *PL*, 85, n.33)

It is clear from these lines that what Rawls interprets in terms of a conception-dependent desire is the teleological relation, internal to deontological theories, between the pure *a priori* principles constitutive of right and a certain reasonable conception of the person regarded by individuals as the final end in the employment of their freedom. These individuals are willing to abide by fair terms of cooperation only insofar as they make this particular conception of society their practical end in a Kantian sense. The same teleological structure underlies all Kant-inspired deontological theories, such as that of Thomas Scanlon. When Scanlon places at the basis of his account of moral motivation a "desire to be able to justify one's actions to others on grounds they could not reasonably reject," what he means is that moral agents are inclined to act in ways for which they genuinely believe that an adequate justification exists, even if other individuals in fact may not recognize this justification (Scanlon 1982, 116).[6] Agents are not, in other words, moved by the desire to be in actual agreement with others but rather by the desire to live up to their own rational standard, which requires acting only in ways that are justifiable to others. This principle-dependent desire is an integral part of the idea of a person who is reasonable in her behavior. The difference between Scanlon and Rawls lies in the nature of the conception that gives rise to conception-dependent desires. While Scanlon would agree with Kant that this desire is enjoined *a priori* upon us by reason and that it is revealed to us through our experience of duty, Rawls wants to argue that citizens contingently inherit this desire from their common political culture:

> if it is asked how principle- and conception-dependent desires become elements in people's motivational sets in the first place, then the superficial answer [...] is that they are learned from the public political culture. [...] How these conceptions and ideals enter into the public culture itself and often stay there, that is a long and different story.
>
> (*PL*, 85, n.33)

In this passage, Rawls reaffirms his commitment to the practical approach to political justification and at the same time admits that simply saying that people's desire to act in ways that express their reasonable nature in grounded in their public political culture is a "superficial" and ultimately unsatisfying answer. To be meaningful, this answer must be supported by a thoroughgoing account of how this desire became an integral part of the public political culture in question. Unfortunately, this account is nowhere to be found in the writings of the leading advocates of political liberalism. Rawls limits himself to recounting the historical landmarks that have punctuated the emergence of political liberalism in modern Europe (*PL*, xxvi–xxix). But this rather simplistic historical account cannot constitute the sought-after explanation insofar as it is not supported by a rationale enabling us to understand why European history evolved in this way. In the absence of this rationale, we can only agree with Williams that liberalism in general, and political liberalism in particular, "has a poor account, or in many cases no account, of the cognitive status of its own history. [...][It] cannot plausibly explain, adequately to its moral pretensions, why, when, and by whom it has been accepted and rejected" (2005: 9).

The analysis presented in this chapter allows going one step further and claiming that political liberalism simply cannot provide the sought-after explanation because it would then become apparent that it is neither freestanding nor autonomous in the relevant sense. It would appear that the presumed autonomy of liberal political morality is nothing but a sophisticated façade hiding a deeper commitment to a Kantian form of moral autonomy. Rawls's appeal to the notion of reasonableness – and its global analogue, decency – marks the importation into the political sphere of a specifically Western epistemic standard, which holds that normative principles must be determined by reference to the ideal of autonomous life, an ideal which recommends, in substance, to live up to the standard set by one's own rational nature. So the answer to the question "Are political conceptions of justice parochial?" is ultimately positive, at least when considered from the angle of the motivation that actors may have to adopt in politics a reasonable attitude in the Rawlsian sense.

Conclusion

Some may object that expecting Rawls to provide a full-fledged moral psychology containing the conceptual resources necessary to answer the question of motivation is misunderstanding the nature of his project. As Onora O'Neill, for example, has rightly emphasized, his political liberalism "does not aim to justify principles [...] by showing that individuals with a certain motivational structure will come to agree on them" (O'Neill 1997, 417). His aim is rather to justify those principles by showing that they are "the most appropriate principles" for individuals sharing a certain conception of the citizen and society (*PL*, 22) – what O'Neill calls a "common political identity" (O'Neill 1997, 420). Rawls himself makes this point clearly when describing his moral psychology as "philosophical, not psychological" (*PL*, 86). This phrase suggests that his account of the moral psychology of Western citizens is based on a consideration of their philosophical beliefs rather than their natural psychological traits. Of course, Rawls does not deny that human nature imposes certain constraints on the type of moral psychology that political actors can develop. But he considers that human nature does not determine all the aspects of the moral psychology they may endorse. In his view, human beings enjoy a certain freedom in developing the moral psychology that best corresponds to their political identity. It is within that space of freedom that he develops his own moral psychology, which he conceives as the best interpretation of the moral psychology that citizens sharing a liberal-democratic political identity must have. In line with the epistemic standard specific to the political approach, the validity of that conception does not depend on whether it is supported by a theoretically coherent account of the motivation that citizens may have in upholding it but rather "on whether [they] can apply and affirm its principles and ideals in political life" (*PL*, 87).

Without denying the specificity of Rawls's moral psychology, I have tried to show in this chapter, against those who regard his approach as philosophically satisfactory, that the question of motivation cannot be so easily bypassed. Before accounting for the willingness of reasonable citizens to endorse a given political conception of justice, one must be able to specify the reasons why they are inclined to look for such an overlapping consensus rather than to adopt a more familiar strategy, such as negotiating a *modus vivendi*. These are reasons they must also share as part of their common political culture, but which are distinct from the substantive reasons leading them to endorse a specific conception of justice. To see this, it is useful to distinguish between two senses in which a political culture can be said to be homogeneous. The political culture of Western democracies, for example, is both epistemically homogeneous, in that all citizens agree on the basic conditions of valid practical reasoning, and substantively homogeneous, in that they share the same basic conceptions of the citizen and of social cooperation. It is from epistemic homogeneity rather than substantive homogeneity that the willingness to uphold a political conception of justice in common arises.

Unmindful of this distinction, O'Neill and several others in her wake consider that "Rawls assumes too much in building his account of public reason on an account of citizens' shared sense of political identity" (1997, 422; Talisse 2005; Voice 2005). But I hope to have shown that, more fundamentally than a certain political identity, what citizens must share, if they are to uphold in common a political conception of justice, is a distinctively Kantian sense of their rational nature as imposing normative constraints on their public conduct – what Rawls himself calls "the constraints of having a morality" (*JF*, 63). It is indeed a fundamental assumption of Kantian constructivism – at least in its Rawlsian interpretation – that rational beings engaged in a procedure of construction such as the categorical imperative or the original position are conscious that the resulting principles are nothing but the expression of their rational nature (*CP*, 303–358). This consciousness and the motivation it generates to uphold the principles in question is what make them truly reasonable. So if there is, in the final analysis, a sense in which Rawls assumes "too much," it is not by presupposing that all citizens share the same political identity but rather by assuming that they share the meta-ethical belief that what makes our normative principles normative is the fact that they reflect our rational nature. Because this assumption necessarily underpins the strictly political approach to justice, all political conceptions of global justice are ultimately parochial.

Notes

1 For ease of read, references to John Rawls' writings use their abbreviated titles rather than the author's name and the date of publication. See the reference section at the end of this chapter for the full references.

2 Following traditional scholarly practice, all citations from Kant are to the relevant volume and page of the standard Prussian Academy edition of his works (Kant, Immanuel. 1900 ff. *Kant's gesammelte Schriften*. Berlin: Walter de Gruyter).

3 In line with common usage, I take "public reason liberalism" to encompass all the Rawlsian and neo-Rawlsian forms of liberalism relying on a principle of public justification to solve the problem posed by the diversity of worldviews to political justification (cf. Gaus 2015; Wendt 2019).

4 Some remarks on the role played by conception-dependent desires in political liberalism can nevertheless be found in Krause (2008, 209, n.17) and Ci (2006, 154–155).

5 For more detailed discussions of this distinction and Rawls's understanding of it, see Vallentyne (1987), Kymlicka (1988), Freeman (1994), and Ronzoni (2010).
6 Note that Scanlon later rejected this account of human motivation (see Scanlon 1998, 6ff.).

References

Americks, Karl. 2006. *Kant and the Historical Turn: Philosophy as Critical Interpretation.* Oxford: Oxford University Press.

Bai, Tongdong. 2015. "A Criticism of Later Rawls and a Defense of a Decent (Confucian) People." In *The Philosophical Challenge from China*, edited by Brian Bruya, 101–120. Cambridge, MA: The MIT Press.

Barry, Brian. 1998. "International Society from a Cosmopolitan Perspective." In *International Society: Diverse Ethical Perspectives*, edited by David Mapel and Terry Nardin, 144–163. Princeton, NJ: Princeton University Press.

Beitz, Charles. 1979. *International Relations and Political Theory.* Princeton, NJ: Princeton University Press.

Beitz, Charles. 1983. "Cosmopolitan Ideals and National Sentiment." *The Journal of Philosophy* 80 (10): 591–600.

Bell, Duncan. 2019. *Empire, Race and Global Justice.* Cambridge: Cambridge University Press.

Chimakonam, Jonathan. 2017. "African Philosophy and Global Epistemic Injustice." *Journal of Global Ethics* 13 (2): 120–137.

Ci, Jiwei. 2006. *The Two Faces of Justice.* Cambridge, MA: Harvard University Press.

Flikschuh, Katrin. 2017. "Should African Thinkers Engage in the Global Justice Debate?" *Philosophical Papers* 46 (1): 33–58.

Flikschuh, Katrin. 2018. *What is Orientation in Global Thinking? A Kantian Inquiry.* Cambridge: Cambridge University Press.

Freeman, Samuel. 1994. "Utilitarianism, Deontology, and the Priority of the Right." *Philosophy & Public Affairs* 23: 321–322.

Freeman, Samuel. 2006. "The Law of Peoples, Social Cooperation, Human Rights, and Distributive Justice." *Social Philosophy and Policy* 23 (1): 29–68.

Freeman, Samuel. 2007. *Rawls.* London: Routledge.

Gaus, Gerald. 1995. "The Rational, the Reasonable and Justification." *The Journal of Political Philosophy* 3 (3): 234–258.

Gaus, Gerald. 2015. "Public Reason Liberalism." In *The Cambridge Companion to Liberalism,* edited by Steven Wall, 112–140. Cambridge: Cambridge University Press.

Graness, Anke. 2015. "Is the Debate on 'Global Justice' a Global One? Some Considerations in View of Modern Philosophy in Africa." *Journal of Global Ethics* 11 (1): 126–140.

Habermas, Jürgen. 1995. "Reconciliation through the Public Use of Reason: Remarks on John Rawls's Political Liberalism." *Journal of Philosophy* 92 (3): 109–131.

Huang, Yushun. 2016. *Voice from the East: The Chinese Theory of Justice.* Beijing: Paths International.

James, Aaron. 2012. *Fairness in Practice: A Social Contract for a Global Economy.* Oxford: Oxford University Press.

Kant, Immanuel. 1997/1781–1787. *Critique of Pure Reason* (*KrV*, V: 5–252). Translated and edited by Paul Guyer and Allen Wood. Cambridge: Cambridge University Press.
Kant, Immanuel. 2012/1785. *Groundwork of the Metaphysics of Morals* (*G*, IV: 387–463). Translated by Mary Gregor and edited by Jens Timmermann. Cambridge: Cambridge University Press.
Kant, Immanuel. 1997/1788. *Critique of Practical Reason* (*KpV*, V: 1–164). Translated and edited by Mary Gregor. Cambridge: Cambridge University Press.
Kant, Immanuel. 1996/1797. *The Metaphysics of Morals* (*MS*, VI: 205–355, 373–493). Translated and edited by Mary Gregor. Cambridge: Cambridge University Press.
Kant, Immanuel. 1997/1775–1784; 1784–1785; 1793–1794. *Lectures on Ethics* (*LE*, XXVII). Translated and edited by Jerome Schneewind and Peter Heath. Cambridge: Cambridge University Press.
Kaufman, Alexander. 2013. "Political Liberalism, Constructivism, and Global Justice." *Journal of Moral Philosophy* 10 (5): 621–644.
Kohn, Margaret. 2013. "Postcolonialism and Global Justice." *Journal of Global Ethics* 9 (2): 187–200.
Krause, Sharon. 2008. *Civil Passions: Moral Sentiment and Democratic Deliberation*. Princeton, NJ: Princeton University Press.
Kymlicka, Will. 1988. "Rawls on Teleology and Deontology." *Philosophy & Public Affairs* 17: 173–190.
Maffettone, Sebastiano and Aakash Singh Rathore, eds. 2012. *Global Justice. Critical Perspectives*. London: Routledge.
Martin, Rex and David Reidy, eds. 2006. *Rawls's Law of Peoples: A Realistic Utopia?* London: Wiley-Blackwell.
Masaka, Dennis. 2017. "'Global Justice' and the Suppressed Epistemologies of the Indigenous People of Africa." *Philosophical Papers* 46 (1): 59–84.
McCarty, Richard. 1994. "Motivation and Moral Choice in Kant's Theory of Rational Agency." *Kant-Studien* 85: 15–31.
Metz, Thaddeus. 2014. "Harmonizing Global Ethics in the Future: A Proposal to Add South and East to West." *Journal of Global Ethics* 10 (2): 146–155.
Moellendorf, Darrell. 1996. "Constructing the Law of Peoples." *Pacific Philosophical Quarterly* 77 (2): 132–154.
Moellendorf, Darrell. 2002. *Cosmopolitan Justice*. New York: Perseus.
Nussbaum, Martha. 2015. "Political Liberalism and Global Justice." *Journal of Global Ethics* 11 (1): 68–79.
O'Neill, Onora. 1997. "Political Liberalism and Public Reason: A Critical Notice of John Rawls, Political Liberalism." *Philosophical Review* 106 (3):411–428.
Parekh, Bhikhu. 1992. "The Cultural Particularity of Liberal Democracy." *Political Studies* XL: 160–175.
Pogge, Thomas. 1989. *Realizing Rawls*. Ithaca, NY: Cornell University Press.
Pogge, Thomas. 1992. "Cosmopolitanism and Sovereignty." *Ethics* 103 (1): 48–75.
Porter, Thomas. 2012. "Rawls, Reasonableness, and International Toleration." *Politics, Philosophy & Economics* 11 (4): 382–414.
Rao, Rahul. 2012. "Postcolonial Cosmopolitanism." In *The Democratic Predicament: Cultural Diversity in Europe and India*, edited by Jyotirmaya Tripathy and Sudarsan Padmanabhan, 165–187. London: Routledge.
Rawls, John. 1996/1993. *Political Liberalism* (*PL*). Second edition. New York: Columbia University Press.

Rawls, John. 1999/1971. *A Theory of Justice* (*TJ*). Revised edition. Cambridge, MA: Harvard University Press.

Rawls, John. 1999a. *Collected Papers* (*CP*). Edited by Samuel Freeman. Cambridge, MA: Harvard University Press.

Rawls, John. 1999b. *The Law of Peoples: with "The Idea of Public Reason Revisited"* (*LP*). Cambridge, MA: Harvard University Press.

Rawls, John. 2000. *Lectures on the History of Moral Philosophy* (*LHMP*). Edited by Barbara Herman. Cambridge, MA: Harvard University Press.

Rawls, John. 2001. *Justice as Fairness: A Restatement* (*JF*). Edited by Erin Kelly. Cambridge, MA: Harvard University Press.

Raz, Joseph. 1990. "Facing Diversity: The Case of Epistemic Abstinence", *Philosophy & Public Affairs* 19 (1): 3–46.

Ronzoni, Miriam. 2010. "Teleology, Deontology, and the Priority of the Right: On Some Unappreciated Distinctions." *Ethical Theory and Moral Practice* 13 (4): 453–472.

Rossi, Enzo. 2014. "Legitimacy, Democracy and Public Justification: Rawls' Political Liberalism vs Gaus' Justificatory Liberalism." *Res Publica* 20 (1): 9–25.

Scanlon, Thomas. 1982. "Contractualism and Utilitarianism." In *Utilitarianism and Beyond*, edited by Amartya Sen and Bernard Williams, 103–128. Cambridge: Cambridge University Press.

Scanlon, Thomas. 1998. *What We Owe to Each Other*. Cambridge, MA: Harvard University Press.

Shapcott, Richard. 2017. "Global Justice: Shaped Rather than Found." *International Relations* 32 (1): 104–123.

Talisse, Robert. 2005. "Dilemmas of Public Reason: Pluralism, Polarization, and Instability." In *The Legacy of John Rawls*, edited by Thom Brooks and Fabian Freyenhagen, 107–123. New York: Continuum.

Tan, Kok-Chor. 2000. *Toleration, Diversity, and Global Justice*. University Park, PA: The Pennsylvania State University Press.

Tiffany, Evan. 2006. "How Kantian Must Kantian Constructivist Be?" *Inquiry: An Interdisciplinary Journal of Philosophy* 49 (6): 524–546.

Tong, Zhichao. 2017. "The Law of Peoples as Inclusive International Justice." *Journal of International Political Theory* 13 (2): 181–195.

Vallentyne, Peter. 1987. "The Teleological/Deontological Distinction." *Journal of Value Inquiry* 21 (1): 21–32.

Voice, Paul. 2004. "Global Justice and the Challenge of Radical Pluralism." *Theoria* 51 (2): 15–28.

Weithman, Paul. 2010. *Why Political Liberalism? On John Rawls's Political Turn*. Oxford: Oxford University Press.

Wenar, Leif. 1995. "Political Liberalism: *An Internal Critique*." *Ethics* 106 (1): 32–62.

Wenar, Leif. 2016. *Blood Oil. Tyrants, Violence, and the Rules That Run the World*. Oxford: Oxford University Press.

Wendt, Fabian. 2019. "Rescuing Public Justification from Public Reason Liberalism." In *Oxford Studies in Political Philosophy*, edited by David Sobel, Peter Vallentyne, and Steven Wall, Vol. 5, forthcoming. Oxford: Oxford University Press.

Williams, Bernard. 2005. "Realism in Political Theory." In *In the Beginning Was the Deed: Realism and Moralism in Political Argument*, 1–17. Princeton, NJ: Princeton University Press.

Williams, Huw and Carl Death. 2016. *Global Justice: The Basics*. London: Routledge.

Part 2

Contextual appraisal

4 Anticipating global justice

Confucianism and Mohism in Classical China

George Tsai

Introduction

Two striking and conflicting trends mark our current global social order. The first trend is tied to the dramatic technological advancements that have facilitated profound economic, communicative, and political integration and interdependence between members of the global population. These forces of globalization have led to the emergence of, and deepening philosophical interest in, the ideals of global justice and cosmopolitanism. At the level of practice and institutions, there has been, in the last several decades, the continued development and elaboration of international organizations and norm-setting bodies that function to structure, organize, and regulate global economic, technological, and political activity.

At the same time, in the face of the forces of globalization and the emergence of the ideals of global justice and cosmopolitanism, we also observe, more recently, a second trend in the rise of nationalistic, anti-globalist, more traditional political outlooks. In the politics across the US, Western Europe, and Latin America, we find growing intolerance of non-citizens, rejection of globalist ideals and concerns, and the re-emergence of authoritarian political leaders. Many such leaders have come into power by riding waves of populist, nationalist, and anti-globalist sentiment. We see politicians win elections on the basis of campaigns organized around the notion that those who have been in power have illegitimately subordinated their countries' best interests for those of foreigners. And we see newly elected leaders call for the upending of a range of large-scale international efforts: a collective defense system such as NATO; political-economic arrangement like the European Union; and financial institutions like the International Monetary Fund, World Bank, and World Trade Organization.

Among the many issues raised by these conflicting global and nationalistic tendencies are a variety of questions about the source, content, and scope of our moral and political responsibilities. One particularly pressing question we face in the current political climate is that of how we should conceive of our own moral and political responsibilities to diverse classes of people: to our children and families, to our friends and neighbors, to our fellow citizens, and, of course, to those large numbers of people who "live beyond the borders"—fellow human beings and members of the global community.

My aim in this chapter is to suggest that this question and set of concerns about how we should conceive of our own moral and political responsibilities to different people near and far is not necessarily a new one and that it appears in an earlier form in the classical philosophical debates of the pre-Qin or Warring States era of Classical China. This is the historical period demarcated roughly as the time between the death of Confucius in 479 B.C. to the founding of the Qin dynasty in 221 B.C.

In recent years, scholars have begun to reflect on whether, and how, Classical Chinese philosophical perspectives bear on contemporary discussions of justice. For example, Joseph Chan has argued that pre-Qin Chinese societies share with other societies characteristics that, according to contemporary theorists, give rise to circumstances of social justice. In particular, he argues that the philosophical writings of the Confucian figures Mencius and Xunzi can be understood as a response to social justice "issues such as poverty, differentiation of social roles and functions, inequality of income and status, and the distributive role of government" (Chan 2009, 269). Discussions such as Chan's have, however, focused principally on *social* (or *domestic*) justice and have not examined the possible bearing of these perspectives on discussions of *global* (or *international*) justice.

In what follows, I want direct attention to the theoretical affinities between some Classical Chinese philosophical perspectives and contemporary discussions of *global* justice. More specifically, I shall suggest that the debates between the Confucians and Mohists – followers of the teachings of Confucius and Mozi, representing the two most prominent schools of thought during the Classical period – about what we owe to others mirror and anticipate aspects of debates in contemporary moral and political philosophy concerning our responsibilities to other people and concerning the proper scope of application of norms of justice. In making apparent parallels between debates and strands of thought in Classical Chinese thought, on the one hand, and recent Western philosophical discussions of cosmopolitanism and global justice, on the other, my hope is that scholars in the Chinese (and, more widely, East Asian) traditions will begin to take greater interest in the philosophical issues of global justice.

Confucians and Mohists on *Ren* 仁

My point of entry is *ren* 仁, a central ethical notion in Classical Chinese thought. The term has been translated variously as "benevolence," "humaneness," and "goodness." Kwong-loi Shun writes that there are at least two different views concerning the root meaning of the character *ren*. According to one view of *ren*, "the character originally referred to the quality that makes someone a distinctive member of an aristocratic clan." According to a different view, "it originally had the meaning of love, especially the kindness of rulers to their subjects" (Shun 2002, 53). What is important for our purposes is not necessarily which view is correct but that, on both widely accepted views, *ren* is used to refer to a desirable ethical ideal or quality.

Though both Confucians and Mohists treat *ren* as a central ethical ideal, they offer interestingly different interpretations of it. Even among Confucians, there exists somewhat varying interpretations of the term. In the *Analects*, it is sometimes described alongside other desirable qualities, such as wisdom and courage (*Analects* 9.29; 14.4; 14.28). But in the same work, *ren* is also sometimes described as involving other desirable qualities such as feelings of love or affection for fellow human beings (*Analects* 12.22). Elsewhere in the work, *ren* is referred to as the consummation of personal ethical excellence. For example, "A man who finds benevolence attractive cannot be surpassed" 好仁者, 無以尚之 (*Analects* 4:6; Lau 1979, 72–73).

A distinctive feature of the Confucian understanding of *ren* is that it is taken to involve "graded compassion" (i.e., compassion that should be stronger for family members than for strangers). For example, "The feeling of compassion is the sprout of benevolence" 惻隱之心, 仁之端也 (*Mencius* 2A6; Van Norden 2008, 47); "Treating one's parents as parents is benevolence. … There is nothing else to do but extend [this] to the world" 親親, 仁也 … 無他, 達之天下也 (*Mencius* 7A15; Van Norden 2008, 175). Against this interpretation of *ren*, the Mohists – who were critical of Confucian thought – interpreted *ren* to mean "universal love" (i.e., equal compassion for each human): "It is the business of the benevolent man to try to promote what is beneficial to the world and to eliminate what is harmful" 仁人之事者, 必務求興天下之利, 除天下之害 (*Mozi* 16; Watson 2003, 41).

The contrasting interpretations of *ren* by the Confucians and Mohists manifests the deep tension that exists between the Confucian ethical view that recommends *graded* love or compassion and the Mohist ethical view that recommends *universal* love or compassion. I want to now elaborate on this tension before going on to suggest that it anticipates aspects of debates in contemporary moral and political philosophy concerning our responsibilities to other people.

Confucians on "graded love"

The role of the family and the ideal of filial piety are absolutely central in Confucian ethics. The centrality of the family is brought out in the importance placed on Confucian rituals such as ancestor worship and mourning practices. As David Wong has noted, the prominence of the family is one of Confucianism's most distinctive features (Wong 2008). Similarly, Yu-Wei Hsieh writes that "one can hardly understand Chinese ethics, and to some extent even Chinese political activities, if he cannot grasp the true import of this filial doctrine with its practical application in Chinese society" (Hsieh 1967, 167).

Part of the reason why Confucians placed such importance on the family is because they appreciated the role of the family in moral education and development. For the Confucians, one's ethical concerns, dispositions, values, and priorities are developed out of, and shaped by, one's family. As Mencius says, "Among babes in arms there are none that do not know how to love their parents. When they grow older, there are none that do not know to revere their elder brothers" 孩提之童, 無不知愛其親者, 及其長也, 無不知敬其兄也 (*Mengzi* 7A15; Van Norden 2008, 175). He also says that the "beginning of *yi* 義" – translated as "meaning," "significance," "righteousness," "rightness," "right," "principle," "integrity," and sometimes "just" or "justice" – is among the "four sprouts" that constitute the good dispositions (*xing* 性) human beings are born with (*Mencius* 2A6; 6A6; 7A21). The Confucian idea that part of the importance of the family resides in its role in moral education and development anticipates the more recent notion found in the *communitarian* view in contemporary philosophy that people's social identity – their sense of what's good and valuable and worthwhile in life – comes from their links to a particular place.

Notably, the Confucians conceived of the family not in egalitarian but in hierarchical terms. In traditional Confucianism, wives are understood to be subordinate to husbands, children are subordinate to their parents, and younger siblings are subordinate to elder siblings. Individuals within a family thus find themselves fitting into certain relationship-roles, and attached to these roles are certain responsibilities, obligations, expectations, and benefits. For example, parents and elder siblings have responsibilities to nurture and take care of the younger members of the family; the younger members, in turn, are expected to be devoted and obedient.

The centrality of the family in Confucianism is connected to the specific Confucian doctrine of *graded love* or *compassion* (sometimes also referred to as *differentiated caring*), which I earlier mentioned. According to this doctrine, one should have greater concern for those who are bound to one by special relationships, such as those between ruler and minister, father and son, husband and wife, elder and younger brother, and between friends. This doctrine is brought out in the following famous passage from the *Analects*:

> 葉公語孔子曰：「吾黨有直躬者，其父攘羊，而子證之。」孔子曰：「吾黨之直者異於是。父為子隱，子為父隱，直在其中矣。」
>
> The Duke of She said to Confucius, "Among my people there is one we call 'Upright Gong.' When his father stole a sheep, he reported him to the authorities."
>
> Confucius replied, "Among my people, those we consider 'upright' are different from this: fathers cover up for their sons, and sons cover up for their fathers. 'Uprightness' is to be found in this".
>
> (*Analects* 13:18; Slingerland 2003, 147)

From a purely impartial perspective, it seems that one is required to treat the thieving father as any other person and so to report the person to the authorities. However, Confucius praises the son who "covers up" for the thieving father in this case, suggesting that there is virtue in treating differentially, on the basis of the special relationship that might (or might not) obtain between one and the other person.

We find a similar example in the *Mencius*. In one passage (7A35), Mencius is presented with the following hypothetical case: Suppose that the father of the venerated sage king Shun were to commit murder, would Shun use his power to shield his father from prosecution? Mencius claims that Shun could neither allow his father to stand trial nor actively block his prosecution. Instead, Shun would abdicate the throne and secretly flee to the coast with his father, living out his years in happiness and without regret. Elsewhere (5A3), Mencius approves of Shun granting his morally depraved brother a fief and enriching him because doing so discharged Shun's filial obligation to ennoble his own family.

Roger Ames and David Hall have raised the worry that Confucianism, with its "graduated love and responsibility" and "intense family loyalties" might lead inevitability to provincialism and parochialism. They write that "Chinese culture has traditionally been plagued with abuses that arise because of the fine line that keeps social order beginning at home separate from nepotism, personal loyalties from special privilege, deference to excellence from elitism, appropriate respect from graft" (Hall and Ames 1987, 308).

For the Confucians, then, one has greater obligations toward those who are bound to oneself by community, friendship, and especially kinship. In addition to these greater moral obligations, one should also have stronger emotional attachment to those to whom one bears a special relationship. I believe the Confucian idea of "graded love" bears interesting relations to the contemporary moral philosophical idea of associative or special duties: duties that the members of significant social groups and the participants in close personal relationships have toward one another.

Mohists on impartial concern (*jian'ai* 兼愛)

Against the Confucian outlook, Mozi argued that the ritual practices that the Confucians emphasized as importantly tied to fulfilling one's family obligations were often pointless and economically wasteful. Mozi rejected the Confucian doctrine of "graded love," advocating instead the doctrine of *impartial concern* or *universal love* (*jian'ai* 兼愛). The doctrine of impartial concern holds that one ought to be concerned for the welfare of people in a spirit of "impartial concern" that does not make distinctions between self and other, associates and strangers. According to the doctrine of impartial concern, one should have equal concern for all. That is, the doctrine asks people to love the family members of others as much as they love their own family members. Moreover, the doctrine holds that one has equal moral obligations to all. That is, one is morally obligated to promote the welfare of every person, regardless of any special relation a person might have with oneself.

There are, of course, more and less demanding readings of the doctrine of impartial concern. On the very demanding end of the spectrum, the doctrine might be interpreted to require people to strive to benefit strangers to the same extent as they benefit themselves and their loved ones. There is a good question here whether this view can be completely coherent, as there may be certain forms of benefit that depend on the existence of differential treatment between self and loved ones, on the one hand, and others and strangers, on the other. On the less demanding end, the doctrine might be interpreted only to require that people refrain from harming others and strangers to the same extent in which they avoid harms to themselves and their loved ones. An intermediate reading, which Hui-chieh Loy has suggested, holds that people ought (to seek) to help strangers with urgent needs as much as they do associates and themselves (Loy 2013, 487).

The Mohists argued for the doctrine by appealing to considerations of "Heaven's Will" as well as "good consequences of the world." That is, they justified the doctrine of impartial concern on the grounds that it realizes Heaven's Will and that it furthers peace and promotes welfare of the world. Indeed, the Mohists argued that people's failure to live up to the doctrine is the source of the word's social problems and conflicts. For the Mohists, it is the tendency to act *partially* – the tendency to act on the basis of a greater regard for their own interests and the interests of their loved ones, over that of strangers (non-intimates) – that accounts for the widespread fact that people benefit themselves and their loved ones at the expense of strangers. In other words, the partiality at the root of the Confucian outlook is the source of social ills, and the doctrine of "impartial concern" has the potential to reverse the social ills if (enough) people adopt it.

Cosmopolitanism and global responsibility

I want to now develop the suggestion that the Mohist *jian'ai* doctrine can be understood as a forerunner to the contemporary conceptions of cosmopolitanism and global justice. The English term *cosmopolitanism* comes from the Greek word *kosmopolites*, which means citizen of the cosmos, of the world. The core idea of cosmopolitanism is the idea that each individual is a citizen of the world, and owes allegiance, as Martha Nussbaum has put it, "to the worldwide community of human beings" (Nussbaum 2002, 4).

Although many contemporary theorists have put forward views that they describe as cosmopolitan, there is some divergence in the content of these views, as well as in their subject matter. To some people, cosmopolitanism is primarily a view about *sovereignty*. To others, it is primarily a view about *culture* and *identity*. To many philosophers, however, it is primarily a view about *justice*, and in recent years, there has been a proliferation of philosophical work on the topic of "global justice." Global justice theorists usually distinguish between *political* and *moral* cosmopolitanism.[1] Political cosmopolitanism is the view that political communities should not be territorially limited in their scope or that supranational political institutions are legitimate bearers of political authority. Moral cosmopolitanism is the view that our conception of global justice must accommodate the fundamental belief that all human beings are of equal moral importance. What all of these views have in common – what makes them cosmopolitan views – is the notion that any adequate political conception for our time must in some way comprehend the world as a whole.

For the cosmopolitan, it is appropriate to raise questions about justice on a world scale, taking into account all human beings and populations in the world. However, very few philosophers have advocated for the development of the kind of global state that would give the idea of "world citizenship" literal application.[2] Still, the thought of one as a citizen of the world is supposed to make a *political difference* in transforming one's understanding of the normative significance of one's particular interpersonal relationships and group affiliations. For the cosmopolitan about justice, the idea of world citizenship means that the norms of justice must ultimately be seen as governing the relations of all human beings to each other and not merely as applying within individual societies or bounded groups of other kinds. For the cosmopolitan, we are all collectively responsible for one another: the world itself represents a sort of single moral community.

The thought that one is fundamentally a citizen of the world may lead one to the thought that there is no legitimate moral basis for preferring the desires and interests of the people nearest to one to those who might need one's help who are located far away. That is, one might think that there may be no justifiable reason to prioritize the needs and concerns of family and compatriots over strangers in distant parts of the world who may be living in poverty and suffering from malnutrition. Indeed, the contemporary philosopher Peter Singer argues that what a responsible citizen of the world should do is take seriously that all human needs matter.[3] For Singer, people in developed countries have a responsibility – a demanding obligation – to help poor people in developing countries on a general principle of responsiveness to neediness as such, regardless of one's relationship to the global poor. Considering the prevalence of extreme poverty in the world and the amount of preventable suffering and death, the affluent have a moral obligation to provide aid to the poor irrespective of whether they are compatriots or foreigners. Radically, this would involve some of the people in the West giving most of their wealth and income to charity organizations such as Oxfam and UNICEF to save people's lives, particularly those suffering from severe poverty, disease, and malnutrition (Singer 1972; Unger 1996).[4]

There are interesting parallels that can be drawn between Singer's utilitarian-based cosmopolitanism and Mohism, with its consequentialist orientation and commitment to the *jian'ai* doctrine. Indeed, one way in which this is brought out is in the fact that both Singer and the Mohists defend a very demanding conception of morality.

> 嘿則思，言則誨，動則事，使三者代御，必為聖人。必去喜，去怒，去樂，去悲，去愛，而用仁義。手足口鼻耳，從事於義，必為聖人。
>
> When silent, ponder; when speaking, instruct; when acting, work. Make these three alternate and surely you will be a sage. You must eliminate happiness and eliminate anger, eliminate joy and eliminate sorrow, eliminate fondness and eliminate dislike, and use benevolence and righteousness. Your hands, feet, mouth, nose, and ears undertaking righteousness, surely you will be a sage.
>
> (*Mozi* 47; Fraser 2015)

As the passage brings out, the Mohists emphasize a life of complete devotion to moral duty, where this means that one may have to eliminate happiness, joy, and fondness. For the Mohists, if satisfying basic material needs is sufficient to secure our welfare, then once those needs are met, we have little worthwhile to do but help others.

There is also much in common between the Mohist argument for the *ji-an'ai* doctrine and Singer's argument that our duties to others should not be determined by their proximity to us. Both the Mohists, on the one hand, and Singer, on the other, argue that simply because some people are geographically or psychologically distant from one, their needs should not matter less to us than those that are not distant. In other words, our duties to strangers across the globe are just as weighty and stringent as those to our loved ones, family members, and neighbors.

We can contrast the cosmopolitan perspective on global justice with what I shall call a *traditional* perspective. This perspective holds that individuals have greater moral responsibilities toward certain members of the global population than toward others. More precisely, the traditional view holds that the norms of justice apply primarily within bounded social groups comprising some subset of the global population. These social groups are bounded by some shared common history, culture, language, or ethnicity. For the traditionalist, then, there are limits to the scope of an individual's moral responsibilities, and an individual's responsibilities do not hold equally to all others in the world. Insofar as the Confucians adhere to the doctrine of "graded love," we can think of them as being traditionalists.

Against the traditionalists, the cosmopolitans hold a more expansive conception of individual responsibility. Cosmopolitans oppose the notion that there should be principled restrictions on the scope of an adequate conception of justice. They oppose the traditional view that the principles of distributive justice can properly be applied only within sufficiently cohesive social groups: groups that share a common history, culture, language, or ethnicity. Insofar as the Mohists advocate instead the doctrine of *impartial concern* or *universal love* (*jian'ai*), we can think of them as being cosmopolitans of a sort.

Cosmopolitanism and partiality

One way to consider the issue between the cosmopolitan and the traditionalists is in terms of the following question: what kinds of normative reasons can one have for devoting special concern to those individuals with whom one has special relationships consisting in co-membership in a group bounded by shared common history, culture, language, or ethnicity? For the cosmopolitan, one's status as a world citizen has to be seen as in some sense fundamental. But does this mean, then, that directing special concern to those in one's group is necessarily morally unjustified for the cosmopolitan?

One way to answer this question assumes that if such special concern is to be morally justified, it has to be justified on the basis of the ideal of world citizenship itself. This is the view that Martha Nussbaum defends. Nussbaum writes that "[n]one of the major thinkers in the cosmopolitan tradition denied that we can and should give special attention to our own families and to our own ties of religious and national belonging." According to Nussbaum, cosmopolitans believe "that it is right to give the local an additional measure of concern" and "the primary reason a cosmopolitan should have for this is not that the local is better per se, but rather that this is the only sensible way to do good" (Nussbaum 2002, 135–136).

One reading of Nussbaum's thought is that if each of us devotes our special attention to our own children, this is the most effective way of apportioning our benevolence and more effective than if each of us directly attempts to divide our attention equally among all the children of the world. But in devoting special attention to our own children, we must not suppose that our own children are more worthy of attention than other children. In other words, special attention to particular people is morally defensible since, and only because, it can be justified by reference to the interests of all human beings considered as equals. Cosmopolitanism, then, implies that particular human relationships and group affiliations never provide independent reasons for action or suffice by themselves to generate special responsibilities to one's intimates and associates.

A different understanding of the cosmopolitan view of special concern is to hold that, in addition to one's relationships and affiliations with particular individuals and groups, one also stands in an ethically significant relation to other human beings in general in virtue of being a citizen of the world. This view does *not* imply that one's special relationships and affiliations need to be justified by reference to the ideal of world citizenship itself or that any legitimate reasons we have for promoting the interests of the people we care specially about must be derivative from the interests of humanity as a whole. Instead, world citizenship is one important form of membership among others, one important source of reasons and responsibilities among others. Cosmopolitanism, on this more moderate interpretation, insists only that one's local attachments and affiliations must always be balanced and constrained by consideration of the interests of other people.

If we are to think of Mohists as a kind of early cosmopolitans, it is not clear which of the two understandings of cosmopolitan special concern that I have just outlined fits in with the Mohists more closely. One the one hand, the Mohist *jian'ai* doctrine – that each of us should be motivated impartially by equal concern for all regardless of one's relationship to them and that one's behavior conforms to the standard of "regarding others as though regarding oneself" – shares with supposition in the first cosmopolitan interpretation described above that the interests of all human beings should be considered as equal and that one's own children are no more worthy of attention than other children. On the other hand, the Mohists believed that one's local attachments and affiliations (such as family members and loved ones) must always be balanced and constrained by consideration of the interests of other people. In taking seriously the interests of those non-intimates that are in need in this way, the Mohists have something in common with the second cosmopolitan interpretation.

Rawls and global justice

In the previous section, I described the issue between the cosmopolitan and the traditionalist in terms of *justice*: Is there anything that the members of an individual society owe each other, as a matter of justice, that they do not owe to non-members? Here, the concept of justice is a distributive notion, concerning how benefits and burdens should be distributed to members (of a society, of the world population) according to certain normative principles. The disagreement between cosmopolitan advocates of global justice and advocates of more traditional, anti-globalist views of justice might also be framed in terms of the proper scope of the principles of justice in the individual society or the world as a whole.

Since much of the terms of the contemporary global justice debate – the debate concerning whether norms of justice apply only within an individual society or to the world as a whole – comes out of responses to John Rawls's *A Theory of Justice*, it will be useful to discuss briefly some of the main ideas of Rawls's theory. In the opening pages of *A Theory of Justice*, Rawls claimed that "justice is the first virtue of social institutions, as truth is of systems of thought" (Rawls 1971, 3). In making this claim, Rawls elevated the concept of justice above other important political ideas such as liberty, law, equality, power, rights, obligation, security, democracy, and the state. For Rawls, justice is the paramount virtue of social institutions in that whatever other virtues such institutions might possess, they are unacceptable if unjust. For example, a society might be wealthy and stable, but these attributes count for naught if those institutions are unjust.

The role of justice is to define "the appropriate distribution of the benefits and burdens of cooperation" (Rawls 1971, 4). The primary subject of justice, according to Rawls, is the "basic structure" of society: "the way in which major social institutions distribute fundamental rights and duties and determine the division of advantages from social cooperation" (Rawls 1971: 6). One source of the idea that the principles of distributive justice should be extended to the global level comes out of responses to Rawls's emphasis on "the basic structure of society" as the primary subject of justice. By "the basic structure of society," Rawls refers to a society's major social, political, and economic institutions. One of the reasons why Rawls focused almost exclusively on the basic structure in developing his two principles of justice is because he appreciated its deep role in shaping people's life prospects, including how well or poorly they fare economically. Some proponents of global justice (but, importantly, not Rawls himself) have argued that the increasingly complex global economy also has a deep impact on the lives and prospects of people worldwide and that it is therefore essential that institutions and bodies that ground the rules of the economy should be regulated by principles of justice (Pogge 2008).[5]

Rawls argued that distribution of wealth and income in society is unjust if they are unduly determined by "morally arbitrary" factors, such as whether one is born into an affluent or poor family. Some proponents of global justice have argued that there exist enormous disparities in wealth in different societies in the world and that some of these disparities stem from factors, such as differences in countries' natural resource endowments, which are at least as morally arbitrary as the factors that Rawls identified. It is also morally arbitrary whether someone happens to be born in an affluent society or a poor one – the country of one's birth is not something morally deserved or merited. Thus, these proponents of global justice (which do not include Rawls himself) argue that, if it is unjust to have the distribution of income and wealth within a society be unduly influenced by morally arbitrary factors, then it is also unjust to have the global economic distribution be influenced by such factors.[6]

I have been focusing in particular on two Rawlsian ideas that have played important roles in the development of the cosmopolitan position in global justice discussion. The first idea is that the "primary subject of justice" is the "basic structure" of an individual society, which comprises a society's major social, political, and economic institutions. The second idea is that a just society cannot permit the distribution of income and wealth to be influenced by morally arbitrary factors such as people's native abilities or the social circumstances into which they are born. I want to now discuss the commonalities between these Rawlsian ideas that have been influential in developing the cosmopolitan position on global justice, on the one hand, and ideas in Confucian and Mohist thought, on the other. More specifically, I shall make two claims: (1) that the rationale for the Confucians emphasis on the family in their ethical outlook has something in common with Rawls emphasis on the basic structure of society in his theory of justice and (2) that the Mohist *jian'ai* doctrine has something in common with the argument, made by some cosmopolitans, that national boundaries are morally arbitrary from the standpoint of justice made. I shall take these two points in turn.

First, recall that for Rawls, principles of distributive justice apply to not the global distribution of income and wealth as a whole but rather the basic structure of each society taken one at a time. Some cosmopolitans have objected to Rawls by arguing that something like his theory of distributive justice should apply globally. Rawls's main reason for focusing on the basic structure is because its effects in shaping people's life prospects are so profound. Individuals born into different social positions have different expectations in life, some of them more favorable than others. Rawls appreciated that a social system shapes deeply people's desires, aspirations, and expectations. It shapes the kinds of persons they are and want to be.

There is a way in which the Confucian normative emphasis on the family is broadly similar to Rawls's emphasis on the basic structure, in that both emphases derive from an appreciation of what is taken to be among the most central social structures in shaping human lives: the family in the Confucian case, the individual (non-global) society in Rawls's case. That is, I believe this Rawlsian emphasis on the application of the norms of justice to the basic structure given the immense role it plays in shaping people's lives has something in common with the Confucian concern with the family, as the Confucians too applied norms of ritual propriety (*li* 禮) to the family, on the grounds that the family played a formative role in shaping people's desires, aspirations, expectations, and character. Just as Rawlsians believe that the basic structure should be regulated by a conception of justice, given the significant role it plays in shaping people's lives, Confucians believe that the family ought to be regulated by norms of ritual propriety, given the significant role that it plays in shaping people's lives.[7]

Second, recall that for Rawls, a just society cannot permit the distribution of income and wealth to be influenced by morally arbitrary factors such as people's native abilities or the social circumstances into which they are born. Some cosmopolitans have drawn on this Rawlsian idea of moral arbitrariness to argue that national boundaries are equally arbitrary from the standpoint of justice: as a matter of justice, the accident of where one is born should have no effect on one's economic prospects.

I believe Rawls's appeal to the idea of moral arbitrariness in the individual society – an idea that some advocates of global justice have tried to extend to the whole as a whole – has something in common with the Mohists *jian'ai* doctrine. Recall, that the *jian'ai* doctrine holds that one ought to be concerned for the welfare of people in a spirit of "impartial concern" that does not make distinctions between self and other, associates and strangers. At the root of the Mohist thought that people ought to have concern for their own family members as well as non-family members is a recognition of the moral arbitrariness of social distance. For the Mohist, every person's welfare matters, regardless of any special relation a person might have with oneself, and for many contemporary philosophers, appreciation of just this idea has been one important path toward the development of a concern with global justice.

Conclusion

To summarize, I have argued that the philosophical question about how we should understand our moral and political responsibilities to different people is not necessarily a new one and that it has appeared in an earlier form in the philosophical debates between the Confucians and Mohists. In striking respects, their debates about our obligations to others mirror and anticipate aspects of debates in contemporary Western analytic philosophy about our responsibilities to other people and about the proper scope of application of norms of justice.[8]

Notes

1 On this distinction, see Beitz (2005).
2 One who has is Luis Cabrera, who makes a moral argument for world government. See Cabrera (2014).
3 Singer's argument relies on two premises. The first is that affluent individuals should contribute a much greater proportion of their resources to aid those who are suffering from poverty, disease, and malnutrition. The second is that all individuals have far-reaching duties to prevent harm and alleviate suffering.
4 It is worth noting that utilitarian or consequentialist cosmopolitanism of the sort advocated by Singer is not widely defended in the global justice debate, for many global theorists ground their views on non-consequentialist assumptions. For an overview of current cosmopolitan trends, see Caney (2010).
5 Rawls famously insisted that his principles of justice be applied solely to the basic structure of an individual society rather than to the world as a whole.
6 My discussion of Rawls's work may suggest that he neglected issues of global justice. It would be unfair and inaccurate to draw this conclusion, despite the fact that he explicitly rejected the notion of applying his principles of distributive justice globally. Instead, Rawls argued that relations among societies are governed by the "law of peoples" (Rawls 2001). The law of peoples sets out principles of justice to govern international relations, but they are not principles of distributive justice. In other words, they do not concern themselves with the distribution of income and wealth per se but instead presuppose the existence of separate societies within which distributive principles do apply. In his discussion of the law of peoples, Rawls claims that wealthier societies have a duty to assist what he calls "burdened societies."
7 Interestingly, Rawls himself did not take the family to be part of the basic structure. For discussion of the proper "site" of distributive justice, see the discussion between Gerald A. Cohen (1997), Liam Murphy (1998), and Thomas Pogge (2000). For feminist criticisms of Rawls's exclusion of the family from the basic structure, see Okin (1994).

8 The ideas in this article developed out of conversations that took place during the Routledge Conference on "Global Justice" at Sun Yat-sen University, Zhuhai campus, during May 19–20, 2018. I am grateful to Jun-Hyeok Kwak for organizing this conference and to the participants for stimulating discussion of issues of global justice in the East Asian context. I also thank Hugo El Kholi for the helpful comments he provided on an earlier draft and Michael Dufresne for his assistance in preparing the bibliography.

References

Beitz, Charles. 2005. "Cosmopolitanism and Global Justice." *Journal of Ethics* 9(1/2): 11–27.

Cabrera, Luis. 2014. *Political Theory of Global Justice. A Cosmopolitan Case for the World State*. London: Routledge.

Caney, Simon. 2010. "Cosmopolitanism." In Duncan Bell, ed., *Ethics and World Politics*. Oxford: Oxford University Press, 146–163.

Chan, Joseph. 2009. "Is there a Confucian Perspective on Social Justice?" In Takashi Shogimen and Cary J. Nederman, eds., *Western Political Thought in Dialogue with Asia*. Lanham, MD: Lexington, 261–277.

Cohen, Gerald A. 1997 "Where the Action is: On the Site of Distributive Justice." *Philosophy and Public Affairs* 26(1): 3–30.

Confucius. 2003. *Analects: With Selections from Traditional Commentaries*. Translated by Edward Slingerland. Indianapolis: Hackett Publishing.

Fraser, Chris. 2015. "Mohism." In E. N. Zalta, ed., *Stanford Encyclopedia of Philosophy*, Winter 2015 Edition. https://stanford.library.sydney.edu.au/archives/sum2016/entries/mohism/

Hall, David and Roger Ames. 1987. *Thinking Through Confucius*. Albany: State University of New York Press.

Hsieh, Yu-Wei. 1967. "Filial Piety and Chinese Society." In Charles A. Moore, ed., *The Chinese Mind: Essentials of Chinese Philosophy and Culture*. Honolulu: University of Hawaii Press, 167–187.

Loy, Hui-cheh. 2013. "On the Argument for *Jian'ai*." *Dao* 12 (4): 487–504.

Mengzi. 2008. *Mengzi: With Selections from Traditional Commentaries*. Translated by Bryan Van Norden. Indianapolis: Hackett Publishing.

Mozi. 2003. *Mozi: Basic Writings*. Translated by Burton Watson. New York: Columbia University Press.

Murphy, Liam. 1998. "Institutions and the Demands of Justice." *Philosophy and Public Affairs* 27(4): 251–291.

Nussbaum, Martha. 2002. *For Love of Country?* Edited by Joshua Cohen. Boston, MA: Beacon Press.

Okin, Susan Moller. 1994. "Political Liberalism, Justice, and Gender." *Ethics* 105(1): 23–43.

Pogge, Thomas. 2000. "On the Site of Distributive Justice: Reflections on Cohen and Murphy." *Philosophy and Public Affairs* 29(2): 137–169.

Pogge, Thomas. 2008. *World Poverty and Human Rights*. Malden, MA: Polity Press.

Rawls, John. 1971. *A Theory of Justice*. Cambridge, MA: Belknap Press of Harvard University Press.

Rawls, John. 2001. *The Law of Peoples: With "The Idea of Public Reason Revisited."* New York: Harvard University Press.

Shun, Kwong-loi. 2002. "*Ren* 仁 and *Li* 禮 in the *Analects*." In Bryan Van Norden, ed., *Confucius and the Analects: New Essays*. Oxford: Oxford University Press, 53–72.
Singer, Peter. 1972. "Famine, Affluence, and Morality." *Philosophy & Public Affair* 1: 229–243.
Unger, Peter. 1996. *Living High and Letting Die: Our Illusion of Innocence.* Oxford: Oxford University Press.
Wong, David. 2008. "Chinese Ethics." In Edward N. Zalta, ed., *Stanford Encyclopedia of Philosophy*, Fall 2008 Edition. https://plato.stanford.edu/archives/fall2008/entries/ethics-chinese/

5 Chinese political culture and the international order

Li Shaomeng

Introduction

As China's presence looms larger and larger on the global stage, the world looks at China with uneasy expectations and apprehensions. What kind of international strategies will China adopt? How will China's domestic situation affect its global choices? And more specifically, what role will China play in humanity's struggle for international order? This chapter assumes that a nation's political culture can serve as a good indicator of its international policies and strategies,[1] and it aims to decipher some important elements of Chinese political culture for the purpose of understanding current and future Chinese contribution to global governance.

Strong nations tend to project their political culture not only onto other nations, but also onto the international order more widely. Such a familiar phenomenon in human history served as at least a partial motive of tension if not aggression in, for example, the Greco-Persian Wars and the Cold War, two cases of the perennial conflict between the East and the West. Another factor to consider, perhaps as powerful as the first, is that the international environment and the international norms in or next to which a country abides also impact the political culture of even strong nations. It may not be an accident that the ideas of state sovereignty, international law, the rule of law, and limited government were all developed in a European multi-state system. In contrast, China, before its forced engagement with the West beginning in the middle 19th century, had only negligible exposure to alternative forms of political organization, accustomed as it was to viewing itself as the center of the civilized world, without feeling the necessity to deal with other countries in an international forum.[2] This difference would prove to have lasting consequences for both China and the world in the working out of the contemporary international order.

Political cultures tend to live longer than particular political structures. This gives us a good reason to take political culture seriously as we try to understand the long-term prospects of a nation.[3] To fully appreciate the merits of any culture, we have to understand its historical background. Cultures produce and make available choices with respect to the values guiding people's choices, while historical backgrounds concern the various options available in the first place for people to make choices. Especially when we compare different cultures, historical background can be crucial for a fair understanding of the differences in values.

John Rawls famously argued that the stability of a constitutional democracy requires a political culture to support an overlapping consensus over certain core conceptions of justice.[4] This is also true, I believe, for the stability of authoritarian regimes, whose ability to persist also requires support from particular political cultures. A further question can be asked about whether a system of international order itself requires a corresponding global political culture to support it, but obviously it is beyond the scope of this chapter.

Chinese political culture

For over two thousand years, Chinese people have lived under authoritarian regimes. For much of that time, Confucianism in its various iterations provided the official ideology for these regimes.[5] This tradition of political culture poses a very distinctive problem for contemporary Chinese intellectuals: given that the Chinese revolutions of the 20th century have made many monarchical elements of Confucianism obsolete, then if authoritarianism is necessary for the continued survival of the Chinese political order, what kind of philosophy will be capable of sustaining the stability of an authoritarian regime today?

Two major solutions have so far been proposed: one calls for the revival of a Confucianism that can appropriately speak to a modernized and continuously modernizing China, and the other calls for the adoption of some Western versions of authoritarianism. Because these two solutions are innocuous to the current political situation, Chinese philosophers laboring for either of these two solutions have gained prestigious status in the Chinese academy over the course of the last three decades. There is, however, a third proposed solution, one that inclines toward liberal democracy. No matter that this solution is popular, perhaps even the most popular among the three: because it is apparently in contradiction with the Chinese reality, it has been largely sidelined.[6]

Still, we can ask an altogether different question: does authoritarianism need philosophy at all and in the first place? Aren't authoritarian regimes running on force and force only? At least in the West, those philosophers in favor of authoritarianism rarely enjoyed guardianship in authoritarian regimes. Plato, Machiavelli, Hobbes, Schmitt, and Strauss have been very popular among Chinese intellectuals in recent years, but in their own days, their names were scarcely honored, nor did later Western authoritarian regimes call on them for ideological guidance or justification.

The history of China tells a different story. Confucius and many later generations of Confucian philosophers have been honored by virtually every major dynasty. From ancient to late Imperial China, Confucian writings have been systematically used to justify dynastic political order, educate the people, and prepare the literati or scholar-gentry class to serve the dynasties.[7] Several Chinese dynasties lasted more than 200 years primarily because, as many argue, they depended on the Confucian system of values, deeply integrated in both literary education and the imperial examinations, to supply themselves with educated talents and ideological loyalty.

Such an enduring alliance between dynastic rulers and Confucian intellectuals is perhaps the most salient fact that distinguishes China from the West in terms of political culture.[8] The only comparable intellectual resource in the history of the West is the Catholic church and its well-educated clergy, yet due to the political divisions of Western Europe during medieval times, the Catholic church was able to sustain its own independent bases of power within which it harbored its own independent ambitions, and it often functioned as a check on royal and aristocratic powers. The early modern era even witnessed powerful branches of the church that dared to challenge political establishments, and Protestantism became a major catalyst for breaking the monopoly over political power by the military and political classes. Religious wars prompted by Protestantism were also a formative factor behind the evolution of the European or Westphalian system of nation-states and the modern Western domestic and international orders.[9]

Authoritarianism in China never confronted checks in such ways and therefore it was able to develop into absolute extremes. As a result of authoritarian rule over the course of more than two thousand years, an exclusive understanding of power politics has been time and again reinforced in Chinese political culture. Three propositions or attitudes about power saliently stand out: power is intrinsically good and commands honor and respect; power is best when concentrated and centralized; and political competition is but the real-time play of power politics in which the ends justify the means.

One might argue that this formulation is exaggerated in the face of traditional Chinese teachings that are full of moralistic commands about holding one's principles when confronted with afflicting realities, and Confucians believed that the benevolent will ultimately prevail. But in reality, this emphasis on justice and benevolence has all-too-often been ignored or even twisted to the effect that whoever wins must in fact be the champion of justice and benevolence (Lin 2003). It is fair to say that Chinese political culture, especially at the popular level of culture, is motivated more by hidden realism than by apparent moralism.

If we compare these theses with contemporary liberalism, the Sino-European contrast will be even more transparent. Against authoritarianism, liberalism asserts three antitheses: power is intrinsically evil and corruptive; power should be divided and dispersed; political competition should follow neutral and impartial rules. These principles are not always honored in Western countries, of course, but they are the pillar ideals behind the institutional structures of a modern Western society. Due to strong Western influences in recent four decades, China is inching toward these principles as ideals simultaneously with the development of associated institutions, but to succeed in this historic effort requires smashing through many barriers, especially the long tradition of its authoritarian political culture.

This is not to say that Chinese minds are completely unfamiliar with rule-based politics. The original Confucianism, for example, devoted efforts to put a touch of civility on the rampant power politics. This is so partly because its earliest spokesmen, especially Confucius and Mencius, had as their ideals a feudal political order in which different kingdoms coexist and international politics was an unavoidable fact of life. When hereditary nobles fought and checked each other, there were rules of engagement at play. But unfortunately, such a feudal tradition was later lost in the centralized dynasties, and the original Confucianism was also reinterpreted to be more congruent with authoritarian regimes.

For a few centuries after the Qin unification in 221 BC, "bureaucracy" (*junxian* 郡縣) and "feudalism" (*fengjian* 封建) were locked in battle as the two main competing ideals for Chinese dynastic politics. Nevertheless, with the forward movements of history, the feudal ideal gradually phased out, while centralized bureaucracy and its authoritarian tendency took the dominant position. The Manchu take-over of China (1644) in the founding of the Qing dynasty compelled many great thinkers of the time to reflect on the plight of Chinese culture, and they came to a consensus that China was so easily lost to foreign rule precisely because of the abandonment of feudalism. This observation seems to confirm Machiavelli's observation that a feudal country is more difficult to conquer than a centralized kingdom.[10] In other words, China paid a very high price for its political culture of authoritarianism, that is, the periodical collapses of the entire political order and the recurring foreign occupations and take-overs of the whole country.[11]

Does China have an authoritarian tradition?

Judgments about history usually reflect, and fluctuate with, judgments about reality. This is especially true when it comes to judging the main characteristics of Chinese political culture. One hundred years ago, the May Fourth Movement (1919) presented a very negative picture of the Chinese past, and after that, an entire generation of intellectuals had been trying to achieve modernity by a thorough critique and refusal of the Chinese authoritarian tradition.[12] China has been rising in recent decades, and consequently, many Chinese intellectuals have adopted a more positive attitude toward the Chinese tradition and expressed a deep regret about the May Fourth Movement. In their view, China is becoming great again exactly because it had a very good tradition of authoritarian yet benevolent governance, and such a tradition cannot be judged by Western standards, let alone be replaced by Western ideologies.[13]

In this chapter, I am not attempting to judge the Chinese political culture by the Western standards; anyway, such a judgment would not make much difference if we recognize the staying power of political culture. My intent here is rather to describe Chinese political culture through a comparison to Western political culture. This comparison can assist in giving definition to the central doctrine of Confucianism, the dominant tradition of Chinese political culture, which is respect for superiors, ultimately for the sovereign. According to Confucianism, the sovereign power is the key to order and stability. Chinese political order is constructed from above: first there is the sovereign ruler, and afterward all lower levels of power positions will be filled with his agents. Officials on every level get their powers from their superiors, and the sovereign ruler sits at the top; they answer to no one other than their superiors, who ultimately answer to the sovereign ruler (Pines 2012; Liu 2014). Such a principle of organization leaves people of lower positions no option to reject or replace their superiors.

Compared to the West, China does not have any historical memory of democratic election, symbolically represented by Classical Athens, or republican checks and balances, symbolically represented by Classical Rome. As a result, the bravest imagination of a Confucian is to hope the ruler to be virtuous and benevolent. Moral education and self-cultivation are the paramount instruments of Confucian moral and political philosophy. Instead of developing institutional checks against the ruler, Confucians deposit their hope for a good political order in the "moderation," or "temperance" (*zhongyong* 中庸), of a benevolent ruler. Such is also the general mentality of the educated intellectuals, whose main goal is to achieve such a moderation or benevolence in themselves as empowered bureaucrats and in the king as the absolute ruler. Institutional checks and balances were used to some extent in the imperial system but in a completely reversed direction, that is, mainly to monitor the bureaucrats and to safeguard the sovereign power.[14]

Throughout the long history of Chinese authoritarian regimes, Chinese people have been impelled to cultivate in themselves a mentality of obedience and submission. Other than military insurrection, which is a life and death choice, Chinese people had no institutional means to effect social reform in the direction of justice. With no alternatives when they suffer injustice, Chinese people are simply accustomed to praising the authority or begging from it (Hirschman 1970). There is a shortage of public morality and public spirit, since the people are completely bereft of self-confidence when it comes to enforcing or challenging social norms. Fatalist apathy is very common and well justified. It is actually the common trait of Daoism and Chinese Buddhism, the two ideologies besides Confucianism, and arguably the safe haven for the crushed and the downtrodden.[15]

While the modern Western mind is fascinated with individual rights, the Chinese mind is highly dependent on government authority. In the history of Chinese political philosophy, the analogy between paternal power and political power has been ubiquitous and convincing, to such an extent that it was widely used in daily discourses. It is a fact that you cannot choose your parents, so you had better obey and respect them. It is also a fact that you cannot choose your rulers, so you had better obey and respect them. Filial piety and political loyalty are not just the default choice but also a duty (Yang 2017, 187–203).

Duties enjoy priority over rights, if there are any rights at all.[16] Ancestral worship, arguably the most salient characteristic of Chinese culture, lends further weight to the priority of duties. We owe our very existence to our parents and to our ancestors. As a result of this fact, we also owe duties and respect to our parents and ancestors. Analogously, we owe our existence to the government, which is the provider of civil order and the guarantor of the peaceful production of material means necessary for life. This fact entails duties toward the government on the side of the people.

Such discourses that derive duties from preceding facts do not work for the concept of rights. The very life and existence of each person depends on other people and on some sort of social institutions. Even as adults, people still get their wealth, opportunities, and rights from a network of social institutions, social organizations, and social relations, such as markets, shared knowledge and technologies, public services, etc. These are undeniable facts, which constitute the conditions for any meaningful human life. To argue from these facts, individual human beings always owe something to society before they can own anything, including rights.

As a result, duty-centered moral and political doctrines are universally appealing in most cultures, and perhaps only with the development of social contract theories could we challenge and reverse its logic. Both Locke and Rousseau claimed that political power is neither analogous to nor derived from paternal power[17]; therefore the authority of the parents, even if well established, cannot provide legitimacy to the authority of the government. The legitimacy of government power can only come from the voluntary consent of the ruled, who had equal rights in the state of nature already and can contract with each other to delegate their rights to a neutral public power empowered to defend them. Somehow, by way of this hypothetical state of freedom and equality, a normative discourse of rights was established.

The discourse on duties, on the other hand, will almost inevitably lead to some form of authoritarianism and even give a normative force to it. Authoritarianism is not a simple claim of "might is right"; it can also be developed into a delicate morality of duties. The history of China proves that authoritarianism does have this normative power and did produce positive effects. China was perhaps the first society to develop the institutions of a modern state. While modern states began to take shape in Europe only around the 17th century, China's first centralized state was established in 221 BC, if not earlier. Compared to political cultures like the Indian tradition, in which local governance was the default tendency, Chinese people were able to rebuild the unified state time and again after the periodic collapses of political order. To some extent, this too is the achievement of an authoritarian political culture.[18]

The problem with strong authoritarian cultures is that the discourse of rights can hardly emerge. In the history of China, individuals had little opportunity to claim property rights, religious liberties, or the freedom of expression. Obligations, not rights, are the foundation of the Chinese identity. Such a way of thinking is not only the result of authoritarian regimes; it also gives legitimacy and stability to authoritarianism just as liberal ideas of rights and dignity lend legitimacy and stability to a modern democracy.

The Chinese fascination with power politics: domestic and international

Authoritarians are likely to interpret every human relationship as a power game, in which agents are mainly motivated by power and interests, and reasons for action based on principle are nothing but an excuse.[19] A liberal political culture, on the other hand, values compromise, toleration, and overlapping consensus over common principles and values; an authoritarian political culture focuses on the question of who has more power or who is about to win. Hobbes's conception of the sovereign speaks well for the authoritarian concern: without the highest authority vested in one who wields arbitrary power to enforce the natural laws, the incessant urge for power will lead individuals only to mutual destruction. Without authoritarianism, everything is permitted, and there is no such thing as injustice or justice.

Xunzi, a famous Confucian who lived at the end of the Warring States period (475 BC–221 BC), also emphasizes such a necessity:

> The lord occupies the most exalted position in the state, and the father occupies the most exalted position in the family. When the most exalted position is held by one person alone, there will be order, but if held by two people, there will be chaos. From ancient times to the present there has not yet been a case where two people who both occupy the most exalted position and contend for greater authority can last for long.
>
> (Xunzi 2014, chapter 14)

Age-old Chinese political wisdom insists that sovereign power can only reside in one single position or agent. Hobbes's arguments lead to the same conclusion. The greatest danger an authoritarian regime can face is the very possibility of challenges to its sovereign power.

In the Chinese universe, "politics" (*zhengzhi* 政治) usually means "power politics," and it typically refers to command or compliance, enemy or friend, life or death. Unlike Hannah Arendt's definition of politics as the engagement with a plurality of voices and actions, the Chinese understanding of the term leaves very little space for rational argument among equals. It is motivated by interest calculation and manipulated by different forms of coercion. In fact, it was this understanding of politics that made the Chinese mind so receptive to Marxist ideas.[20] Marx, after all, also believed that the political institutions of the state and the ideologies of religion and culture were nothing but superstructural reflections of the economic interests of the dominant classes. Therefore, instead of being influenced by Western political culture through Marxism, the Chinese adoption of Marxist ideology has only been reinforcing Chinese conceptions of power politics.

The discourse on global justice or global order has so far been met with general suspicion in China, both from the academy and from the public.[21] Given the cosmopolitan tradition in China's long history, this attitude is especially perplexing. But there is another side to the Chinese political culture, which is the fascination with power politics. The Chinese people, made powerless by repressive regimes coupled with a recent history of diplomatic isolation, domination, and humiliation, are particularly sensitive to injustice, but they are also cynical about the willingness of political and economic elites to sincerely promote justice. Such a perspective of power politics is even more salient in the Chinese understanding of the international arena which, according to many Chinese people, is only a battlefield of national interests.

In the domestic domain, Chinese people are also fascinated by the imagination of power struggles and conspiracies, even though, or perhaps because, they only have very limited channels to learn inside news about the power game. Authoritarianism or absolutism figures prominently in this imagination, since all power struggles are expected by the Chinese mind to end up with the winner terminating the loser, being a zero-sum game. This is a pity because in the actual world, especially in the Western world, power games can have a happier ending. Compromise can be negotiated, and powers can be checked by other powers. The balance of power, both in power structures and social formations, is perhaps the secret for the European success.

It will not be too much of an exaggeration to say that the modern global order emerged from the expansion of the European system of nation-states. The most conspicuous fact about the history of Europe is that it never reunited again after the fall of the Roman Empire in the 5th century AD. This sustained condition of separation and competition not only gave birth to incessant feudal wars; it also made the idea of international law possible and the idea of the rule of law fruitful.[22] Interspersed with short periods of imperial unification under the Frankish Empire and the Holy Roman Empire, Europe was almost always immersed in a multi-state system. This historical experience is not just different from the Chinese experience; it might be a very unique and exceptional experience in the history of all human civilizations.

To understand the idea of state authority in France, or to understand the idea of liberalism in England, it is often necessary to understand the political, religious, and cultural background of the whole European continent. China, on the other hand, has maintained its political order only in relation to itself. The Chinese empire was formed and developed against a background of other, "barbarian" states hugging it on almost every landlocked side and corner of its borders, but in the eyes of Chinese intellectuals and rulers, those "barbarian" states had no claims to sovereignty or legitimate authority demanding mutual respect. To them, the "barbarian" regimes could not be counted as actual human political achievements, nor did they present any valid political alternatives to be taken seriously.[23] They simply marked the limits or the boundaries of political civilization. As Confucius once said, "The barbarians may have their kings, but they live in a state of chaos worse than when we don't have kings."[24]

If you view politics as but a game of power, you would create a fertile ground for conspiracy theories, which sometimes lead to certain level of paranoia.[25] Many examples of tragic paranoia, which usually ended in massive bloodshed, can be found in the history of China. Mutual fear, mutual distrust, and mutual suspicion work together to create such scenarios, the recurrence of which suggests a structural pattern beyond personality issues. It can be called an internal Thucydides's Trap,[26] with a zero-sum competition over the sovereign power.

China and the West: two extremes of political cultures

China is still living its tradition, and the Chinese tradition, if we push for a single word answer, is authoritarianism. The early modern European concept of authoritarianism (absolutism) is a good starting point for us to understand the cultural divide between China and the West, and this is so not just because mutual understanding can be achieved by calling two different things by the same name; there are also many structural similarities in the two examples. For one thing, the emergence of nation-states in Europe since the Reformation and the fierce competition between states during the Chinese Warring States period are very comparable historical processes, even though they ended up with different results. Histories and ideas can be very different in the European and the Chinese traditions, but if we can unpack the full meaning of this comparison of the two periods separated by 2000 years and by a vast continent of Euro-Asia, we may achieve not only a better understanding of the human struggle for peace and order, but also a reconciliation (Hui 2005; Zhao 2015).

Authoritarianism reflects a mental ideal about the source and the methodology of power, in all its forms. Authoritarianism maintains that there is only one source of power and authority, and all other power agents must view themselves as delegates of the absolute power. The practical incentive to imagine such a power pyramid lies in the scenario of an army in battle against another army. The army with a more unitary command chain will more likely be victorious, and winning a military conflict can be a decisive event in the formative years of a state, especially an ancient one. In any case, the Chinese state was almost always reinvigorated by crucial wars. There are many structural similarities and connections between a Chinese state and a Chinese army (Li 2001).

As a result, passive obedience was encouraged in the minds of Chinese people, and a discourse on rights could hardly be imagined, much less invoked.

We can look at the example of religious liberty for freedom of conscience, which was perhaps the first modern individual liberty that European people earned for themselves in the wake of the Protestant Reformation and the ensuing religious wars. Since government was taken to be the only source of authority in the history of China, various religions had to yield to political power if they were to survive. So even though different religions flourished in China and rarely experienced anything close to a religious war, one religion against another, to that extent we may rightfully claim a Chinese style of religious toleration; nevertheless, all religious communities had to submit to political authority and live under government regulations. Religious activism was strictly contained and, in several cases, led to persecution. Due at least in part to this logic, most religions in China developed a common Chinese characteristic, namely, fatalism.[27] Believers of different religions were told to accept their own destinies and to find peace in their own hearts. In this way, religions worked to the benefit of the political authority, easing social tensions and justifying social hierarchies by spiritual means.

Another challenge that has been well-managed and contained by Chinese authoritarian political culture is the market economy. Because market economy requires certain levels of private property rights, it too can challenge the total control of political power. The development of capitalism in the West, on the other hand, was a driving force behind the social and political movements toward a limited government. Looking at the history of China, however, a puzzling phenomenon can hardly escape our attention: China reached a high level of economic development at a very early stage, characterized by big cities, huge wealth and general abundance, advanced commercial networks and technologies, and intensive international trade. When trade between the West and the East began to boom after the Age of Discovery, China even became a very successful exporter and managed to gain a very competitive ground. Yet capitalism didn't materialize in China, nor did economic freedom lead to political freedom.

The failure of China to develop capitalism despite a very rich history of economic advancement may suggest that capitalism requires a multi-state system in which to incubate. Because the Chinese state was all-powerful and largely isolated from challenges from neighboring states, it always took advantage of this monopoly of power to exploit the society. This tendency is of course not limited to China, nor is it confined to ancient times. Even today the strong hand of government power can stifle a free market economy. It is therefore quite reasonable to count the Chinese deficit in capitalism as one of the consequences of Chinese political culture.

Concluding remarks

In this chapter, I have tried to present my understanding of Chinese political culture by comparing it to Western political culture. Such a comparison can reveal similarities as well as differences, but so far I have been focusing on the major differences. These differences were created in a long historical process and are due to different geo-political environments, different historical paths, and different institutional backgrounds. As such they cannot be easily eliminated in a short time, and can become sources of misunderstanding, mistrust, and conflict. This potential is testified both by historical experience and by current affairs.

But is this the end of the story? Are China and the West both bound to proceed within the terms of a pre-established historical discourse erected around their separate and different political cultures? Or worse, since currently nationalism and power politics seem attractive to many countries, including not a few major powers, is the whole world pivoting toward a new cold war, a balance only to be maintained by mutually assured destruction locked in a *modus vivendi*? Or worse still, will the competition between major powers devolve into a Hobbesian state of nature to end with a single hegemonic sovereignty, just like the tragic conclusion of the Warring States Period in China two thousand years ago but on a global scale?

In view of these differences in political cultures, it is perhaps too early to predict the destiny of humankind. But based on a comparative survey of political cultures in China and in the West, I am tempted to say that the global political culture will ultimately share more characteristics with the Western political culture, in which realistic checks and balances will lead to a certain overlapping consensus over a certain conception of global order and global justice. This is so mainly because the world we see now is an expansion of the world of Europe, in which a single unifier fails to materialize, and as a result, the balance of power would logically lead to a rational discourse of national and global orders.

The very existence of a global system of multiple nations, and the very impossibility of uniting all nations under one single political regime in the near future, may turn out to be the best news for the growth of democratic political culture. So long as there are contending sources of authority on the international stage, pluralism of authority on the domestic level will also become the dominant tendency. The pressure is on those authoritarians who have to face alternatives without and challenges within. It will be more and more difficult to maintain an authoritarian political culture when alternative realities and values are easily available. In this sense, China is moving toward the world, not dragging the world toward itself.

Notes

1 Here I am with the liberals in the field of international relations, who endeavor to develop a more comprehensive and more coherent explanation of the interconnection between domestic politics and international politics. To understand a nation's preferences in its international behavior, it is important to understand its domestic political structures and political values. A more thorough version of liberalism would also study the impact of a nation's international environment on the evolution of its domestic institutions and values (Moravcsik 1997, 513–553).

My gratitude is due to Hugo El Kholi for pointing out this family resemblance and for other thoughtful suggestions.

2 This sense of Chinese cultural superiority had been expressed through, and supported by, three main theses in traditional Chinese thought: Hua-Yi distinction (*hua yi zhi bian* 華夷之辨), the status of the Orthodoxy (*zhengtong lun* 正統論), and the "Hanization" (*hanhua* 漢化) of the minorities.

3 Alexis de Tocqueville, whose famous study of democracy in America focuses not on American political institutions but on American civic culture, is reckoned as the pioneer of modern theories of political culture. A more contemporary scholar of political culture who enjoys great influence is Samuel Huntington, who correctly anticipated that cultural differences would soon be seen to play a much bigger role in international politics than had previously been imagined (Huntington 1996). The term "political culture" is hard to define, since it covers too many aspects of our political life, and usually influences our collective actions through unspoken presumptions. For a recent review of the research on political culture, see Lichterman and Cefai (2006), where they also have to select "a relatively few, prominent lines of thinking on political culture, rather than attempting an exhaustive review." Political culture is important, because "culture structures the way actors create their strategies, perceive their field of action, define their identities and solidarities" (393).

4 For Rawls's discussion of political culture, see Rawls (1997), section 4. Note also that Rawls makes a further differentiation between "public political culture," "non-public political culture," and "background culture."

5 It is undeniable that Legalism was much more authoritarian than Confucianism. But as an ideology, Legalism was discredited immediately after the collapse of Qin Dynasty (207 BC). Later emperors might use Legalism as a hidden weapon, but they dared not to claim their legitimacy on Legalism. On the part of the intellectuals, there was hardly any famous Legalist after Han Fei (280 BC–233 BC), while each dynasty had its own generations of Confucian scholars. At the heart of Chinese authoritarianism, therefore, is Confucianism, not Legalism.

6 For the contemporary revival of Confucian political philosophy, see Jiang (2016); for the adoption of Western authoritarianism or conservatism, see Liu (2013) and Gan (2014); for a contemporary liberal review of Chinese political culture, see Deng (2013).

7 It is arguable that the Five Classics, the foundational texts of Chinese culture, were not the writings of any particular philosophers but the political documents of the earliest three dynasties of China. As Zhang Xuecheng (章學誠, 1738–1801) says at the beginning of his *Wenshi Tongyi* (《文史通義》), "the Six Classics are all histories. Ancient intellectuals did not write books; they did not philosophize beyond practical matters. The Six Classics are all political documents of the ancient kings ("六經皆史也。古人不著書，古人未嘗離事而言理。六經皆先王之政典也。" Zhang 2014). But this point does not negate the fact that later philosophers played an outstanding role in expounding and expanding the teachings of these classics. More important is the fact that the Confucian intellectuals have a long tradition of supporting the stability of the political establishment through interpreting these classics.

8 Benjamin Schwartz has a similar observation: "Confucius' unique dominance as a 'culture hero' is truly exceptional, since there are no exact parallels in any other ancient civilization, although one can find parallels in specific religious traditions, such as Buddhism and Christianity" (Schwartz 1985, 60).

9 To be sure, both Martin Luther and John Calvin encouraged obedience to secular authorities, but in later developments, the Protestant churches in France, England, and other countries ran into conflict with their established rulers. Due to this complicated historical process, Christianity, unlike Confucianism,

did not end up to be a loyal ideological buttress for authoritarian regimes. See Sabine (1973), "The Early Protestant Reformers."

10 Machiavelli (2005), chapter 4. For the rediscoveries of the merits of feudalism by Gu Yanwu (顧炎武, 1613–1682) and Huang Zongxi (黃宗羲, 1610–1695), see Qu (2016). For a more comprehensive clarification of many misunderstandings about Chinese *fengjian* and *junxian*, see Feng (2007).

11 In chapter 3 of *Considerations on Representative Government*, John Stuart Mill also has the observation that a "despotic monarchy" can be more easily conquered (Mill 1977).

12 For a radical critique of Chinese political tradition in the first half of the 20th century, see Hsiao (1979); for a positive review during the same period, see Ch'ien (2012).

13 For recent debates over the Chinese political tradition and the re-evaluation of the May Fourth Movement, see Bai (2012, 2016). For a more comprehensive re-evaluation of the Chinese political tradition as a meritocracy, see Bell (2015).

14 For the lack of institutional checks in Confucianism, see Chan (2014), chapter 2.

15 Hu Shih shared this observation, see Hu (2012), chapter 2. Fatalism is also a theme in Confucianism, which was attacked by Mozi (2010, chapters 35–37).

16 A famous Mainland scholar on Chinese philosophy, Chen Lai, argues that the priority of duties over rights is one of the four main characteristics of Chinese way of thinking. The other three priorities are responsibility over freedom, the group over the individual, and harmony over conflict. He claims that such priorities are positive heritages that should be carried on (Chen 2015).

17 See Locke (2003), book I, chapter 2, and Rousseau (2002), chapter 2. Arguably, Aristotle has already made a distinction between political authority and paternal authority (Aristotle 1998, section 1.12).

18 Francis Fukuyama emphasized this merit of the Chinese tradition and compared it with the Indian tradition. See Fukuyama (2011), chapter 7. Fukuyama also found this Chinese tradition: "Did might then make right for the Chinese? Was the Mandate of Heaven simply an after-the-fact ratification of a power struggle between warlords? To a large extent, it was" (Fukuyama 2011, chapter 20).

19 Hobbes has an even more monist understanding of human motivation: "The passions that most of all cause the differences of wit are principally the more or less desire of power, of riches, of knowledge, and of honour. All which may be reduced to the first, that is, desire of power. For riches, knowledge and honour are but several sorts of power." See Hobbes (1996), chapter VIII, section 15.

20 For a similar critique of Marx, see Arendt (1998, 33).

21 For recent expressions of skepticism against global justice and the related debates, see Tan (2019), Gu (2019), and Liu (2019). Gu Su and Liu Qingping are both liberal intellectuals, so their doubts over global justice can be more representative of the Chinese attitude on this matter.

22 Here I am with Philippe Nemo, who argued that modern Western liberal democracy and the values and practices accompanying it were developed in a long historical process of "a polycentric social order." As Nemo says, "the European reformers of the sixteenth to the twentieth centuries ascertained that a polycentric social order was more efficient in regard to the resolution of the most important social issues than any previously known type of social order."

> Under the impulse of these ideas, which gradually evolved into an explicit model, the great democratic revolutions promoted the doctrine and practice of *intellectual liberalism* (religious tolerance, pluralism in the sciences, schools, the press, and culture in general), *democracy* (pluralism in politics, free elections, and shared and limited-term responsibility of government),

and *economic liberalism* (pluralism in the economic arena). In each case, progress was so significant that it would not be unreasonable to call the phenomenon a new cultural leap forward.

(Nemo 2005, 62–63)

Such a modern development, I believe, was made possible by an even longer history of political separation since the collapse of the Western Roman Empire in the 5th century.

23 Those agricultural civilizations attacked by nomads tended to view this kind of invasion as natural disasters or supernatural punishments; they failed or refused to recognize those nomadic states as alternative forms of political civilization. See Barfield (1989, 25–26).

24 *Analects*, 3.5. ("夷狄之有君不如諸夏之亡也") The English rendition is mine. A recent translation goes like this: "The Yi and Di barbarians, even with their rulers, are still inferior to the Chinese states without their rulers." See Confucius (2003), 18.

25 Hobbes typically names fear and power struggle as ingredients of the paranoid mindset. See Glass (2006). Examples of conspiracy and paranoia can be found in historical events like the Cultural Revolution (1966–1976), during which friends and allies turned very quickly into enemies and traitors. See MacFarquhar and Schoenhals (2006).

26 "Thucydides's Trap" is a concept recently elaborated by Allison (2017), where he describes a possible zero-sum game between China and USA.

27 For a recent discussion of Chinese fatalism, see Solomon (2003, 435–454).

References

Allison, Graham. 2017. *Destined for War: Can America and China Escape Thucydides's Trap?* Boston, MA and New York: Houghton Mifflin Harcourt.

Arendt, Hannah. 1998. *The Human Condition*, 2nd ed. Chicago, IL and London: The University of Chicago Press.

Aristotle. 1998. *Politics*. Trans. by C.D.C. Reeve. Indianapolis and Cambridge, MA: Hackett Publishing Company.

Bai, Tongdong. 2016. "How Did China Become a 'Despotic' Country." *Journal of Chinese Humanities* 2016(5). (白彤东, "中国是如何成为专制国家的？", 《文史哲》, 2016年第5期).

Bai, Tongdong. 2012. *China: The Political Philosophy of the Middle Kingdom*. London: Zed Book.

Barfield, Thomas. 1989. *The Perilous Frontier: Nomadic Empires and China*. Cambridge, MA: Basil Blackwell.

Bell, Daniel A. 2015. *The China Model: Political Meritocracy and the Limits of Democracy*. Princeton, NJ and Oxford: Princeton University Press.

Chan, Joseph. 2014. *Confucian Perfectionism: A Political Philosophy for Modern Times*. Princeton, NJ and Oxford: Princeton University Press.

Chen, Lai. 2015. *Core Values of Chinese Civilization: The Development of Guoxue and Traditional Values*. Beijing: SDX Joint Publishing Company. (《中华文明的核心价值：国学流变与传统价值观》，三联书店，2015).

Ch'ien, Mu. 2012. *Advantages and Disadvantages in Government of Chinese Dynasties*. Beijing: SDX Joint Publishing Company. (钱穆，《中国历代政治得失》，1952，三联书店重印，2012).

Confucius. 2003. *Confucius Analects, With Selections from Traditional Commentaries*. Trans. by Edward Slingerland. Indianapolis and Cambridge, MA: Hackett Publishing Company.

Deng, Xiaomang. 2013. *Lectures on the Comparison of the Cultural Psychologies of China and the West*. Beijing: Renmin Press. (邓晓芒：《中西文化心理比较讲演录》，人民出版社，2013).

Feng, Tianyu. 2007. *An Inspection of the Concept of Fengjian*, 2nd ed. Wuhan: Wuhan University Press. (冯天瑜，《"封建"考论》，第二版，武汉大学出版社，2007年)

Fukuyama, Francis. 2011. *The Origins of Political Order: From Prehuman Times to the French Revolution*. New York: Farrar, Straus and Giroux.

Gan, Yang. 2014. *A New Treatise on Culture, China and the World: Three Traditions Connected*. Beijing: SDX Joint Publishing Company. (甘阳：《文化中国与世界新论：通三统》，三联书店，2014)

Glass, James M. 2006. "Paranoia and Political Philosophy." In *The Oxford Handbook of Political Theory*. Eds. by Dryzek, Honig, and Philips. Oxford: Oxford University Press: 729–749.

Gu, Su. 2019. "Nationalism, Egalitarianism and Global Justice." *Fudan Journal of the Humanities and Social Sciences* 12(2): 263–273.

Hirschman, Albert O. 1970. *Exit, Voice, and Loyalty: Responses to Decline of Firms, Organizations, and States*. Cambridge, MA and London: Harvard University Press.

Hobbes, Thomas. 1996. *Leviathan*. Ed. by J.C.A. Gaskin. Oxford and New York: Oxford University Press.

Hsiao, Kung-chuan. 1979. *A History of Chinese Political Thought*, vol. 1. Trans. by F.W. Mote. Princeton, NJ: Princeton University Press.

Hu, Shih. 2012. *English Writings of Hu Shih*, vol. 2. Ed. by Chih-P'ing Chou. Berlin: Springer.

Hui, Victoria Tin-Bor. 2005. *War and State Formation in Ancient China and Early Modern Europe*. Cambridge: Cambridge University Press.

Huntington, Samuel. 1996. *The Clash of Civilizations and the Remaking of World Order*. New York: Simon & Schuster.

Jiang, Qing. 2016. *A Confucian Constitutional Order: How China's Ancient Past Can Shape Its Political Future*. Princeton, NJ and Oxford: Princeton University Press.

Li, Kaiyuan. 2001. *The Establishment of the Han Empire and the Group of Liu Bang: Studies on the Military Meritocracy*. Beijing: SDX Joint Publishing Company. (李开元，《汉帝国的建立与刘邦集团：军功受益阶层研究》，三联书店，2001).

Lichterman, Paul and Daniel Cefai. 2006. "The Idea of Political Culture." In *The Oxford Handbook of Contextual Political Analysis*, Eds. by Robert Goodin and Charles Tilly. New York: Oxford University Press.

Lin, Anwu (林安梧). 2003. *Misplaced Dao: The Essential Problem of Chinese Political Thought* (道的錯置—中國政治思想的根本困結) Taipei (臺北): Taiwan Xuesheng Shuju (臺灣學生書局).

Liu, Qingping. 2019. "Equal Rights versus Equal Needs: Global Justice or Global Virtues?" *Fudan Journal of the Humanities and Social Sciences* 12(2): 275–291.

Liu, Xiaofeng. 2013. *The Route Marker for Leo Strauss*. Beijing: Huaxia Press. (刘小枫，《施特劳斯的路标》，华夏出版社，2013)

Liu, Zehua. 2014. *A General History of Chinese Political Thought*. Beijing: Renmin University of China Press. (刘泽华，《中国政治思想通史》（综论卷），中国人民大学出版社，2014)

Locke, John. 2003. *Two Treatises of Government*. Ed. by Ian Shapiro. New Haven, CT and London: Yale University Press.

MacFarquhar, Roderick and Michael Schoenhals. 2006. *Mao's Last Revolution*. Cambridge, MA: The Belknap Press of Harvard University Press.

Machiavelli, Niccolò. 2005. *The Prince*. Trans. and ed. by Peter Bondanella. New York: Oxford University Press.

Mill, John S. 1977. *Considerations on Representative Government*. In *The Collected Works of John Stuart Mill*, Ed. by John M. Robson. Toronto: University of Toronto Press, London: Routledge and Kegan Paul, 1963–1991, vol. XIX.

Moravcsik, Andrew. 1997. "Taking Preferences Seriously: A Liberal Theory of International Politics." *International Organization* 51(4): 513–553.

Mozi. 2010. *The Mozi: A Complete Translation*. Trans. by Ian Johnston. New York: Columbia University Press.

Nemo, Philippe. 2005. *What is the West?* Trans. by Kenneth Casler. Pittsburgh, Pennsylvania: Duquesne University Press.

Pines, Yuri. 2012. *The Everlasting Empire: The Political Culture of Ancient China and Its Imperial Legacy*. Princeton, NJ and Oxford: Princeton University Press.

Qu, Jingdong. 2016. "The Dual Government System of Chinese Traditional Society: Feudalism vs. Bureaucracy." *Society* 2016(2). (渠敬东, "中国传统社会的双规治理体系——封建与郡县之辨," 《社会》, 2016年第2期)

Rawls, John. 1997. "The Idea of Public Reason Revisited." Reprinted in John Rawls, *Political Liberalism*. Expanded edition, New York: Columbia University Press, 2005.

Rousseau, Jean Jacques. 2002. *The Social Contract*. Ed. by Susan Dunn. New Haven, CT and London: Yale University Press.

Sabine, George. 1973. *A History of Political Theory*, 4th ed. New Delhi: Oxford and IBH.

Schwartz, Benjamin. 1985. *The World of Thought in Ancient China*. Cambridge, MA and London: Harvard University Press.

Solomon, Robert C. 2003. "On Fate and Fatalism." *Philosophy East and West* 53(4): 435–454.

Tan, Kok-Chor. 2019. "Global Justice, Luck, and Human Needs: Reflections on Gu and Liu." *Fudan Journal of Humanities and Social Sciences* 12(2): 255–261.

Xunzi. 2014. *Xunzi*. Trans. by Eric Hutton. Princeton, NJ and Oxford: Princeton University Press.

Yang, Soon-ja. 2017. "The Reconciliation of Filial Piety and Political Authority in Early China." *Dao: A Journal of Comparative Philosophy* 16(2): 187–203.

Zhang, Xuecheng. 2014. *Wenshi Tongyi*. Beijing: Zhonghua Shuju. (《文史通義校注》, 中華書局, 2014)

Zhao, Dingxin. 2015. *The Confucian-Legalist State: A New Theory of Chinese History*. Oxford: Oxford University Press.

6 State coercion, *tianxia*, and the idea of egalitarian global justice

Tan Ankui

Egalitarian global justice has been one of the most influential ideas originating in Western philosophy but widely discussed and even accepted in today's China. To be more accurate, global justice is a family of ideas among which the most radical and egalitarian one seems to focus on economic redistribution, paying little attention to the justification of coercive power. Various views of coercion have been developed to defend or criticize the idea of egalitarian global justice. In this chapter, I will reveal the particular significance of the legitimation of state power for our thinking about distributive justice in China and other underdeveloped countries. Then I will argue that the decisive point in distributive justice is neither state coercion itself nor the particular type of coercion in operation at the global level but the unique character of dual coercion in state power. This is why the underdeveloped countries, including those which have achieved remarkable success such as China, should meet the moral challenge of legitimizing state power before embracing egalitarian global justice. The dual coercion thesis can, at least, partly explain the failure of the attempt to argue for global justice by reviving the ancient Chinese concept of *tianxia*.

State coercion and its significance for global justice talk in the Chinese context

International human rights instruments and practices since the Second World War have set more limits to the sovereignty of each state, and international humanitarian aid has made certain contributions to the relief of suffering in many places. But each nation-state remains as the recognized sphere within which justice in the distributive sense should be administered. Given this background, the development of the idea of global justice since late the 1970s, inspired by John Rawls's theory of domestic egalitarianism, represents a radical revision. For some philosophers, the proliferation of international, supranational, multinational actors, along with the profound influence of the transnational rules and systematic activities of these actors on the domestic life of national societies indicates that "global" is displacing "international." For Thomas Pogge, this terminological shift also reflects that "the very distinction between the national and international realms is dissolving" (Pogge 2010, 14). If national borders have lost their moral and explanatory significance for distributive justice, then social and economic rights may be or even should be realized universally in the name of justice and enjoy their status as universal human rights proper accordingly.

The aforementioned imagining of egalitarian global justice has sparked a lasting echo in China, at least partly due to the enthusiasm for globalization of many Chinese scholars. Another reason for this is that the idea of global justice recognizes the historical and moral harm brought by foreign powers, such as invasion and colonization, which may partly account for the poverty of some underdeveloped countries. As the members of a nation which suffered such seriously unjust events, it seems natural for us to embrace the compensatory implications of egalitarian global justice. Nevertheless, it will be a great affront if I denied that some scholars accept the idea of global justice out of their reasoned and sincere philosophical belief in individualist universalism. The real problem is that, once you follow the reasoning of global justice proponents (or at least some radical egalitarians), your concern will be concentrated on causality and morality at the global level, and the basic issues of domestic justice may be neglected. Among those basic issues, the justification of state power is the most important in triggering our thinking about justice. Egalitarian global justice talk tends to take it for granted that states are the primary agents for achieving justice or to be blamed for global injustice, leaving the legitimation of state coercion aside.

In this chapter, first and foremost, I will invalidate the derivation of the idea of egalitarian global justice from the causal impacts of the global order on poverty and inequality. It is true that the global poverty and inequality have a causal relationship with the actions of rich countries, but in order to make the citizens of rich countries assume moral responsibility for the actions of their own countries, some qualifications are indispensable to warrant the status of the state as a moral agent. This involves justification of the coercive power of the state, and I will argue that the legitimation of state coercion is the real starting point of Rawlsian egalitarianism. To put it another way, domestic egalitarian distributive justice is merely a product of the attempt to justify the coercive power of the state from the perspective of equal citizenship and equal political autonomy. I will argue that, in spite of the deep impacts and even the coercive character of global institutions and rules, today's global order still lacks a critical element which underpins the reasonableness and necessity of domestic egalitarian distribution. This element is what I will call "dual coercion" or "coercively coercive cooperation."

This argument, if tenable, has some general implications for the global justice debate. But it has a more direct and significant relevance to China and many other underdeveloped countries. During the past four decades, the whole world has witnessed China's rapid economic growth and its expanding influence. It has been widely accepted that the legitimacy of the regime and state power in China largely results from its remarkable economic performance. But since the early 2000s, the Chinese government has attempted to adopt more and more distributive-justice-oriented or equality-directed social policies without substantive political reforms, at least political reforms up to the standard of legitimacy prevailing in Western societies. In this context, more widely shared welfare benefits are provided as if economic inequality in itself was sufficient to warrant the practice of egalitarian distribution. This ongoing story, just like the idea of egalitarian global justice, seems to leave the challenge of coercive state power aside. On the other hand, the logic of egalitarian global justice may help to legitimize this domestic practice by empowering it with morally attractive reasons. But, if my argument is plausible, no underdeveloped or poor country should ever ignore the legitimation of state power when they propose egalitarian (global) justice. Otherwise, they would just be putting the cart before the horse, since the real trigger of egalitarian justice is coercive state power. And my contribution to the argument for the priority of coercive state power, compared to contemporary Western political philosophers such as Thomas Nagel, Michael Blake, and Laura Valentini, as will be revealed in the following, lies in not merely my emphasis on coercion itself but my analysis of the "dual coercion" character of state power. As I will argue, it is this "dual coercion" character, rather than coercion itself, that is decisive for the confining of egalitarian distribution to the sphere of domestic societies.

But when we argue against egalitarian global justice in terms of the distinctiveness of state coercion, especially when we think about this issue in the Chinese context, we have to undertake the burden of examining and responding to an emerging Chinese theory of global justice. For some philosophers, the ancient Chinese concept of "All-under-Heaven" (or *tianxia*) may inspire us to develop a promising alternative approach to global justice, since this concept, as it has historically been imagined and assumed, represents a real supranational vision because of its more culturally inclusive dimension. In the last part of this chapter, I will introduce and analyze the theory of the *tianxia* system newly developed by a celebrated Chinese philosopher, Zhao Tingyang, revealing its potential and limitations for the prospect of egalitarian global justice. This illuminating theory, explicitly aiming at a new institutional scheme for the whole world in the age of globalization and, in this sense, far more radical than the prevailing ideas of global justice, attempts to replace the individual or state-based model of political order in modern Western societies. But the political and institutional dimension of the *tianxia* system is too utopian to be feasible, and its grounding arguments are still too weak. Even if a world government could be established, global libertarianism and egalitarianism would just be two options with equal theoretical and moral cogency. So the final conclusion of my analysis is still pessimistic as to whether ancient Chinese wisdom can give us insights into global egalitarianism. And this, in turn, may help us to reaffirm the moral and political priority of the justification for state coercion.

The culpability of citizens for state actions

Viewed from our everyday moral thinking, justice means something special in the sense that the people, particularly those who are disadvantaged, have "rights" to make corresponding claims. Rights in the proper sense are correlated with specific duty bearers, so they are either universal or negative rights against every other person (and against institutions as a logical extension) or positive rights against those who have particular relationships/interactions with the rights holders. H. L. A. Hart's well-known distinction between general rights and special rights is the widely accepted conceptualization of this (Hart 1955, 183–188). This standard distinction is also applied to the dichotomy between negative and positive duties which separately correspond to the two categories of rights. But there are obviously some other positive duties which have no correlative rights, as exemplified by humanitarian duties.

Given this distinction, poverty and inequality themselves cannot be transformed into rights talk or the discourse of justice without further conditions under which some particular relationships or interactions can be confirmed. So, some proponents of global justice who seek to establish it on a more solid foundation attempt to start from a less controversial conception of human rights, instead of taking poverty and inequality themselves as grounding reasons, so that our positive duties toward those in poverty can be more closely connected with a widely recognized concept of universal negative rights.

As a matter of fact, as the intellectual origin of human rights, the idea of natural rights established in early modern philosophy conceives these rights as the rights of each individual against every other individual. Although from then on it has been a common view that human rights are rights against the government, it is undeniable that the starting point of the idea of natural rights lies in a moral imagination of interpersonal relationships, and the individual-government relationship measured by natural rights is merely a moral and logical extension. Only under this general background can we interpret correctly Kant's formulation of innate rights: "An innate right is that which belongs to everyone by nature, independently of any act that would establish a right" (Kant 1996, 30). A right is innate in the sense that it is not acquired through particular actions. Otherwise, that right can only be accounted as a special right in Hart's sense. An innate right has already existed and played its normative roles among individuals before they become involved in any other particular relationships through particular actions from which further rights and obligations may emerge. Since these rights are not grounded in any particular relationships or particular actions, they are both universal and negative.

As a leading philosopher of global justice, Thomas Pogge realizes that what we can affirm as universal rights are only those negative rights correlated with negative duties. So he attempts to develop an argument for the status of freedom from poverty as a human right based on our common presumption of negative duties the essence of which is the non-injury principle. For this to be possible, he has to give an account of the causes of poverty to reveal that poverty is not a natural or neutral fact but a result of some kind of injury from outside. Pogge attempts to do this within his "new philosophical framework" associated with the expression "global justice," and the core of this framework is "the causal impact of the design of the transnational institutional arrangements upon the conditions of life experienced by human beings worldwide" (Pogge 2010, 19). Based on this, we can approach another decisive consideration in the idea of global justice: "In the modern world, the rules governing economic transactions – both nationally and internationally – are the most important causal determinants of the incidence and depth of poverty" (Pogge 2007, 26).

Then another question should be raised. Is an institution that causally leads to poverty simply unjust? If we want to get "yes," two points are indispensable. First, poverty itself is not merely an evil, but also a reflection of injustice (or to put it in a similar way, poverty is a violation of human rights). Second, causal impacts are in their nature associated with justice, and the concept of causal responsibility implies moral responsibility. Since we have already denied the first point as an unwarranted assertion, we will only focus on the second in the following.

Actually, social life in its nature always produces some unavoidable negative externalities. It is theoretically untenable and practically extravagant to believe that all causal impacts, even negative ones, in this unending causal chain entail some violations of rights. If we look into moral responsibility in this way, nobody could take any action freely, and even nobody should come into this world at all – just imagine how many people a person's birth and later life will affect in various ways! Even negative externalities cannot be accused of violating rights in a general way. As Stéphane Chauvier points out humorously, "even if the beautiful is preferable to the ugly, it seems difficult to speak of a right to see only what is beautiful." So it is logically safe to say that "not all evil inflicted on others, as a negative side effect of social activities, can be held as the violation of a right" (Chauvier 2007, 311). Pogge himself admits that the emphasis on causal impacts

> does not mean that we should hold ourselves responsible for the remote effects of our economic decisions. These effects reverberate around the world and interact with the effects of countless other such decisions and thus cannot be traced, let alone predicted.
>
> (Pogge 2008, 205–206)

Now it is clear that the concept "impact" is too neutral and broad to bear the necessary moral implications.

Some proponents of global justice also emphasize certain compensatory ideas about duty, according to which "culpable causal responsibility establishes that those so responsible have an obligation to compensate those who are in poverty as a result of that culpable conduct as well as to refrain from producing poverty in the first place" (Campbell 2007, 70). Pogge himself uses terms such as "compensatory obligations" (Pogge 2008, 26) too. As a logical problem, compensation can only be understood within the framework of rectificatory justice, which makes no sense without a "prototype" of justice. But the idea of global justice cannot offer such a prototype unless, once again, it holds that freedom from poverty in itself is a positive human right which implies that every person is entitled to living conditions above poverty. Only in this way can the proponents of global justice tell us why the causal responsibility for poverty is "culpable." Given the negative nature of the concept of human rights, this positive conception of human rights can hardly hold.

But Pogge's argument goes deeper. He focuses on the factors that lead to the incidence of poverty. Thus, we have to confront two further questions: Whose actions cause such impacts? And what's wrong with those actions? In the context of global justice, it is the global order that affects the incidence and persistence of poverty. But on the global stage, the main actors are different states and their governments. There is a powerful moral accusation that "the citizens and governments of the affluent countries – whether intentionally or not – are imposing a global institutional order that foreseeably and avoidably reproduces severe and widespread poverty" (Pogge 2008, 207). Even if poverty itself can give us no specific moral teaching, the fact that the order behind it is "imposed" by others obviously has negative moral implications. What follows directly from this moral defect is that the global order should be democratized rather than dominated by a few wealthy and mighty powers so that the "democratic deficit" at the international level may be overcome.[1]

Relative to global justice, the appeal to the democratization of the global order sounds more prudent and morally more reasonable, since it does not demand the positive requirement of distributive justice among states other than the eradication of the domination of mighty powers. If we keep moving forward to global distributive justice, another serious challenge will emerge. When positive duties are assigned to states in the name of justice, these duties can only be fulfilled by the citizens in each state. After all, the resources to be distributed and redistributed are produced by the citizens, although the main actors at the global level are states or governments. So a question comes to the fore: why should citizens take the responsibility for the actions of their state and its government? Some proponents of global justice simply affirm that

> since citizens are collectively responsible for their society's organization and its resulting human-rights record, human rights ultimately make demands upon (especially the more influential) citizens. Persons share

> responsibility for official disrespect of human rights within any coercive institutional order they are involved in upholding.
>
> (Pogge 2008, 70)

For Pogge, this responsibility is "a shared responsibility" (Pogge 2008, 176). But the idea of global justice is both cosmopolitan and individualist, and "the central idea of moral cosmopolitanism is that every human being has a global stature as an ultimate unit of moral concern" (Pogge 2008, 247). From the individualist standpoint, why citizens should be responsible for their government's violations of human rights of people in other countries (let's just assume that these human rights are there and they have been actually violated) is far from self-evident. The question of where the so-called "collective responsibility" and "shared responsibility" arise from still awaits an explanation.

It is undeniable that each state acts on behalf of and in the name of its citizens on the international stage. However, it is not unreasonable for us to ask Pogge to offer us an explanation for how a state is entitled as a moral agent to represent its citizens, since he is a flat-out individualist. It is somewhat surprising that he transfers the institutional (in its essence, national) responsibility to citizens while talks so little about how the institutions of a state themselves should be organized. Pogge just emphasizes that we as citizens "participate in upholding" the institutions of our state and, as far as the badly slanted global order is concerned, "we are materially involved" (Pogge 2008, 139) in its continuous shaping and coercive imposition. But this seems to be too demanding for citizens. By paying taxes and fulfilling their positional duties, citizens might be said to have helped to uphold their domestic institutions, but they might have done so simply out of fear or helplessness. Given this, if their government did wrong in imposing an unjust global order and we just unreflectingly demand that the citizens share the responsibility, we are probably taking a serious moral risk of intensifying the injustice already prevailing in their domestic society. If this happens, the idea of global justice may begin as ethical idealism but end as moral cynicism. Even for those poor people in poor countries,

> if…extreme inequality and poverty is a result of a complex system of domination and exploitation, a focus on only distributive justice may be insufficient and may even harbor the danger of leaving the unjust system basically intact by turning the hitherto dominated into mere claimants and recipients of goods.
>
> (Forst 2001, 175)

For a state or its government to have a moral entitlement to represent its citizens and to act so that the citizens can reasonably be required to share the responsibility for its actions, the primary problem to be resolved is the source and distribution of its power and other resources. That means the focus of our concern should be withdrawn back to the domestic realm, and this follows from the inner logic of global justice because only in this way can we confer on a state and its government the status of a moral agent who can legitimately act in the name of its citizens.

Dual coercion and domestic social justice

One conclusion can be drawn from the previous analysis that the moral precondition of global justice lies in not the causal impacts of global institutions on the poor but the moral entitlement of states as legitimate representatives of their citizens. Our concern for this entitlement arises from a fundamental political fact that states and their governments exercise coercive power over their citizens which in some conditions may reasonably exempt the latter from taking responsibility for the actions of the former.

Each state possesses coercive power, and a domestic cooperative system is necessarily coercive. The lack of this coercive power has been traditionally considered as the decisive characteristic of an international order without a world government. But Pogge rightly emphasizes that "any social order requires a certain degree of coercion (imposition) in its creation and maintenance" (Pogge 2008, 142). In the practice of global order, modern international law has left room for international conventions, and countries who transgress international law or violate international conventions may be sanctioned. But as we have argued previously in Part 2, the moral requirement that naturally follows from the existence of coercive impositions is the democratization of the global order which gives each state an equal voice in the establishment of global institutions. A democratized global order reflects the consent of each party. In addition, consent can play a powerful legitimatizing role here because it implies that each state has, at least in principle, the option to withdraw from the global cooperative system. In spite of the depth of interdependence of all states, the possibility of withdrawing from global cooperation has not in principle been closed. If a state has to participate in cooperation under pressure, then democratization of the global order may be the right solution. In a democratized global order, all those countries who voluntarily play the cooperative game may be understood to have made the choice out of their own interest. Engagement based on self-interest is not evidence for the illegitimacy of the game itself.

But it is a totally different matter as to the domestic order. On the one hand, the parties to a domestic cooperative system are confronted with coercive power. On the other hand, they do not have the same exit mechanism as in global cooperation. An immediate objection may be raised here: Is not migration such an exit mechanism? Apparently it is, but in fact not. When a citizen no longer wants to accept domestic cooperation and chooses to leave, he will be confronted with another state's coercive power. He has no opportunity to live alone. In this sense, at least for an individual in modern times, coercive state power is not a choice at all. Even if a particular group of people in a given state successfully build their own state, the story for each individual is repeated. But in democratized global cooperation, when a state chooses to withdraw, it does not have to face another external coercive power.

A more illuminating but concealed point has often been ignored. Even the conditions for withdrawal from a particular domestic cooperative system are themselves a constituent part of the coercive cooperation, since they are coercively prescribed a priori by the state power. In any cooperative game, withdrawal may be qualified. But in a democratized global order, these qualifications can actually be based on the unanimous consent of all the parties. This is just unimaginable in a domestic system. In one word, (democratized) global cooperation is a game that can in principle be rejected by any single state, whereas national cooperation is a game that individuals must play. So understood, compared to global cooperation, the most distinguishable character of the domestic one lies in not its coercion but its coercive coercion. We may call it "coercively coercive cooperation." It is coercively coercive in two senses: its coercive rules are not up to the individual citizen's choice, and coercive cooperation in some form is always inescapable for individuals (even for immigrants).

This dual coercion is the most worrisome characteristic which distinguishes national cooperation from both every kind of voluntary association and the global order (however much we emphasize interdependence among nations). Owing to this character, state power, in spite of its capacity to protect individual liberties and interests, constitutes the strictest limitations on, even a fundamental negation of, their free will. Given this, the legitimation of state power should be different from that of the global order or associations. It is impossible for the former merely to appeal to actual individual consent to the cooperative system of a state but more plausible to offer each individual good reasons not to withdraw from the system to which they can consent, since it is meaningless in the final analysis to imagine "agree, or withdraw" in the domestic context.

Now I'd like to argue that this is exactly the starting point of Rawls's theory of domestic social justice. Distributive justice is the subject matter of his theory, but why Rawlsian distributive justice? The immediate answer is that it is to regulate the basic structure of a society. But to seek a just basic structure is, for Rawls, to legitimize state power. He clearly articulates the liberal principle or ideal of political legitimacy in his later works as follows: "Our exercise of political power is proper only when we sincerely believe that the reasons we would offer for our political actions…are sufficient, and we also reasonably think that other citizens might also reasonably accept those reasons" (Rawls 1996, 217). This ideal of political legitimacy presupposes that state power as coercive power should be shared equally by each citizen, and the exercise of it requires that citizens should give reasons that they can mutually accept. Although articulated only in his later works, this ideal runs through all Rawls's political thinking. In interpreting his design of the original position and the veil of ignorance, he emphasizes that this design models an initial situation that is fair in which "all are similarly situated and no one is able to design principles to favor his particular condition," and this is why the conception of justice developed in *A Theory of Justice* is called "justice as fairness" (Rawls 1971, 12). Hence there is no doubt that the two principles of justice, as the choice of the parties in the original position, are indeed the outcome of the consideration of political legitimacy.

Based on this egalitarian conception of social justice, each citizen can make valid claims to his fair share of the primary goods within the national society, and these claims are positive rights. It is the legitimation of state power that enables us to take a decisive step forward beyond negative rights and negative duties, and this is what the concept of universal human rights that originated from the concept of natural rights can hardly do. As a critic of egalitarian global justice, Thomas Nagel rightly points out that justice in the distributive sense applies "only to a form of organization that claims political legitimacy and the right to impose decisions by force, and not to a voluntary association or contract among independent parties concerned to advance their common interests" (Nagel 2005, 140). But it is worth mentioning that to emphasize coercion does not necessarily mean denying the point of cooperation for distributive justice. As a matter of fact, without a conception of social cooperation, even domestic distributive justice may be impossible, since the citizens under that condition need not give acceptable reasons to each other at all. This is why another critic of global justice, Michael Blake, goes too far in holding that "coercion, not cooperation, is the sine qua non of distributive justice" (Blake 2001, 289). To put it more exactly, my argument does not deny the necessity of cooperation itself, although it highlights the unique "coercively coercive" character of domestic cooperation. But it must be clarified that what ultimately distinguishes domestic political legitimacy from the legitimacy of the global order lies in the coercively coercive character of state power. Under the background of dual coercion, citizens mutually give reasons acceptable to each other, and the egalitarian rights and duties are the norms that will regulate their mutual relations which are different from those between them and outsiders. As citizens of a particular country, we may still bear some duties to others in other countries, such as humanitarian duties, but they have nothing to do with equal citizenship and are different in both their nature and content. The decisive point is that, at the global level, we cannot reasonably conceive the potential beneficiaries of humanitarian duties as positive rights claimants.

It seems safe to say that my dual coercion argument goes deeper than Thomas Nagel's and Michael Blake's view of coercion. But Laura Valentini re-elaborates the latter view of coercion to argue for, not against, egalitarian global justice (Valentini 2011). She distinguishes between two types of coercion, one of which is interactional and the other systemic. The former is exercised by an individual or collective agent, and the latter is exercised through a system of rules exercised by a sufficiently large number of agents.

Valentini argues that, at the global level, the justification of the former requires the principles regulating interstate interference and that of the latter requires principles of global socioeconomic justice. For Valentini, the function of socioeconomic justice is to justify state coercion by making it compatible with each citizen's freedom, but she complains that the notion of coercion employed by contemporary liberals is too narrow to capture the constraints on freedom that need to be justified. In other words, they pay little attention to global systemic coercion. This criticism is probably valid and even powerful when it is directed at Thomas Nagel's and Michael Blake's views. But in my dual coercion argument, I manifestly affirm that the coercion represented by the international rules, which is different from the domestic coercive power, does exist at the global level.

The crucial disagreement between my argument and Valentini's lies in whether the coercion at the global level can trigger egalitarian justice. In the light of Valentini's understanding of the function of socioeconomic justice, our conceptions of freedom have the last word on this problem. Here lies the most decisive step in Valentini's view. She holds a very broad conception of freedom that is internally related to autonomy and socioeconomic opportunities. This is sufficiently revealed when she talks about the baseline against which to evaluate whether someone's freedom has been restricted. She says,

> Even if more agents are better off (in terms of freedom) under the current system S than under its relevant counterfactual counterpart S′, so long as some of them are better off under S′, S counts as coercive. If some agents' freedom is restricted, they are owed a justification as to why the system is designed in the way it is.
>
> (Valentini 2011, 214)

This positive conception of freedom unreflectively presupposes too much, and it takes the risk that no system of cooperation could be justified at all except a thoroughgoing egalitarian one. On the other hand, even if we hold such a conception of freedom, it is not necessary for the justification of a system to appeal to socioeconomic equality. It is logically imaginable that a democratic procedure for the design of the system may be enough. Valentini attempts to reach the conclusion that "the ***same kind*** of systemic coercion liberals justify domestically by appeal to egalitarian socioeconomic justice also exists internationally" (Valentini 2011, 217). But if my interpretation of John Rawls's theory is plausible, he has not intended to justify domestic coercion "by appeal to" egalitarian justice as if the legitimacy of egalitarian justice itself were unquestionable. For Rawls, pace Valentini, egalitarian justice is not a given starting point but the outcome of his political justification for domestic coercion.

I have defended a particular version of coercion against egalitarian global justice. Based on the above argument, we can now give a brief analysis of two statements in Rawls's theory which are frequently charged by global justice theorists as contradictory to reality. The first is the assumption of a domestic society as a closed system. When Rawls assumes a structure of basic institutions we "enter only by birth and exit only by death" (Rawls 1996, 135–136), he is not intending to deny the possibility of an individual leaving his country. The plausibility of this assumption comes from the fact that the conditions of withdrawal are themselves set coercively by the state and that nobody can escape coercive state power in general. Against this background, it is both reasonable and understandable to assume a state as a closed society when we think about how its basic structure should be organized, since citizenship in this sense is not a cosmopolitan idea. The second is the assumption of a domestic society as "self-sufficient" (Rawls 1971, 4) or "self-contained" (Rawls 1996, 457). Pogge points out that "in the modern world there are no self-contained national societies; a closed background system exists only at the global level" (Pogge 1989, 240–241). In spite of its empirical plausibility, it does not follow from this judgment, based on today's global system, that a country cannot reach self-sufficiency without involving global cooperation and its division of labor. Even if there are some extreme cases, such as the situation of Arctic Eskimos, they can, as Rawls suggests, be resolved in an ad hoc way (Rawls 1999, 108). Nevertheless, this is not a problem of positive rights based on social justice, although our duty to help them may be morally weighty enough. All this considered, since what concerns us is what people can make positive claims to, we are going into the realm of distributive justice which originates from the justification of coercively coercive state power.

In sum, taking the deep interdependence of today's global system as evidence of a global cooperative system is not enough for the extension of Rawlsian distributive justice to the global realm. This invalidates a fundamental claim of global justice as asserted by Charles Beitz:

> If the societies of the world are now to be conceived as open, fully interdependent systems, the world as a whole would fit the description of a scheme of social cooperation, and the arguments for the two principles would apply, a fortiori, at the global level.
>
> (Beitz 1979, 132)

Rawls himself applies the concept of the cooperative system to a wider scope rather than confining it to national societies. For example, he says that the law of peoples must be fair between all the reasonable peoples and effective "in shaping the larger schemes of their cooperation" (Rawls 1999, 12). But he rejects the vision of egalitarian global justice. Given that a domestic cooperative system is a "coercively coercive cooperative system," the global cooperative system, even if it is coercive, cannot be treated in the same way as domestic cooperation should be. And we should not, just as Pogge does, reach the conclusion that the very distinction between the national and international realms is dissolving, if only in that the sovereign-nation-state system has not broken down. Following this, the politically necessary precondition for the extension of Rawlsian social justice to the global realm is the creation of a world government. Even some moderate proponents such as David Miller realizes that "global equality cannot even be properly defined unless we suppose that the peoples of the world come to form a single political unit with common rules governing the holding and use of resources" (Miller 1999, 210). But even the most fervent proponents of global justice are cautious in keeping their distance from the radical claim for a world government. For example, Pogge defines his own theory as "moral cosmopolitanism" as opposed to "legal cosmopolitanism" (Pogge 2008, 175).

Tianxia system: a Chinese alternative approach to global justice?

As I have said in the first section, my argument against egalitarian global justice has some implications for China and other underdeveloped countries. Within a global order without a world government, just like the world we live in today, domestic egalitarian distribution resulting from the legitimation of state coercion enjoys its priority and even prevents us from extending it on a global scale. For many developing countries in pursuit of social justice, the justification of domestic state power should be the primary item on the agenda.

But it might be objected that the above argument is too "Westernized" to be applied in a non-Western context. In fact, in order to break the traditional and moral barriers of states so that global justice can be realized along with the process of globalization, some thinkers turn to ancient Chinese wisdom and its newly developed ideas among which "All-under-Heaven" or *tianxia* system is the most remarkable. As an idea that is tremendously different from and far more inclusive than the nation-state system, this ancient Chinese concept seems to have the potential to broaden our horizons beyond national borders.

Over the past years, a Chinese philosopher of great originality, Zhao Tingyang, has developed a highly inspiring and controversial theoretical imagining of a world order that is based on the revival and adaptation of this ancient Chinese concept. The construction of his theory is presented as an innovative ontological inquiry about the world and world order, and it has already been developed as a comprehensive system that covers many important philosophical, political, and ethical topics. This theory is not directly motivated by the concern for global justice, but we can draw some significant conclusions about it, just as Zhao Tingyang himself has done.

The theoretical construction of the *tianxia* system is also inspired by the reality of globalization. But it is far more radical than the idea of global justice in the sense that it questions the system of nation-states and offers a totally different concept of "world sovereignty." Zhao Tingyang says globalization has changed the way of existence of the world and the nature of the political, and the emerging global politics implies that we need to make the rules, construct the power, distribute interests and resources, narrate history and knowledge in a new way, which requires those political principles and institutions appropriate to it to secure the order of global common life and political legitimacy. The inner logic here is that globalization provokes the problem of internalization of the world which calls for the construction of a new *tianxia* system, and under this new system, the world has world sovereignty acting as a political agent (Zhao 2016, 27).

A crucial point here is that international politics is to be replaced by global politics. For the former, the basic political agent is each nation-state, while for the latter, the world itself. But due to the system of nation-states, modern institutions are by nature domestic, not global or for the whole world. The world in this sense is still a "non-world" (Zhao 2005a, 7), and "the most important political problem is how to construct the world in the political sense, that is, to construct a legitimate political world" (Zhao 2005a, 21). There are no intellectual resources in the Western tradition to meet this challenge, since Western political philosophy is concerned primarily with individual rights and national interests. But the Chinese traditional concept of *tianxia* has the potential to model a new way of thinking beyond nation-states, so that the real human values and the interests of the world can be safeguarded (Zhao 2005a, 16–25).

For Zhao Tingyang, the connotation of *tianxia* has three dimensions. One is geographical, referring to all the lands under Heaven; the second is psychological, referring to the common aspirations of all people; the last is ethical-political, referring to a cosmopolitan ideal or utopia that the whole world is one with world institutions and even a world government.[2] Compared to nation-states, the concept *tianxia* enjoys its superiority due to its all-inclusiveness which corresponds to the oneness of the world. It means there is no place for "the others" in the framework of *tianxia.* According to Zhao Tingyang, "the absence of the others" is a very important principle, and simply because of this principle, *tianxia* could be an effective alternative solution to global justice. The contemporary political order is composed by nation-states, and the nation is regarded as the basic element for state building. It may be a good way to consolidate a community but also an obstacle for global justice. The reason is that the nation itself is exclusive; more specifically, people who don't belong to the nation are always regarded as others and even as enemies. Under such circumstances, the way of dealing with international affairs is conflict, trickery, and war. On the contrary, *tianxia* includes all people so that it can avoid useless confrontation. *Tianxia* guarantees not only the a priori integrity of the world, but also the diversity of history.

But this Chinese traditional concept and its all-inclusiveness may be too empty without a further philosophical basis. Zhao Tingyang deepens his investigation with some metaphysical ideas. The *tianxia* system implies that, metaphysically, coexistence enjoys priority over existence. Accordingly, individual rationality should be supplemented with a new form of "relational rationality" which aims at not the minimization of self-interest but the reduction of mutual injury and the improvement of the coexistence of all. He emphasizes that we need a "second enlightenment" through "relational rationality" (Coicaud 2011, 127). Both these two forms of rationality are indispensable, but, like the logical reference to the priority of coexistence over existence, relational rationality is prior to individual rationality (Zhao 2016, 36). Given this metaphysical thesis, he claims that "there are no individuals (except bodies) without interpersonal relationships" (Zhao 2009, 327). And he believes that the concept of human rights should also be reconstructed on this relational conception of existence.

As a highly imaginative theory, the *tianxia* system is still in progress. Part of Zhao Tingyang's concern is how real global justice can be realized, and he once complained that we are far from it (Coicaud 2011, 127). When it comes to economic distribution, he is, like most proponents of egalitarian global justice, discontented with Rawls's non-egalitarian retreat in *The Law of Peoples*. He says, "When Rawls denies the role of difference principle in the international community, he eliminates international justice and encourages an international community following the law of jungle" (Zhao 2005b, 46). But he says little about distributive justice under the *tianxia* system. On the other hand, he seems far more radical than Thomas Pogge and his followers in that he presents us with not merely a moral but a legal and political picture of the *tianxia* system which leaves room for a world government. In fact, what this theory attempts to offer is an "institutional philosophy" for the political world.

Unfortunately, as an institutional philosophy, this theory gives us no clear account of its institutional dimension except an overbroad statement: "Any institution, if only it can take charge of the interests of the world, secure the world peace, establish the universal cooperation of the world, and can be accepted by all the peoples, may satisfy the theoretical demands of the Tian-xia system" (Zhao 2009, 82). But how are world interests defined? Who has the last word on this definition? Zhao Tingyang seems to be silent about these vital problems. The lack of explicit institutional construction is probably rooted in the nature of the *tianxia* system itself. The superiority of this system, as Zhao Tingyang says, lies in its all-inclusiveness. But now it seems clear that this all-inclusiveness is realized (or is expected to be realized) at the cost of the necessary principles without which we cannot make any evaluation of the world order. Are there any metaphysically or morally true principles that can be revealed by philosophers and that underlie the *tianxia* system? Or will all the individuals or different peoples have the opportunity to deliberate and determine those principles and the institutions corresponding to them? These questions crucially matter for a political theory of the whole world. A leading scholar working in the history of Chinese thought, Ge Zhaoguang, reminds us of the internal cultural Sinocentrism and its distinction between insiders and outsiders in the concept of *tianxia*. He also warns us of the danger of nationalism in the guise of cosmopolitanism when some scholars try to revive this ancient Chinese concept. And what is particularly revealing is that, as a historian, he acutely raises two political and moral questions which we should face with intellectual courage: "Who is the author of the world institution? And who is eligible to evaluate the soundness of it?" (Ge 2015, 31). For these questions, Zhao Tingyang and other followers of the Chinese traditional conception of *tianxia* owe us an answer.

These two problems are in fact parallel to the hidden concerns behind Rawlsian domestic egalitarian justice as revealed above. As I have argued in the third section, the distributive justice of domestic egalitarianism is the product of equal citizenship, and it models the equal political autonomy of each citizen through a contract situation in which they can equally determine the social cooperative principles. The deepest reason why we should achieve such distributive justice is not only because of the mandatory state power, but also and more importantly because of its character of dual coercion. On the contrary, the theory of *tianxia* system offers us no account of the agent who is to specify and evaluate the global institutional arrangements. What's more, once the world government preferred by this institutional philosophy is established, if it ever could be, the most perplexing problem of dual coercion will disappear. In this hypothetical social context, should goods be equally distributed within the scope of the whole world? Is the Rawlsian difference principle still a plausible and desirable option? To put it more incisively, why should egalitarianism enjoy its priority over libertarianism in that imagined world? In such a hypothetical post-nation-state world, coercion by government will still be imposed on each of us, while the coercive coercion which underpins the domestic egalitarian justice nowadays will no longer function. It follows from the dual coercion view that we have no reason to take the extension of egalitarian domestic justice to the whole world for granted even under a world government. Against such a background, egalitarian justice will be, at most, an option among many others. So it is safe to say that the *tianxia* system is not powerful enough to be an alternative approach to the prevailing ideas of egalitarian global justice proposed by Western philosophers. For those underdeveloped countries, such as China and many others in East Asia, the legitimation of state coercion and domestic egalitarian justice are still the primary missions that they should undertake, although they can achieve those goals in their own distinctive ways.

Notes

1 For the discussions of "democratic deficit" at the international level, see B. S. Chimni, 2004, "International Institutions Today: An Imperial Global State in the Making," *European Journal of International Law*, 15, p. 6; Joseph S. Nye Jr, 2001, "Globalization's Democratic Deficit: How to Make International Institutions More Accountable," *Foreign Affairs*, 80, pp. 2–6. Some theorists argue that the international order should be democratized and legitimized by way of some

forms of deliberative democracy; see Steven Wheatley, 2010, *The Democratic Legitimacy of International Law*, Oxford: Hart Publishing Ltd; Micahel Ignatieff, 2001, *Human Rights as Politics and Idolatry*, Princeton, NJ: Princeton University Press, pp. 3–4; Susan Marks, 2000, *The Riddle of All Constitutions: International Law, Democracy and the Critique of Ideology*, Oxford: Oxford University Press, pp. 103–104.

2 For these three dimensions, see Zhao Tingyang, *Meiyou Shijieguan de Shijie* [No World-view for the World], pp. 8–9; Zhao Tingyang, *Tianxi Tixi: Shejie Zhidu Zhexue Daolun* [The All-under-Heaven System: An Introduction of the Philosophy for the World Institution], pp. 41–42; Zhao Tingyang, *Huai Shijie Yanjiu: Zuowei Diyi Zhexue de Zhengzhi Zhexue* [Investigations of the Bad World: Political Philosophy as First Philosophy], pp. 82–83.

References

Beitz, Charles. 1979. *Political Theory and International Relations*, Princeton, NJ: Princeton University Press.

Blake, Michael. 2001. "Distributive Justice, State Coercion, and Autonomy," *Philosophy & Public Affairs*, 30 (3): 257–296.

Campbell, Tom. 2007. "Poverty as a Violation of Human Rights: Inhumanity or Injustice?" in Thomas Pogge ed., *Freedom from Poverty as a Human Rights*, Oxford: Oxford University Press, 55–74.

Chauvier, Stéphane. 2007. "The Right to Basic Resources," in Thomas W. Pogge ed., *Freedom from Poverty as a Human Right*, Oxford: Oxford University Press, 303–322.

Coicaud, Jean-Marc. 2011. "Zhao Tingyang Jiaoshou Fangtanlu [An Interview with Professor Zhao Tingyang]," *Shijie Zhexue*, 6: 122–129.

Forst, Rainer. 2001. "Towards a Critical Theory of Transnational Justice," in Thomas Pogge ed., *Global Justice*, Oxford: Blackwell Publishers, 169–187.

Ge, Zhaoguang. 2015. "'Tian-xia' Imagined: Politics, Thought, and Academics Behind An Utopian Imagination [Dui Tianxia de Xiangxiang: Yige Wutuobang Xiangxiang Beihou de Zhengzhi, Sixiang he Xueshu]," *Si Xiang*, 29: 15–37.

Hart, H. L. A. 1955. "Are There Any Natural Rights?" *The Philosophical Review* 64 (2): 175–191.

Kant, Immanuel. 1996. *The Metaphysics of Morals*, translated and edited by Mary Gregor, Cambridge: Cambridge University Press.

Miller, David. 1999. "Justice and Inequality," in Andrew Hurrell and Ngaire Woods eds., *Inequality, Globalization, and World Politics*, Oxford: Oxford University Press, 187–210.

Nagel, Thomas. 2005. "The Problem of Global Justice." *Philosophy & Public Affairs* 33 (2): 113–147.

Pogge, Thomas. 1989. *Realizing Rawls*, Ithaca, NY: Cornell University Press.

Pogge, Thomas. 2007. "Severe Poverty as a Human Rights Violation," in Thomas Pogge ed., *Freedom from Poverty as a Human Right*, Oxford: Oxford University Press, 11–53.

Pogge, Thomas. 2008. *World Poverty and Human Rights*, 2nd edition, Malden, MA: Polity Press.

Pogge, Thomas. 2010. *Politics as Usual.* Malden, MA: Polity Press.

Rawls, John. 1971. *A Theory of Justice*, Cambridge MA: Harvard University Press.

Rawls, John. 1996. *Political Liberalism*, 2nd edition, New York: Columbia University Press.

Rawls, John. 1999. *The Law of Peoples*, Cambridge MA: Harvard University Press.

Valentini, Laura. 2011. "Coercion and (Global) Justice," *The American Political Science Review*, 105 (1): 205–220.

Zhao, Tingyang. 2005a. *Meiyou Shijieguan de Shijie* [No Worldview for the World], 2nd, Beijing: Zhongguo Renmin Daxue Chubanshe.

Zhao, Tingyang. 2005b. *Tianxi Tixi: Shejie Zhidu Zhexue Daolun* [The All-under-Heaven System: An Introduction of the Philosophy for the World Institution], Nanjing: Jiangsu Jiaoyu Chubanshe.

Zhao, Tingyang. 2009. *Huai Shijie Yanjiu: Zuowei Diyi Zhexue de Zhengzhi Zhexue* [Investigations of the Bad World: Political Philosophy as First Philosophy], Beijing: Zhongguo Renmin Daxue Chubanshe.

Zhao, Tingyang. 2016. *Tianxia de Dangdai Xing* [A Possible World of All-under-heaven System], Beijing: Zhongxin Chubanshe.

Part 3

East Asian insights into global justice

7 All-under-Heaven and liberty

Yu Yih-Soong

Introduction

The pattern of All-under-Heaven (*tianxia* 天下) is a traditional Chinese worldview. Recently it has been widely discussed following Tingyang Zhao's interpretation of it as an alternative to the current world order led by Western nations (Zhao 2009, 6). To some people, the pattern of All-under-Heaven represents China's challenge to the West.[1] But in my view, Zhao's interpretation is not, as it seems, simply a voice for the current rise of China. Despite Zhao's claim that it was the Chinese empire that had provided a successful experience of world unity rather than modern globalization (Zhao 2006, 37), the fact is he also did not recognize any existing country as the center of the world order he was advocating (Zhao 2011, 3). In addition, Zhao's designation of a world government, which aims to replace the United Nations, is not an entirely new modern Chinese version of cosmopolitanism. In fact, a century ago when China was being bullied by a group of imperialist nations, a Chinese reformer named Kang Youwei (康有为 1858–1927) had already laid out the path to world government in detail.

Nonetheless, Zhao's thought is provocative given his complete opposition to the Western view of international politics. This may encourage his readers to think that he is claiming that China and the West are irreconcilable, or the pattern of All-under-Heaven means Chinese hegemony. I believe this is not Zhao's intention, as he has admitted: the pattern of All-under-Heaven is a proposal for the far future, over 200 years distant, and not the solution to the current clash between nations. He has even admitted that he cannot give any prediction as to how it could be progressed (Zhao 2011, 11).

I agree with Zhao that the pattern of All-under-Heaven is valuable as an alternative to the current, typical view of international politics, as it is more inclusive of many cultures. However, I disagree with Zhao because he contrasts the pattern of All-under-Heaven with the concept of liberty. In Chinese history, the pattern of All-under-Heaven is not simply an ideal; it was represented by the institution of the Son of Heaven (i.e., the emperor). I find that Zhao's interpretation is indiscriminate and thus fails to examine the problems of the pattern of All-under-Heaven occurring in history. A hundred years ago, many Chinese reformers had been vehemently accusing the emperor system of making Chinese history stagnant; by doing so, they were also making an appeal to embrace the Western concept of liberty. A representative reformer Kang Youwei had even provided a cosmopolitan theory which related the concept of liberty to Confucianism. In my view, without reconciliation to modern values, the idea of the pattern of All-under-Heaven may well lead to a dominant single superpower appearing in Chinese history, rather than the harmony between nations that Zhao and others (including me) have looked forward to. In this vein, I claim that Kang Youwei's thought can provide a more desirable interpretation of the concept of the pattern of All-under-Heaven than Zhao's.

Accordingly, this chapter mainly considers two issues. Firstly, despite in Zhao's theory the pattern of All-under-Heaven is not an imitation of the Chinese imperial system, it is worth noticing that the realistic basis of his theory implies the dominance of a single superpower with regard to Chinese history. To discuss this issue, I will condense his theory into six features and then reveal their problems one by one in the next section. Secondly, in the section "Kang Youwei on liberty," I will discuss how Kang Youwei combined the notion of the right to self-mastery with the Confucian concept of empathy and thus how this may suggest an egalitarian progression toward world government.

The problems in Zhao's theory

According to Zhao, the pattern of All-under-Heaven is a traditional Chinese concept which had brought long periods of peace and stability to society in many dynasties of the Chinese empire (Zhao 2006, 36). The concept means that a good institution must be applicable at all political levels; that is to say, within the descending order from world government to nation-states then to families, all levels must follow family ethics (Zhao 2009, 13). This is exactly the Confucian principle which designates how the Chinese empire operated for thousands of years. The ancient Chinese people expected the emperor and every official to extend benevolence in the manner of a good parent; conversely, the people were expected to show filial piety and loyalty in the manner of good children. Simply put, Zhao's interpretation of the pattern of All-under-Heaven adheres to the traditional Chinese idea of the "co-construction of family and state (*jia-guo-tong-gou* 家国同构)." The difference is that Zhao replaced "emperor" with "world government" as the highest political level within the pattern.

Zhao has noted that only the Zhou dynasty (1046 BC–256 BC) had put the pattern of All-under-Heaven into fully fledged practice (Zhao 2009, 8). This means, in Zhao's interpretation, that Chinese feudalism is better than the Chinese centralism after the Qin dynasty as a representation of the pattern of All-under-Heaven. With respect to modern reality, this means the pattern of All-under-Heaven is a world order in which all the nation-states can co-establish a world government, but each of them retains a series of autonomous rights. Zhao has admitted that Chinese feudalism "waned because it was too good to exist" (Zhao 2009, 9). In the traditional Chinese narrative, the age of feudalism represents the Golden era, just as its waning reveals moral decline: the world had come to need a central government to end disputes between states. Zhao has not given any answer as to the means we would use to restore the Golden Era in modern international politics. He simply lays out the features of the pattern of All-under-Heaven. In this section, I will summarize them into six features, and then I will reveal that, with regard to Chinese history, these six features imply the dominance of a single superpower acting as their realistic basis.

The six features

Zhao contrasts the pattern of All-under-Heaven with the United Nations. He claims that the United Nations represents a type of fundamentalism, one which aims to universalize every nation as a copy of Western modernity. Zhao views the result as only enhancing the system of nations/states rather than a world government (Zhao 2006, 37–38). In his own words: "All-under-Heaven presupposes the Oneness of the world, and the oneness shows itself in all its diversities" (37). This means, in the pattern of All-under-Heaven, all the nations, or all the people of the world, are allowed to keep their local identity, even their idiosyncrasies, and the rule of the world government is entirely based on the voluntary consent of all the people (Ibid: 39).

The six features provided by Zhao explain how the pattern of All-under-Heaven is different from the Western understanding of international politics and what is meant by "voluntary consent."

Firstly, world government must be based on the general will of the world; this means that world government can satisfy all the people with good governance, instead of satisfying the interests of the majority (30).

Secondly, the world government must view affairs and problems from a world-wide viewpoint, instead of a national viewpoint; this means that the world government views the world as a single family, instead of a society of states (Ibid: 30–31).

Thirdly, the legitimacy of world government is proved by what it does instead of what it is. This means that the observation of social trends or preferences proves the legitimacy of world government, rather than statistical methods, such as democratic elections (31–32).

Fourthly, the virtue of world government is understood in terms of family harmony, rather than the concept of liberty. This means that world government deals with relations between people to proclaim their co-existence, rather than dealing with every individual proclaiming defense of their liberty (33).

Fifthly, the co-existence created by world government is understood in terms of the absolute of otherness, instead of in terms of subjectivity. The ethical principle of this is the negative representation of the Bible's rule, and accordingly it admits everyone may legitimately choose a different life.

As the Bible's rule states it, "do unto others as you would have them do unto you"; and Zhao has rewritten this as: "never do to others what the other would not want you to do to them" (35).

Sixthly, world government upholds a consensual game rather than a fair game to create a harmonious world order. The consensual game is defined by two strategies: (1) Confucian Equilibrium: the players share their fortune together, which means X benefits if Y also benefits, and loses if Y loses; (2) Confucian Improvement: the player needs to promote the other's fulfillment to attain her own fulfillment, which means that X attains fulfillment if Y also attains fulfillment (Zhao 2009, 15).

Thus, the pattern of All-under-Heaven requires a non-elected world government, which promises to create harmony between differences instead of a unity of sameness, and under its rule, every nation-state is led to have the mutually beneficial game instead of the competitive-fair game. The question is: is there a realistic basis upon which this world government could exist?

The realistic basis

Normally, a political theory is considered utopian if the realization of the political order it advocates cannot be imagined in existing reality. According to this standard, the pattern of All-under-Heaven is obviously utopian. It is hardly to be imagined that all existing nation-states, based as they are on self-interested motives, would unanimously follow a single leadership, i.e., a non-elected world government, but somehow this receives the voluntary consent of all the people in the world. However, according to Zhao, the pattern of All-under-Heaven is not entirely impossible. As Zhao has noted, it had been partly realized in Chinese centralism and fully realized in Chinese feudalism. Therefore, if the pattern of All-under-Heaven requires a realistic basis to explain how world government could exist, then the clue to it can only be found in Chinese history instead of current reality.

Notably, from the Zhou dynasty until the Qing dynasty, all of the united governments throughout 3,000 years were established at the end of a full-scale war: either the civil wars between the numerous local powers or the overall invasion by the northern nomads. This implies that the world government in Zhao's pattern of All-under-Heaven is a single dominant superpower that can end world war.

According to Zhao's explanation of the traditional Chinese view, the rectitude of the emperor is proved on two bases: one is that the emperor can save the people from a terrible situation; the other is that he can maintain the world according to the order that most of the people want (Zhao 2006, 31). Zhao's explanation is well fitted to Chinese history. Given that losses during the Chinese civil wars were always over half the population,[2] it is obvious that the ruler who could end the civil war, rebuild the central government, and unite the whole country must have received the people's unanimous support; by the same token, he does not need an election to prove his rectitude. This explains the realistic basis of the first and third features of world government elaborated by Zhao. But the problem is that it requires that the ruler really is and continues to be the single dominant superpower. Otherwise, the empire will gradually collapse into civil war,[3] or be conquered by northern nomads.[4]

In Zhao's description, world government promises to create harmony between differences in the world-wide viewpoint. And Zhao illustrates this with the Mongolian and the Manchurian reigns, given that they were admitted by the Chinese people to be the successor of the Mandate of Heaven without discrimination (Zhao 2006, 32). The problem is that according to the most widely known Chinese historian, i.e., Qian Mu (钱穆 1895–1990), the Mongolian and Manchurian reigns in China in practice represented colonialism and imperialism (Ch'ien 1982, 100, 137).[5] Qian proved this with the fact that the discrimination policies applied during the Mongolian and Manchurian reigns in different areas or on different ethnicities were actually intended to make their control of the Chinese easier. For example, the Mongolian reign utilized a system of Provinces to geographically demarcate the Chinese conquest, thereby preventing the Chinese from organizing a self-sufficient military base (101).[6] Another example, the Manchurian reign set up a special office to deal exclusively with Mongolian affairs, and Chinese officials were forbidden to be recruited into it; this policy was intended to guarantee the advantages of the alliance of the Manchurian and Mongolian tribes to the majority ethnic Hans (Ibid: 137).[7]

That is to say, the co-existence between different ethnicities that the Chinese emperor intended to maintain was not purely out of concern for the welfare of the people; the other reason behind this was that the emperor was exploiting the differences in order to dissipate the people's strength and, by doing so, he was capable of maintaining a single dominance over his mass of subjects. This explains the realistic basis of the second, fourth, and fifth features of world government elaborated by Zhao.

Zhao does not give an example of the last feature, which says that the world government must promote the mutually beneficial game between the people. Undoubtedly, this feature is rooted in Confucian teachings about rites (*li* 礼). However, according to the paradigmatic account, which is illustrated by Xunzi (荀子), the order of rites is virtually a hierarchical society.[8] Xunzi suggests that the rites originated from setting the measure and ratio to regulate humanity's endless desires; they distinguish who shall receive more and who shall receive less; and thus disorderly contests between people provoked by their desires can be prevented. In Xunzi's words, the rites regulate:

> the gradations of rank according to nobility or baseness, disparities between the privileges of old and young, and modes of identification to match these with poverty or wealth, insignificance or importance.
>
> (Knoblock 1994, 56)

If the mutually beneficial game is feasible, Xunzi's illustration tells us that the rule of this game is virtually the rites of a hierarchical society. Furthermore, the rites require a single dominating power, i.e., the Son of Heaven to guarantee that they will be observed by all members of the hierarchy; otherwise this will inevitably be challenged by a rising of the stronger men. This is the realistic basis which explains the sixth feature of world government elaborated by Zhao.

In my view, Zhao's complete opposition to the Western concept of liberty has undermined the desirability of the pattern of All-under-Heaven. As I have illustrated above, with regard to Chinese history, Zhao's descriptions of a world government imply a single dominant superpower. Of course, such a dominant superpower does not necessarily lead to irrational or arbitrary control over the world. However, if the worst case happened, given that such a superpower is unelected, the people can only bear it, or initiate a world war to challenge it. Nonetheless, the pattern of All-under-Heaven itself is a traditional idea commonly inherited by the Chinese, therefore its interpretation ought to be opened to others' appraisal. In the next section, I will argue that with Zhao's (or our) predecessor, i.e., Kang Youwei's ideas, the pattern of All-under-Heaven can be combined with the concept of liberty. And on this ground, world government can be progressed peacefully, in an egalitarian way.

Kang Youwei on liberty

Kang Youwei was the very first person who laid out the agenda of Chinese modernization. Right after the Qing dynasty had been defeated by Japan in 1895, Kang began publicly advocating and interpreting Confucianism to embrace the Western conception of liberty.[9] Given that his interpretation is based on his criticism of Chinese despotism, this explains the problems within the traditional concept of the pattern of All-under-Heaven. Moreover, he did not simply apply the conception of liberty to advocate China's constitutional reform; he went further and directed it to advocating a one-world society. Actually, Kang was the first Chinese philosopher to have elaborated a comprehensive theory of cosmopolitanism in modern times. With reference to Kang's ideas, we can see not only the grounds on which the Chinese cosmopolitan view should and could embrace the conception of liberty, but also the reasoning by which the pattern of All-under-Heaven could imply a liberal as well as an egalitarian world society. Given that Kang always contended that the concept of liberty went together with the term the "right to self-mastery," I will first adduce my arguments about its meaning. Then, I will turn to illustrate, through his notion of the right to self-mastery, how Kang advocated progress toward a world government.

Right to self-mastery

The right to self-mastery is my translation of the Chinese term 自主之权 (*Zi-zhu-zhi-quan*) used by Kang.[10] Literally, *Zi-Zhu*, apart from self-mastery, can be translated as self-rule, or self-determination. I take the first given that it exclusively implies two images.

The first image is the egalitarian state without a hierarchy. As advisor to the emperor, Kang was not allowed to bluntly apply the metaphor of the slave-master in his arguments; nonetheless, he did explain his idea with a phrase from the *Book of Change*: "no leader among the dragons" (*Qun-Long-Wu-Shou* 群龙无首). This signifies Kang's opposition to traditional Chinese political culture; in Kang's writings, he looks toward an egalitarian society without the division into ruling and ruled (Kang 1991, 473). The second image is the idea of "true-self," which particularly signifies humanity's empathetic nature; this is based on Kang's preoccupation with his Confucian background. In Kang's writing, the failure to function is signified by barbarism or the annihilation of humanity (*ren-dao-mie-jue* 人道灭绝).

Noticeably, Kang's notion of the right to self-mastery should not be understood in its literal English meaning. The image of true-self in Kang's thinking is defined in terms of Confucian ethics rather than rationalism; as a result, his notion of the right to self-mastery is not equivalent to self-control or the positive liberty discussed by Isaiah Berlin. In short, in Kang's idea, the right to self-mastery is tactical instead of deontological, and it leads to collective instead of individual self-realization. To make this clear, the comparison with the English general understanding of self-mastery is inevitable. In the following, I will give a brief outline of the context behind Kang's reception of the concept of liberty, and then I will apply Isaiah Berlin's and Charles Taylor's reflections to make the comparison with Kang's notion.

Kang's reception of the concept of liberty is his immediate reaction to China's defeat in the First Sino-Japanese War (1894–1895). He attributed that defeat to the constitutional monarchy of Japan, for the reason that such a monarchy could be held to have produced a more efficient and stronger government than the despotic system of China. In his fourth petition sent to the Guangxu emperor (光绪皇帝 1871–1908), Kang contended that the superiority of the West is because the European countries had gone through many long-term wars between themselves; therefore, threats from other nations had driven the West to develop institutions that are efficient in motivating and uniting the people to struggle for common goals (Kang 1991, 149–150).

In comparison, Kang contended that as China had always needed to worry about civil disruption rather than threats from neighbors, this had therefore driven China to confining political power to the emperor and officials. As a result of this, the connection between locals and the center had been weakened, and the people's willingness to contribute their talents for common goals had been obstructed (150–151).

Kang's criticism is highly relevant to the problems with the traditional concept of the pattern of All-under-Heaven. His criticism suggests that a world government may well intend to confine resources to its own control, rather than investing in guarding the autonomous development of the nation-states. This moral hazard is conditioned within the structure of the pattern of All-under-Heaven itself. Nevertheless, the autonomy of nation-states would increase the risk of internal disruption to the rule of world government. Chinese history had proved this probability.

Kang's advocacy of Chinese political modernization and world government were focused on promoting the people's right to self-mastery. To be clear, Kang's reception of the notion of the right to self-mastery from Western thought is because he had seen his people being restrained from making a collective contribution, instead of being made to suffer under the coercion of a despotic system. Relying on his Confucian background, he thus defined the image of true-self in terms of empathy, instead of rationality. Accordingly, he identified the right to self-mastery as the political condition which allows the people to make a contribution, rather than acquiring freedom from suppression. To illustrate these subtle differences, I need to set out a formula for deduction to make the comparison with Berlin's idea of self-mastery.

I think that a reasonable notion of freedom must have been based on the assumption of a human psychological trait, and this assumption must have, accordingly, led to the specific goal of freedom. In terms of this, different notions of freedom can be commonly elucidated with the same formula for deduction. This is the formula: given that humanity suffers from X, ethically humanity should have freedom from X; and so politically, humanity should have the right to freedom from X.

In Berlin's idea, self-mastery is the kernel of positive liberty, which is distinguished from negative liberty (Berlin 1969, 15–35). With my formula, Berlin's narratives of negative liberty and positive liberty can be summarized as follows: (1) negative liberty: given that humanity is suffering from *being interfered with*, ethically humanity should have freedom from *being interfered with*; and so politically, humanity should have the right to be free from *being interfered with*. (2) Positive liberty: given that humanity is suffering from *failing to be its own master*, ethically humanity should have freedom from *failing to be its own master*; and so politically, humanity should have the right to be free from *failing to be its own master*.

Noticeably, Berlin's idea of self-mastery is equivalent to self-control, because he viewed the nature of suffering to be external coercion, and his image of true-self is the disciplined self (Berlin 1969, 20, 24). In comparison, Kang viewed it in three different ways. Firstly, in Kang's view, the suffering comes instead from internal misery, which is derived from humanity's empathetic nature; he illustrated this by indicating how much he was suffering from seeing others suffer from various kinds of tragedies (Kang 1994, 9–10). Secondly, he adhered to Mencius's idea of "the heart of not bearing to see others suffer,"[11] and thus he viewed the image of true-self as the willingness to extend empathy or benevolence (*Ren* 仁) (Kang 1994, 3–4). Thirdly, he considered the nature of tragedy to be caused by inequality, and thus he considered that the extension of empathy in practice means to eliminate the various kinds of inequality existing in the world (Kang 1994, 11).

With regards to these three differences, using my formula, Kang's notion of liberty can be summarized thus: the reason for human suffering is suffering from *seeing inequality*; therefore ethically, humanity should have freedom from *seeing inequality*; and so politically, humanity should have the right to be free from *seeing inequality*. Given that the act of *seeing inequality* is voluntary rather than coerced, such a narrative might be perplexing. However, in the Confucian idea, the extension of empathy is the natural course which signifies humanity's innate endowment; therefore, Kang considered that suffering from seeing inequality cannot be isolated. In his metaphor, it is likewise the reactionary perception of external things:

> Master Kang then says: If [a thing be] external to myself, how can I have knowledge [of it], how can I feel affection [for it]? Since I have a body, then I share with coexisting bodies that which permeates the air of Heaven, permeates the matter of Earth, permeates the breath of Man [...] Hence, if men sever what constitutes their compassionate love, their human-ness will be annihilated. Those whose [human-ness] has been annihilated cease to be civilized, and return to barbarism.
>
> (Kang 1994, 4; Thompson 1958, 64)

Kang considered that suffering from seeing inequalities is the essential psychological trait that defines liberty; by the same token, he considered that the act of removing inequalities is the essential objective of the right to self-mastery. So to speak, in Kang's view, the willingness to contribute for the common good is one of humanity's desires given its empathetic nature (9). Noticeably, as Berlin had likewise determined, the right to self-mastery in Kang's idea leads to a collective realization as well. However, given that Kang's image of true-self is defined according to feeling, in this case empathy, the promotion of the right to self-mastery in Kang's theory is tactical and not deontological. To elaborate upon this difference, I will apply Charles Taylor's criticism of Berlin to make the comparison.

In Berlin's view, negative liberty is more desirable than positive liberty, because the latter would entail authoritarian social control in the name of collective true-self-realization; in contrast, the former admits the truth that everyone shall find her own way to pursue her own goals (Berlin 1969: 33). With regard to Berlin's evaluation, Taylor's criticism is that liberty in practice is indivisible, there is no clear-cut division into negative and positive. According to Taylor's argument, positive liberty cannot be excluded, because it is required to evaluate whether the absence of external obstacles is really significant for us (Taylor 1997, 422). Taylor indicated that the true-self is not necessarily defined as an ontological principle; in common sense, the image of true-self may be opposed to the irrational self or to the self-indulgent slave of desire (425). In these terms, positive liberty is required to identify what should be restrained; that is, some external restraints are needed to restrict the irrational self in order to give humanity greater freedom; for example, pedestrian crosswalks exist to give pedestrians freedom from the risk of traffic accidents (Ibid: 422).

Taylor's image of true-self is personal rather than collective; it can be varied depending on the agent's social situation and internal reasons (421). Accordingly, everyone has different forms of self-realization or different kinds of self-mastery. Kang's image of true-self is the same as Taylor's on the grounds that it is personal, given that empathy is essentially a kind of feeling instead of an ontological principle and also the opposite of empathy is the fettered desire rather than a false thought (or ideology). But Kang's image of true-self is different from Taylor's as well, given that the self-realization in Kang's image must be collective. This is because the extension of empathy is generally a moral principle. However, it should not be misunderstood that Kang's notion of the right to self-mastery is necessarily deontological.

Noticeably, empathy itself is the feeling that puts first the other's feeling rather than one's own thoughts. Kang did note that the perception of what constitutes inequalities varies between people, and therefore he emphasized that the radical removal of inequalities, which disregards the diversity of social circumstance and the complexity of social conditions, would cause more suffering to the people. Kang articulated this truth with the metaphor of the medicine that will cause death if the patient's physical condition is disregarded (Kang 2007c, 553).

That is, Kang was suggesting that the promotion of the right to self-mastery must be a gradually evolving progress, instead of a radical revolution. His notion of the right to self-mastery is legitimate when it is tailored in accordance with different social conditions, while at the same time, it is oriented toward a desirable but tentatively infeasible world. For example, despite Kang admitting that democracy is a polity of a higher order, he nevertheless resolutely advocated a constitutional monarchy. This seems contradictory, but the fact is that Kang had seen that in his times, China needed the monarch to act as a traditional authority to unite the whole country, and the call for democracy would have plunged China into civil war (Kang 2007b, 312–313).

Another example: with his notion of the right to self-mastery, Kang could be both a nationalist and a cosmopolitan simultaneously. He endeavored to make China powerful, but he yearned for a one-world society as well. In Kang's thought, the promotion of the right to self-mastery meant increasing one's chance to contribute for the common good with one's own empathetic nature; therefore this ought not be confined to one's own country but needs to be extended to the world ethically (Kang 1994, 5–6). In the same vein, Kang's endeavor for China is because he could not bear to see his country unequal to the West and Japan; in the meantime, this does not conflict with his hope for an egalitarian world.

In conclusion, Kang's notions of the promotion of the right to self-mastery, as well as the realization of true-self, are tactical while needing to be collective. Given that Kang's concept of liberty is tied up with Confucianism, inevitably his cosmopolitan view inherited the traditional concept of the pattern of All-under-Heaven. But it is different in that it suggests an egalitarian progress toward world government while embracing the concept of liberty.

Progress toward world government

With his notion of the right to self-mastery, Kang laid out a social evolution from the domestic to the cosmopolitan level: despotic system → constitutional monarchy → democracy → one-world government; it signifies increasing the fulfillment of the people's right to self-mastery, as well as the decrease of social inequalities.[12] In contrast to Zhao's understanding of the pattern of All-under-Heaven, Kang's designation of world government does not imply the dominance of a single superpower; instead, it suggests a global union of nations. In the following, I will elaborate on the psychological and realistic bases upon which Kang contended for progress toward world government.

The psychological basis is that empathy is humanity's inseparable feeling; it cannot be isolated. In Confucianism, "the heart of not bearing to see others suffer" is the root of humanity's benevolence. Given that it is humanity's inherent endowment, its extension must be in due course universal if unobstructed by selfish desire. In these terms, the realization of true-self is equivalent to making a contribution for others without boundaries. In Kang's view, the extension of benevolence is equivalent to the promotion of the right to self-mastery, as they both lead to the common good instead of self-interest: "benevolence must have required removing the forces restraining and suppressing, to enable everyone equally to have self-mastery" (Kang 1991, 17). This explains how the people would willingly play the mutually beneficial game, instead of the fair-opportunity game; in other words, the reason that the people would willingly choose to have world government rather than a society of states.

On the other hand, the realistic basis is that the promotion of the right to self-mastery will bring about the development of the nation as well as the removal of social inequalities. To elaborate this, I need to narrate Kang's whole schedule of the progress toward world government. Given that Kang saw that the right to self-mastery would allow the people to contribute for the common good, he expected that its promotion would lead the society of states to result in world unity (Kang 1994, 87–88). Note that Kang could not have foreseen the movement for decolonization and independence which arose twenty years after his death. Despite his expectation being definitely historically incorrect, it has its own reasons.

Kang's expectation divided the progress toward world government into two grand stages: an international balance of power, then a global alliance. The occurrence of the international balance of power is expected in four sub-stages (see 91–93). (1) Both big and small despotic nations would be swallowed up or colonized by the constitutional nations, if they do not initiate constitutional reform, for example, Russia in 1910s. (2) The people in small constitutional nations with their right to self-mastery will unite into a big nation, or, say, a federation, for the sake of competing with the big nations. (3) Consequently, all constitutional nations will unite into a bigger nation. (4) Eventually, all surviving nations are constitutional, while simultaneously, their forces are in equilibrium with each other.

The next occurrence is the global alliance, which is also expected in four sub-stages (see 93–94). (1) The result of war is very difficult to anticipate given the international balance of power; as a result, the people will not allow the government to declare war against any other nation. (2) Given that war has no reason to be declared, all the nations will come together for an agreement on disarmament. (3) And the peaceful worldly exchange will drive the integration of ethics and the laws of the nations. (4) Eventually, given that the people in possession of their right to self-mastery tend to remove inequalities, the acceleration of world integration will bring the people to urge the establishment of the world government by election.

Kang's expectation indicates that with the promotion of the right to self-mastery, the world government could be called into being by the people voluntarily in a peaceful process. It does not suggest a single superpower whose righteousness is based on the assumption that it can end world war, as the change of dynasty in Chinese history had told. In this sense, the concept of liberty, rejected by Zhao, is necessary to be included in the pattern of All-under-Heaven. In other words, the third and fourth features elaborated by Zhao need to and could be rectified by Kang's thought.

Furthermore, with regards to the other four features elaborated by Zhao, Kang's ideas could provide a psychological basis which will make them more persuasive. Given that world government results from the promotion of the right to self-mastery, accordingly the instructive principles of world government should be deduced from the realization of true-self, i.e., benevolence. Given that the extension of benevolence has no boundary, the world government would tend to satisfy all the people rather than just the majority (first feature) and view the world as a single family (second feature). On the other hand, benevolence arises from empathy; therefore, the world government would tend to put forth the other's feeling rather than its own thoughts (fifth feature). In the same vein, the people in the world government, with their adherence to the right to self-mastery, will intend to remove inequalities for others; if they put this into practice, it means they are playing the mutually beneficial game (sixth feature).

Conclusion

In general, traditional Chinese ethics always emphasized moral inclusivism and social egalitarianism; therefore, much of traditional Chinese political thought naturally inclines toward cosmopolitanism.[13] It is no surprise that

Kang's and Zhao's understandings of the concept of the pattern of All-under-Heaven share numerous ideas, as they are both heirs to the same cultural tradition, especially the influence of Confucianism. Nevertheless, Kang differs from Zhao in his reception of the Western concept of liberty, and he further reconciles this with Mencius's idea of "the heart of not bearing to see others suffer." My study has revealed the reasons whereby the pattern of All-under-Heaven needs to and can be compatible with the concept of liberty.

It is true my study might not sufficiently answer a fully practical way of progress to world government, given that the idea of world government is virtually incompatible with the typical view of world politics now current, namely a society of states. However, at least my study may help to make clear that the cosmopolitan view based on Chinese history does not necessarily imply either Chinese hegemony or a complete opposition to Western ideas.

Notes

1 For example, William A. Callahan thinks that the pattern of All-under-Heaven serves to enhance "China's soft power as a source of a universally valid model of world politics" (Callahan 2008: 759).

2 During the civil war before the Han dynasty, half the population was lost (ten million); during the era of the three kingdoms, four-fifths was lost; before the Tang dynasty, two-thirds; and before the Song dynasty, four-fifths. See the information in Jin (1984: 150–152).

3 For example, Zhou, Qin (221 BC–207 BC), Han (202 BC–220 AD), and Tang dynasties (618 AD–907 AD).

4 For example, Song (960 AD–1279 AD) and Ming dynasties (1368 AD–1644 AD).

5 The English translation of Qian Mu's study deleted some content which discusses colonialism and imperialism, owing to Qian illustrating his discussion with the dominance of Britain over Hong Kong. The original Chinese work can be seen in Qian (2001).

6 In Chinese, the term "the system of Provinces" is 行省制度; it has been continuously adopted by Chinese governments, even to date.

7 The special office is named *li-fan-yuan* (理藩院).

8 See the "Discourse on Ritual Principles (礼论)" in *Xunzi*; the English terms and quote I use to illustrate Xunzi's thoughts are in accordance with John Knoblock's translation; I simply note the pages of his book: Knoblock (1994, 49–73).

9 Kang Youwei is a controversial figure in Chinese history; this is owing to the fact that he suggested not only having a constitutional monarchy, but also establishing a Confucian church. Nonetheless his thought has always been debated in Chinese academia. Especially in recent times, a group of scholars in mainland China are advocating "back to Kang Youwei" to find a new way to China's political reform, see Tang (2015, 15). In English studies, the most comprehensive work is by Kung-chuan Hsiao, see Hsiao (1975).

10 Kang's discussion of liberty in his writings is a tactic for his political advocacy; therefore, he would vary the terms he used with regard to different issues. For example, he would apply the "right to self-determination" (*Zi-Li-Zhi-Quan* 自立之权) to the issue of freedom of marriage (Kang 1994: 89) or the "rights of the people" (*Min-Quan* 民权) to the issue of freedom of political participation (Kang 2007b: 475). Nonetheless, "self-mastery" is the earliest and most frequent term he used; the earliest occurrence is in 实理公法全书, which is believed to have been written during 1888–1890. For the book, see Kang (2007a, 146).

11 In Chinese: *bu-ren-ren-zhi-xin* 不忍人之心..
12 Kang even discussed progress to decrease all kinds of inequalities radically, his so-called "Nine Boundaries (*jiu-jie* 九界)", inclusive of classes, races, gender, families, property, places, species (Kang is suggesting animal rights, too), and, last, the enjoyment of life (Kang 1994).
13 See Ding (2012, 93–94).

References

Berlin, Isaiah. 1969. "Two Concepts of Liberty." In Isaiah Berlin, ed. *Four Essays on Liberty*, 15–35. Oxford: Oxford University Press.

Callahan, William A. 2008. "Chinese Visions of World Order: Post-Hegemonic or a New Hegemony?" *International Studies Review* 10(4), 749–761.

Ch'ien, Mu. 1982. *Traditional Government in Imperial China: A Critical Analysis*. Translated by Chun-tu Hsueh and George O. Totten. Hong Kong: The Chinese University of Hong Kong.

Ding, John Zijiang. 2012. "Transformative Modes of Chinese Cosmopolitanism: A Historical Comparison." *Journal of East-West Thought* 2(December), 89–112.

Hsiao, Kung-chuan. 1975. *A Modern China and a New World: K'ang Yu-wei, Reformer and Utopian, 1858–1927*. Seattle: University of Washington Press.

Jin, Guantao. 1984. *Zai li shi de biao xiang bei hou I*. Sichuan: Si chuan ren min chu ban she.

Kang, Youwei. 1991. *Kang Youwei Zheng Lun Ji*, Tang Zhijun, ed. Beijing: Zhong hua shu ju.

Kang, Youwei. 2007a. *Kang Youwei Quan Ji*, Jiang Yihua and Zhang Rongxiao, eds., vol. 1. Beijing: Zhong guo ren min da xue chu ban she.

Kang, Youwei. 2007b. *Kang Youwei Quan Ji*, Jiang Yihua and Zhang Rongxiao, eds., vol. 6. Beijing: Zhong guo ren min da xue chu ban she.

Kang, Youwei. 2007c. *Kang Youwei Quan Ji*, Jiang Yihua and Zhang Rongxiao, eds., vol. 5. Beijing: Zhong guo ren min da xue chu ban she.

Knoblock, John. 1994. *Xunzi: A Translation and Study of the Complete Works*, vol. 3. Stanford, CA: Stanford University Press.

Qian, Mu. 2001. *Zhong Guo Li Dai Zheng Zhi De Shi*. Beijing: Sheng huo du shu xin zhi san lian shu dian.

Tang, Wenming. 2015. "Hui dao Kang Youwei yu lu tai xin ru jia zhi zheng." *Zhong-Hua-Du-Shu-Bao*, May 20, 15.

Taylor, Charles. 1997. "What's Wrong with Negative Liberty." In Robert E. Goodin and Philip Pettit, eds. *Contemporary Political Philosophy: An Anthology*, 418–428. Oxford: Blackwell Publishers.

Thompson, Laurence G. 1958. *Ta T'ung Shu: The One-World Philosophy of K'ang Yu-wei*. London: George Allen & Unwin Ltd.

Zhao, Tingyang. 2006. "Rethinking Empire from a Chinese Concept of 'All-under-Heaven' (*Tian-xia* 天下)." *Social Identities* 12(1), 29–41.

Zhao, Tingyang. 2009. "A Political World Philosophy in terms of All-under-Heaven (Tian-xia)." *Diogenes* 56(1), 5–18.

Zhao, Tingyang. 2011. *Tian Xia Ti Xi: Shi Jie Zhi Du Zhe Xue Dao Lun*. Beijing: Zhong guo ren min da xue chu ban she.

8 A Confucian "Law of Peoples"

Mencius's thought on global justice[1]

Wang Binfan

Introduction

Ancient China is widely known as an everlasting empire with a history very different from Europe. This perception might be generally true after the Qin Dynasty, the first dynasty of imperial China, was established in 221 BC. However, before this crucial moment, over approximately 550 years of the Spring and Autumn and the Warring State periods (770 BC–221 BC), numerous states[2] competed for the central plains of China (*zhongyuan*), which was the whole world for them then. Some scholars, therefore, regard this period as presenting an ancient model of international relations because the whole world was anarchic, and diplomatic policy influenced the fate of states.[3] It is also worth mentioning that at that time, states practiced different schools of thought (e.g., Confucianism, Mohism, and Legalism) as guidance for governance, which influenced both domestic and interstate policies.[4] Confucius (551 BC–479 BC) and Mencius (372 BC–289 BC) both lived during this period and, like many other theorists, spent most of their lives traveling from state to state attempting to persuade rulers to adopt Confucianism as a political ideology.

Unfortunately, Confucianism was not very attractive in these highly competitive circumstances, and the Qin Dynasty (established by the Qin state) embraced the guidance of legalism. However, this first dynasty of imperial China only lasted for fifteen years. After its collapse, the Han Dynasty (206 BC–220 AD) selected Confucianism as its official ideology, a choice followed and reinforced by most succeeding dynasties. It, therefore, is fair to say that Confucianism guided both the domestic ruling and the global governance of imperial China. In other words, if we think ancient China had its own theory of global justice for over nearly 2,000 years,[5] Confucianism was undoubtedly the mainstream doctrine, which started with Confucius's and Mencius's thoughts and practices.

This chapter explores Mencius's thoughts on global justice, especially his emphasis on benevolence as the primary principle and the Confucian Law of Peoples. Although Confucius certainly was the origin of Confucianism, Mencius developed Confucius's thought to deal with a more competitive and anarchic world[6] and left more detailed texts for discussion. By reviewing Mencius's thought through the lens of John Rawls's theoretical framework,[7] we will see that Mencius's principle of global justice is different from the premises of the Westphalian system treating all states as equal and from the logic of realism understanding international relations as merely domination or the balance of power.

Benevolence as the principle of global justice

In Confucianism, benevolence is the core virtue in moral self-cultivation and relates to the understanding of justice. Benevolence does not mean only the will to do good (the Western general understanding) but establishes the moral ideal for the gentleman (*junzi*) who is very different from the petty person (*xiaoren*) who only cares about self-interest. Since ancient China was mostly ruled by one emperor, whether the ruler could be benevolent undoubtedly influenced political governance, and a state with a benevolent ruler is usually regarded as under benevolent governance. However, such an understanding narrows the context of benevolence, especially when considering Mencius, whose thoughts on benevolence neither concern only the ruler's personality nor stop at the state level. Benevolence demands coherent development from individual goodness toward global governance not only as an individual virtue but also as a principle of justice (or a political ideal) for states to follow. Mencius's concept of benevolent governance develops the meaning of benevolence as a political virtue and encourages states to pursue some degree of global unity to ensure the peace and normative uniformity of the world. Such an emphasis blurs the normative significance of state boundaries and makes benevolence the main principle of global justice.

However, it has been questioned whether the discussion on benevolence has a part to play in contemporary debates on global justice or whether Confucianism has a theory of justice. This is because contemporary discussions on justice are mainly based on Rawls's theory, whose understanding of individual and states follows the Western liberal tradition. In these discussions, justice only concerns the principles of distribution and related institutional design and has no connection to individual virtue or the creation of a well-ordered, hierarchical society based on rites, as emphasized by Confucianism.[8] However, the meaning of justice should not be limited to the modern liberal conception, which treats moral self-cultivation as random individual choice and holds that the normative principles of political theory can only refer to elements of social design, such as distribution. Broadly speaking, justice means things that are normatively good, and the Western history of thought offers a variety of theories on justice not related to distribution. To enrich the resources for discussion, therefore, contemporary discussions on justice (such as global justice) should be more open to non-Western and pre-modern theories. The former is even more critical because we live in an era of globalization when any theory of global justice should be able to apply to the whole world and its diverse culture and traditions. As Cline (2007) points out, Confucianism and Rawlsian theories should learn from each other, and comparative political philosophy (also the field of this chapter) provides an excellent approach to deepen our understanding of both views, which, in turn, benefits the development of our sense of justice.

Let us start with the individual level. What does benevolence mean as an individual virtue (or moral ideal)? In *Analects*, Confucius argues that the essence of benevolence consists of "restraining yourself and returning to the rites" (12.1)[9] and "caring for others" (12.22).[10] The latter is an attitude toward others, while the former requires that one refrain from impolite behavior and instead follow the Confucian rites, which mainly regulate the relationships between different social identities (e.g., parents and children, elder and younger brothers, and rulers and ministers). Putting them both together, Confucius declares that "desiring to take his stand, one who is benevolent helps others to take their stand; wanting to realize himself, he helps others to realize themselves" (6.30).

However, what does "others" mean in Confucian thought? This point needs clarification because Confucianism considers people's specific identities rather than treating them as the same or equal beings. In *Analects* and *Mencius*, we can see two principles to understand who others are. First, Confucianism understands others through a system of hierarchy rather than the concept of equality. As Mencius states, the

> gentleman (*junzi*) loves living things without being benevolent toward them and is benevolent toward the people without being affectionate. That he is affectionate toward his family is what allows him to be benevolent toward the people and loving toward creatures.
>
> (7A45)

Benevolence then is a virtue practiced toward other human beings, not living things in general, and the gentleman who has the virtue of benevolence treats family, non-family members, and non-human living things differently. These principles reinforce that family relationships are important checks on the gentleman's behavior. In other words, the family is the basic unit of society and the starting point for the gentleman's self-cultivation. In *The Great Learning*, a crucial text indicating Confucius's thought, a famous Confucian motto declares the value of "cultivating personal life, regulating family, ruling state and making all under heaven (*tianxia*) in peace." This motto describes the process of individual self-development from personal life[11] to family regulation, then to governance of the state and peace-seeking for the world. In other words, by putting benevolence into practice, the gentleman contributes to improving the state of the family, state, and world step by step. The gentleman must first be a good family member before he can participate in governance at higher levels.

Here, however, arises a practical question: What if a person who would like to become a gentleman unfortunately loses family members – to take an extreme case, becomes an orphan? If one has no opportunity for family regulation due to, for example, unfortunate accidents outside one's control, can one, according to *The Great Learning*, still go through the process of self-development to practice benevolence and participate in political activities to improve governance?[12] Confucianism certainly highlights the importance of family relationships and their influence on political practice, but a short passage in *Analects* reminds us that we should not understand family relationships too strictly:

> Anxiously, Sima Niu remarked, "Everyone has brothers. I alone have none." Zixia replied, "I have heard it said, 'Life and death are governed by fate. Wealth and honor are determined by Heaven.' A gentleman is respectful and free of errors. He is reverent and ritually proper in his dealings with others. In this way, everyone within the Four Seas is his brother. How could a gentleman be concerned about not having brothers?"
>
> (12.5)

Although Sima Niu is unfortunate because of his missing family relationships, Zixia, one of Confucius's most famous students, reminds us that the way the gentleman deals with others might change their normative identity from strangers to non-strangers and make others of similar age one's brothers. In other words, the absence of a blood relationship is not an insurmountable obstacle for an unfortunate person such as Sima Niu to practice benevolence and become a gentleman. To fully follow the principle of benevolence, one can (perhaps should) treat other people of similar age as one's brothers and sisters, other people in the younger generation as one's children, and other people in the older generation as one's father and mother. The Confucian understanding of a gentleman is not a narrow-minded, family-loving person but one who cares for strangers based on the principle of benevolence. It is worth asking whether this principle is so universal that every gentleman should treat everyone in the world as his family members, but it at least reminds us that blood relationship can be broadened when we "return to rites" (12.1). Another point we should not miss in Zixia's response is his reference to "the Four Seas" when discussing strangers because this phrase means the whole world, including all states. The second principle to understanding "others," therefore, is that neither blood relationships nor state boundaries are the stable conditions excluding any person from the normative hierarchical system in which the family is the basic model.

Such clarification of benevolence at the individual level is important not only because it solves a problem for people in unfortunate circumstance but also because referring to benevolent governance urges the rulers and ministers of states to practice benevolence as a political ideal. Mencius argues that "there is a common expression, '*tianxia*, the state, the family.' *Tianxia* has its basis in the state, the state in the family, and the family in one's own self" (4A5). This statement relates to the motto in *The Great Learning* discussed earlier and indicates the validity of the motto when placed in reverse sequence: Good global governance is based on good domestic ruling, which, in turn, is based on good family regulation and then self-restraint. By practicing benevolence, strangers can become family members, so when governed well, a state and the whole world (*tianxia*) can be understood as a family in a larger scope. More specifically, for Mencius, the ruler should practice benevolent governance to

> reduce punishment and taxation, get the people to plough deeply and weed promptly, and get the able-bodied men learn, in their spare time, to be good sons and good younger brothers, loyal to their ruler and true to their word, so that they will, in the family, serve their fathers and elder brothers, and outside the family, serve their elders and superiors. (1A5)

Benevolent governance thus is more than an analogy of the ruler regulating the big family in good order. We should also see that by reconciling policies of punishment, tax, agriculture, and more, benevolent governance builds a well-ordered society that provides good conditions for more people to practice benevolence and affection. Mencius, therefore, insists that such a state will not be defeated, even with only "a territory of 100 li square" (1A5), because a united community in which people share the same ideal of governance has unimaginable power.

Considering the reality of the time, Mencius admits that benevolent governance is not the only way to rule if the governor is only eager to gain possession of a state. However, if a ruler wishes to succeed in competitive international relations, benevolent government becomes necessary because state boundaries do not pose obstacles that stop the influence of benevolent governance.[13] In the case of Sima Niu, the gentleman who practices benevolence can treat "everyone within the Four Seas" of similar ages as his brothers and sisters. Accordingly, citizens who are gentlemen should not treat foreigners differently simply because they live outside the state boundaries. Mencius, therefore, believes that widely practiced benevolence, the blurring of state boundaries, and the convenience of migration then make well-ordered states highly attractive to many people, directly leading to heavy immigration. In ancient times, when agriculture heavily relied on human labor, and war heavily relied on the number of soldiers, such developments would directly strengthen the state's power, making it much more difficult to defeat in war. As Confucius states, the ideal governing is to attempt to ensure that "those near to you are pleased, and those who are far from you are drawn closer" (13.16). Mencius describes these conditions drawing migrants "just as water flows downwards" (1A6), the power of which is unstoppable.

For both practical and normative reasons, therefore, benevolent governance should become the principle of global justice, and states that follow this principle will become models for the world.

Before we can use benevolence as a basis for exploring Mencius's view of the world, I would like to further clarify two more points about benevolent governance. First, although during Mencius's time, all states were ruled by individual rulers (monarchies or tyranny), and Confucian rites crucial to the principle of benevolence promoted a hierarchical understanding of human society, these circumstances do not mean that benevolent governance cannot apply to other regimes. In other words, states that choose benevolent governance can be ruled by one, few, many, or all. For example, when discussing the success of Shun, a sage king in Confucianism, at governing the whole world, Confucius also emphasizes the roles of five ministers.[14] A regime might determine the domestic institutional design and the process of policy making, while benevolent governance focuses on the creation of an attractive social order giving everyone opportunities to practice Confucian rites. This clarification is important for benevolent governance because it is seriously misleading to think that benevolent governance relies only on the individual ruler's practice of benevolence. As discussed, all gentlemen should overcome the narrow-minded understanding of family based on blood relationships and contribute to a well-ordered benevolent society, and we have no reason to ignore the influence of virtues and ideals spreading in such a community such as civil society. Although most states were ruled by one man during Mencius's time, the Confucian ideal of benevolent governance is not confined to that system.

Second, although Mencius frequently cites practical benefits (e.g., attracting migration to strengthen the state) to persuade rulers to practice benevolent governance, it is also misleading to think that Confucianism supports benevolence primarily for instrumental reasons. Similar to the distinction between the gentleman and the petty man at the individual level, benevolent governance as a governing principle recalls the Hua–Yi distinction (the Sino–barbarian dichotomy) in Chinese tradition, which determines the legitimacy of rulers, especially for those who would like to govern the whole world. As some studies have pointed out, the Hua and Yi identities are related to race, geography, and civilization, but only civilization (which demands choosing benevolent governance) can be regarded as so necessary and crucial as to be named Hua (Tang 2011). Every state, therefore, has the opportunity to become a model of the world regardless of location and the race of citizens. For example, Mencius points out that the sage kings Shun and King Wen of Zhou were born as barbarians based on race and geography, but by embracing benevolent governance, they transformed from Yi to civilized Hua, making them models (4B1). Moreover, this distinction emphasizes a normative requirement for those who desire to become decent participants and even leaders in global governance. We are reminded that benevolent governance does not tend to accustom states to jungle law in international relations but calls for them to change it and create a well-ordered world.

Five kinds of states (peoples) in the world

Taking benevolence as the principle of global justice, we can apply it as a criterion to divide the states under Heaven into two categories, and those states that choose benevolent governance certainly should be stronger. However, Mencius's conversation with some rulers shows that in a highly competitive world, some states still felt hesitant to choose benevolent governance because there is another factor that could not be ignored: force. In Mencius's time, those states were uncertain about the benefit of benevolent governance because they had lost in wars against states with strong military power[15] and feared attacks by other states.[16]

Benevolent governance is not the only method of ruling, so it is possible that a ruler might find a working strategy to make the state powerful in force without practicing benevolent governance. In this case, the ruler does not choose to be benevolent or aim to build a society in which people follow the Confucian rites. For example, one of the main reasons for the strength of the Qin state was its continuous war with indigenous minorities in western China. If the attractiveness of benevolent governance represents states' soft power (Nye 1990), force represents states' hard power, and of course, we have no reason to doubt states' capacity for survival if they focus on strengthening their hard power. To take the categorization of states in the world seriously, therefore, Mencius proposes the distinction between kingly rule (*Wang*) and hegemony (*Ba*):

> One who uses force while borrowing from benevolence is enacting hegemonic rule (*Ba*), but to do so he must first be the ruler of a state of considerable size. One who puts benevolence into effect through the transforming influence of virtue is enacting kingly rule (*Wang*), and his success will not depend on the size of his state.
>
> (2A3)

Mencius sees force and benevolence as two approaches states can choose to pursue global governance. Size is the third factor that should also be taken into consideration. Based on these three factors, there exist five kinds of states (peoples) in the world:

1. States (peoples) that choose benevolent governance and are large;
2. States (peoples) that choose benevolent governance but are not large;
3. States (peoples) that use force while borrowing from benevolence and are large;
4. States (peoples) that use force while borrowing from benevolence but are not large;
5. States (peoples) that use force without borrowing from benevolence.

Before analyzing specific kinds of states, two points should be clarified. First, it is apparent that this typology resembles Rawls's (1999, 4) theory in

The Law of Peoples. Rawls (1999, 25–30) discusses the people rather than the state because the people lack traditional sovereignty, and the state with sovereignty might become an obstacle to achieve global justice. As discussed, sovereignty was not emphasized in ancient times, so we can also call Mencius's thought on global justice "the Law of Peoples." However, ancient China called political communities *guo*, which is usually translated as "state," so I will ignore the difference between the "people" and the "state" and continue using "state" in the following discussion for convenience. Rawls's theory has been embraced based on the belief it can contribute to global governance in the contemporary world, not because we should push the state to become the people but because it establishes some principles for the system of states, which remains the basic framework of the world. Thus, as long as other theories that borrow from Rawls's category accept the system of states (rather than non-state actors or a world government) as their basis, the difference between the people and the state might not be significant,[17] and following convention, we can use the word "state" to prevent potential misunderstandings.

Second, from Mencius's explanation of hegemony (*Ba*), we realize that he makes a further distinction between those who do not choose benevolent governance. Some states that believe in force still might choose to "borrow from benevolence"; otherwise, those states belong to the fifth kind as uncivilized ones. To understand what the concept of *Ba* has meant historically, we can find representative examples of states that won hegemony during the Spring and Autumn period. As mentioned in footnote 5, during the Spring and Autumn period, Zhou still had legitimacy as a nominal central authority, and states shared responsibilities to protect Zhou when necessary. Considering the ruler analogy, showing respect and providing protection to Zhou's authority was a requirement of benevolence, and those who chose benevolent governance could help strengthen Zhou's power. In contrast, states (e.g., Qi, Jin, Chu, and Qin) that won hegemony sought to strengthen themselves instead of Zhou. However, they never relinquished their respect or their responsibilities toward Zhou – which is why the motto of "honoring the king and driving off the barbarians" (*zunwang rangyi*) stated by Duke Huan of Qi was widely accepted. Therefore, for Mencius, "borrowing from benevolence" marks the distinction between hegemon and barbarian, and thus states that would like to participate in global governance should superficially follow the principles of benevolent governance, even if they do so without any inner motivation. To draw a parallel with Rawls's theory, states that use force while borrowing from benevolence are like "decent peoples," who are different from "outlaw states," which are similar to the fifth kind of states in Mencius's categories.[18]

Now we can continue to discuss specific kind of states. The distinction between the first and second kinds of states does often arise in Mencius's thought because he thinks that the size of states does not influence their success as long as they choose kingly rule.[19] However, in a further discussion,

Mencius clarifies that there are ideal and non-ideal situations, and in non-ideal circumstances, the size of states also matters. That is why we see two kinds of states here. The third kind of state relies on force to rule as it has large territories and at least superficially follows the principle of benevolence. The fourth kind of state also believes in force as the primary method but is burdened because its limited territory limits its force. The fifth kind of state no longer cares about benevolence and is very brutal and cruel, which is usually called Yi in Chinese tradition, referring to barbarian people who consistently use force to threaten other states regardless of the justification (or lack thereof).

It is worth mentioning that states choosing kingly rule also have the capacity to use force because Confucianism never promotes radical anti-war attitude (the motto of Mohism during Mencius's time) and views the military as always necessary for just wars of self-defense or other interventions.[20] However, the first two kinds of states use force very cautiously in particular circumstances, while the three other kinds of states employ force as their primary method of handling international relations.

A Confucian Law of Peoples

Compared to other lines of ancient Chinese thought (e.g., Legalism and the Military school) and modern Western thought (e.g., realism and liberalism), Confucianism is sometimes regarded as too idealistic to be realized.[21] Considering Mencius's belief that "a benevolent man has no match in *tianxia*" (7B3), such comment should not be treated as totally unfair. However, that does not mean that Confucianism has no connection to reality. Indeed, Mencius never said that benevolent governance would always be undefeatable. If there is a conflict between a state choosing benevolent governance and a state believing in force, which will win, supposing they are similar in size? To answer this question, Mencius introduces both ideal and non-ideal circumstances as different premises of the Confucian "Law of Peoples":

> When the Way (*Dao*) prevails in the world, those of small virtue serve those of great virtue, and those of small ability serve those of great ability. When the Way does not prevail in the world, the small serve the great, and the weak serve the strong. Both of these are owing to Heaven. Those who follow Heaven are preserved, while those who rebel against Heaven perish.
>
> (4A7)

From this text, we learn that Heaven and the Way determine the circumstances, ideal or non-ideal, in which we live. Both Heaven and the Way are complex concepts in Confucianism, but it is at least clear that personal behavior does not easily influence them. When the Way prevails, and general circumstances are ideal, virtue (benevolence) becomes the determinant in global governance; otherwise, force matters more. Mencius kindly reminds us that we cannot choose whether the Way prevails; what we can do is only to follow Heaven. In other words, based on different premises, there are ideal and non-ideal theories of the Confucian Law of Peoples.[22]

In ideal theory, virtue (benevolence) acts as the determinant (but force still matters), so if there is a conflict between force and benevolence, states choosing benevolent governance will ultimately win. However, in non-ideal theory, force matters more, so the world might be dominated by one or more hegemons that belong to the third or even the fifth kind of states, and the states that embrace benevolence might face miserable fates. Mencius does not tell us how to understand the situation in which we live because we cannot fully understand the Way or Heaven. Considering Confucius and Mencius's yearning for ancient dynasties when sage kings ruled, we can be certain that they lived under non-ideal circumstances in which ideal theory was not put into practice.

Ideal theory – when benevolence acts as the determinant

When benevolence matters most in global governance, there is no clear distinction between the first and second kind of states. Without harsh threats from states using force, the attractiveness of benevolent governance makes the first and second kinds of states models for the world, which other kinds of states may choose to follow. Confucius describes such a tendency as "analogous to the Pole Star: it simply remains in its place and receives the homage of the myriad lesser stars" (2.1). Mencius cites the example of Tang and King Wen of Zhou to demonstrate how a small state can "use virtue to make people submit" (2A3). In ideal theory, force still matters, so it is possible that distant people (who could not experience the beauty of well-ordered Confucian community) and states that believe in force might not follow those model states. However, these are not major challenges because a benevolent state could "simply refine [its] culture and virtue in order to attract them [people in other states]. Once [it has] attracted then, [it] should make them content" (16.1). Benevolent states refine the culture and political virtue to maintain the good order of domestic and global governance, so they always have opportunities to attract people who live in the three other kinds of states. Consequently, as a stable norm, benevolence will gradually influence states that have not yet become benevolent and might draw more migrants to model states, thereby strengthening them.

However, what if some states ignore these good influences and continue to rule cruelly? What if other states deliberately attack benevolent states? These two situations recall Mencius's theory of just war, which has been discussed elsewhere (Bell 2006; Bai 2013). To briefly summarize it, Mencius sets strict standards for when a military intervention to prevent or stop cruel rulers can be justified. A representative example is Tang's war against the Lord of Ge (3B5). Such a just war will receive support from all under Heaven, and even people living in non-benevolent states will wish the justified war to come and change their lives. In the case of self-defense, Mencius agrees with Confucius's call to "requite injury with uprightness" (14.34) and argues that when facing a threat from cruel states, all citizens will unite strongly together to defend benevolence as a valuable virtue. In ideal theory, benevolence always has stronger power than force, and winning such a fight should not be difficult, while with the support of people from both sides, the war should not even lead to many deaths.[23]

To conclude, in the ideal situation, states choosing benevolent governance, regardless of size, will attract migrants from other states and increase their power. In case of threats from cruel states, the first two kinds of states can always defend themselves and even wage just wars of intervention in non-benevolent states when necessary. The success of such wars is guaranteed by the superiority of well-ordered society based on Confucian rites, as well as benevolence's attractiveness as a political ideal for even enemies. When such a Law of Peoples regulates the world, what will be the destination of global governance? Will the whole world ultimately unite into one state?

The answer is not clear. Mencius does argue that *tianxia* "can be settled through unity" (1A6), but he leaves many possibilities to explain what unity means. Mencius regards both the Shang Dynasty and the Zhou Dynasty as ideal models of global governance, but their pictures of the world are different – the Shang Dynasty is a united political community, while the Zhou Dynasty is not. This difference indicates that the final picture of the ideal world could be diverse (one united state or a system of many states). The Warring State period was different from ancient dynasties because it had many states competing for survival, and it was highly possible that there was more than one benevolent state.[24] After ideal states defeat non-benevolent states (peacefully or military), what relationship should we expect between them? They clearly have no reason to fight with each other, but that does not mean they will unite into one state simply because they have the same political ideal. Considering this vague answer, we can only say that in ideal theory, global governance will be led by states choosing benevolent governance, and with benevolence as a stable norm, the whole world (*tianxia*) will enjoy peace and eventually be settled through some sort of unity. Such unity could mean one united state governing all under Heaven or, more probably, a system of states embracing the uniformity of benevolence but remaining different in other factors (e.g., race, culture, and regime).

Non-ideal theory – when force matters more

No matter how we evaluate the power of benevolent governance, it is unreasonable to deny that when encountering overwhelming force, weaker states – even if they choose benevolent governance – will be defeated. This view is the premise of non-ideal theory. Embracing the potential power gained from force, the third and fifth kinds of states that tend to use force will strongly threaten the survival of states choosing benevolent governance, especially those small in size (states of the second kind). However, even in the non-ideal situation, benevolent governance will remain attractive to most people, who want to live in a well-ordered society, if possible. However, these good states are easily defeated in war, so it is difficult to declare whether they can become models of the world and enjoy continuous migration coming to strengthen their power. We cannot expect their survival all the time due to their small size or population: "Benevolence overcomes non-benevolence just as water overcomes fire. Those today who practice benevolence do it as if they were using a cup of water to put out the fire consuming a cartload of firewood" (6A18).

In contrast to the many examples Mencius raises in ideal theory (small states that practice benevolent governance always survive and even eventually govern the world), his views on reality are much less optimistic. In a dialogue with Duke Wen of Teng, who worries about the threats from the large states of Qi and Chu, Mencius refers to the ancient conflict between King Tai and the Di people (a neighboring minority state of the fifth kind) and provides some conservative advice (1B13, 1B14, 1B15). King Tai ruled a small, typical benevolent state (the second kind), and Duke Wen worries whether Teng would be strong enough to defend itself if he accepts Mencius's advice and becomes another King Tai. Mencius advises military strategies (e.g., digging moats and building walls) but also states that if the enemy is too strong, giving up and retreating is acceptable in order to wait for the right time when "the Way prevails" (perhaps even the next generation) to fight back.[25] Unlike in ideal theory, states choosing benevolent governance (especially the second kind of state) are vulnerable because solid interpersonal relationships do not generate undefeatable power. Choosing benevolent governance, therefore, does not guarantee states' survival. The whole world will not be very peaceful as well-ordered states struggle, and states that tend to use force apply the jungle law to compete with each other.

Considering the weakness of small benevolent states and the possible absence of large benevolent states,[26] we should pay some attention to the role of the third kind of states, which at least "borrow from benevolence," as a defense against the threat from the even worse fifth kind of states (barbarian or Yi). Commenting on Guan Zhong, who served as the prime minister of Duke Huan, Confucius admits that "to this day, the people continue to enjoy the benefits of his achievements" (14.17). Both Confucius and Mencius are aware that Duke Huan's rule is not benevolent, but his strong state was still important because it used force to defeat Yi. Otherwise, "we would all be wearing out hairs loose and fastening our garments on the left" (14.17) – in other words, uncivilized, without any Confucian rites.

To conclude, in the non-ideal situation, the whole world struggles amid intense tensions and potential long-term conflicts between benevolence and force, and the possible failure of benevolent states makes unity an unreachable future. In extreme cases, when the third or the fifth kind of states is strong enough, it is even possible that all benevolent states will perish, just as Qin unified all other states at the end of Warring State Periods and established a new dynasty. However, Mencius points out that such success is undoubtedly short-lived because "when one uses force to make people submit, they do not submit in their hearts but only because their strength is insufficient" (2A3). History also supports the validity of this judgment – the Qin Dynasty only lasted for fifteen years, and its successor, the Han Dynasty, switched back to Confucianism and explicitly blamed Qin for not practicing benevolent governance.[27]

Conclusion

In Confucianism, the individual is never viewed as an isolated subject independent of all others. Instead, to understand personal identity in the system of social hierarchy, one engages in the process of moral self-cultivation by practicing benevolence, which helps one find proper position in the family, state, and world. We have seen that Mencius mostly accepts Confucius's understanding of benevolence as both a moral and a political ideal but extends its development, especially in his discussion on international relations and global justice. Although the Warring State period was not ideal for such a good thought to be widely accepted and practiced, this political ideal later became the primary resource for many dynasties to maintain their positions as models in the world and to establish proper relationships with neighboring states and minorities.

Mencius's thought differs from Westphalian system, which takes equality and sovereignty as its basic premises, because he introduces a hierarchical system based on the distinction between kingly rule (*Wang*) and hegemony (*Ba*). Mencius's ideas also differ from realism as a modern theory of international relations, which understands the balance or dominance of power (primarily physical power or force) as the basic principle of international relations. Even if force sometimes temporarily determines the fate of states choosing benevolent governance, this situation neither lasts long nor changes the attractiveness of benevolence as the ultimate ideal. Consequently, Mencius names the "Five Ba" (the leaders of the feudal lords in Spring and Autumn period) "offenders against the Three Kings" and the feudal lords of his time "offenders against the Five Ba" (6B7). Moreover, he sharply criticizes ministers whose only concerns are about conquering more lands and gathering more wealth (6B9) without building a benevolent social order which is beneficial both internally and externally. Although the age of Three Kings might not be the only ideal model for the global order, the Confucian Law of Peoples still urges building a well-ordered international society.

Realism and the logic of power domination have become popular explanations in contemporary international relations, but political theorists generally are not satisfied with them and seek to introduce normative principles to prevent harsh, tragic conflicts, such as the two World Wars. For those who accept the interactions of states as a basic picture of global governance, Rawls's *The Law of Peoples* follows the logic of liberalism and provides an excellent framework for discussing global justice. Sharing some structural similarities with this famous contemporary theory, Mencius's thought reveals how an ideal global order could value benevolence rather than liberal democracy as the primary goodness. Despite some difficulties in theory and practice, this Confucian "Law of Peoples" contributes more non-Western resources and possibilities to the current discussion on global justice.

Notes

1 Earlier version of this chapter was presented as a paper at the Routledge Conference on "Global Justice in East Asian Context," at the Department of Philosophy (Zhuhai), Sun Yat-sen University. I thank Professor Jun-Hyeok Kwak's invitation as well as all the participants who gave feedback on the paper. I also thank Zhang Biao, Hugo El Kholi, Stephen Angle, Daniel Bell, and Joseph Carens who read the earlier version and provided valuable comments. All feedback and comments helped improve this paper significantly. The study of global justice in East Asian context was firstly introduced to the Western readership by Zhao Tingyang (2005, 2016), but his work mainly refers to ancient Chinese thought (not only Confucianism) to reconstruct a theory of *tianxia* (all-under-heaven) for contemporary world, while this chapter focuses on the exploration of Mencius's thought to reinterpret ancient tradition and its implications.

2 The concept of the state undoubtedly is modern, and many ancient political communities might not fully meet its definition. However, I describe these political subjects in ancient China as states because they were independent communities that governed specific areas, and most often, there was no prior authority that could interfere with their governance or interactions. Whether these subjects can be regarded as having sovereignty in the modern sense is worth discussion, but they were not so different from states today, so using this modern concept enables contemporary audiences to understand ancient thought and practices.

3 See Schwartz (1968) and Hui (2005). Schwartz argues that the multi-state system in ancient China resembles fifteenth- and sixteenth-century Europe, and Hui's work not only explains why this period can fit into the study of international relations but also reveals why China eventually achieved unity as a whole, while early modern Europe failed to do so.

4 In ancient China, political ideology influenced both domestic and "international" policies not only because there was no clear distinction between domestic governance and diplomacy but also because the state was not the boundary for the practice of normative principles. I later explain in detail why this is also true for Confucianism. We can argue this might also be true for the Western world. For example, Kant's thinking on liberalism influences both domestic regimes and international peace-seeking practices. See Oneal and Russett (1999).

5 It can be questioned why there was a theory of "global justice" in ancient China. Confucius's and Mencius's thoughts were put into practice in an anarchic "world," and even during the period of the long-lasting empire, China had to deal with many neighbor states (e.g., ancient Korea, Japan, and Vietnam), as well as Arab and European states later.

6 Although Chinese history from 770 BC to 221 BC is usually treated as a whole, differences exist between the Spring and Autumn period (when Confucius lived)

and the Warring State period (when Mencius lived). The Spring and Autumn period saw a nominal central political authority called Zhou, whose legitimacy could not be violated by any other states. Although Zhou (called Eastern Zhou in Chinese history) could not influence political practices in other states, its nominal status still enabled it to require protection from others when necessary and stop clear unjust wars. In the Warring State period, although Eastern Zhou did not die out until 256 BC, it lost any control of other states, which made wars much more frequent and crueller. From Mencius's conversation with rulers, we can see how dangerous the fate of small states was then.

7 Mencius's theory shares structural similarities with Rawls's *The Law of Peoples*, especially the typology of states and the distinction between ideal and non-ideal theory. However, this chapter will mainly focus on Mencius's rather than the comparison between Mencius's and Rawls's thoughts on global justice.

8 Chan (2014) argues that it is possible to explore distributive justice in the Confucian view on society, and Xiao (1997), Wang (2009) and Tan (2014) explore Confucius's and Mencius's thoughts to see whether some concepts (such as Yi) could contribute to contemporary discussion of justice. All these studies could be treated as an alternative to this debate. I have no disagreement with such reinterpretation or reconstruction, but I would like to emphasize that it is the discussion of justice, not Confucianism, that should be more open to alternatives. Angle (2012) summarizes some contemporary expressions of Confucianism that could relate to justice.

9 All translations of texts in *Analects* or *Mencius* are based on the versions listed in bibliography, with minor revisions.

10 This certainly is Confucius's thought, but Mencius is not commonly recognized as having a different understanding of benevolence as individual virtue than Confucius.

11 Here, personal life refers to self-cultivation as a gentleman, not being a good citizen of the state or the world.

12 I use "he" here because in ancient times, self-cultivation through family regulation and political governance certainly referred only to men. Whether it could be modified to include women or whether Confucianism had another process of self-cultivation for women are open questions, but due to space limitations, I leave them for later discussion.

13 Mencius claims that "there are cases of a ruthless man gaining possession of a state, but it has never happened that such a man gained possession of *tianxia*" (7B13).

14 As Mencius claims, "Shun had five ministers, and the world was well governed" (8.20).

15 This is the worry of King Hui of Liang, who lost wars against Qi in the east, Qin in the west, and Chu in the south. See Mencius (1A5).

16 This is the question from Wan Zhang, who doubts whether as a small state, Song can practice benevolent governance while defending itself against attack from Qi and Chu. See Mencius (3B5).

17 Another contemporary theorist who borrows from Rawls's framework is Philip Pettit, and he also calls his theory a republican Law of Peoples. However, other than embracing this well-known concept, he does not emphasize the difference between the people and the state. See Pettit (2010).

18 Certainly, Mencius's theory is very different from Rawls's, and this comparison might cause further disagreement. I refer to Rawls's theory here simply because his framework is well known to many audiences, and we do find a similar typology in Mencius's thought.

19 The most famous evidence is the statement that "a territory of a hundred li square is sufficient to enable its ruler to become Wang (a true king)" (1A5).

20 Scholars do not disagree on the justification for self-defense war. However, regarding other types of just wars, some scholars do not think Mencius would approve of so-called humanitarian interventions; see Hagen (2016).

21 This is because Western tradition regards moral self-cultivation, which is crucial to Confucianism, as a random individual choice and tends to think that self-cultivation is not as reliable as institutional design or law. Chinese thought such as legalism shares such ideas to some extent.

22 The distinction between ideal and non-ideal theory was introduced by Rawls (1999, 4–5). Chan's (2014, 4–5) work on Confucianism also refers to the distinction (Chan 2014, 4–5). Mencius's usage here, though, is different from both. For Rawls, ideal theory works only for well-ordered regimes (liberal or decent), so we need non-ideal theory to deal with other regimes. Chan argues for using the regulative ideal in the Kantian sense to test whether Confucian ideals (such as the grand union and the small tranquility) can be achieved in non-ideal circumstances. However, for Mencius, ideal and non-ideal theory correspond to two kinds of worlds that have different premises.

23 Mencius claims that "when the one who was most benevolent attacked the one most devoid of benevolence, how could it have been possible that 'the blood flowed so that it floated the pestles of the mortars'?" (7B3).

24 Ironically, Mencius's life experiences tend to prove that it is also highly possible that there is no benevolent state at all because rulers regard Confucianism as too ideal or the pressure to survive is too high for some states to be brave enough to choose benevolent governance.

25 Mencius, though, also points out that if such a ruler must escape, people may follow him because of the attractiveness of benevolence. See Mencius (1B15).

26 Based on non-ideal theory, if one state believing in benevolence enters into a conflict with another state using force, and the states are similar in size, the latter should win, which means that even the first kind of states (large states with benevolent rulers) can be defeated or even perish. However, Chinese history indicates that when the circumstances are non-ideal, it is highly possible there will be no large, well-ordered, benevolent states. For example, from the collapse of the Zhou Dynasty, we have not seen states of the first kind for more than 500 years (the whole Spring and Autumn and the Warring State periods, in addition to the short-lived Qin Dynasty).

27 A famous text is *The Faults of Qin* written by Han poet and statesman Jia Yi.

References

Angle, Stephen C. 2012. "Confucianism: Contemporary Expressions." In *The Wiley-Blackwell Companion to Religion and Social Justice*, edited by Michael Palmer and Stanley Burgess, 93–109. Malden, MA: Wiley-Blackwell.

Bai, Tongdong. 2013. "Benevolent Right beyond Human Right—Mencius's Theory of Just War." *Social Science* 1: 131–139.

Bell, Daniel. 2006. *Beyond Liberal Democracy: Political Thinking for an East Asian Context*. Princeton, NJ: Princeton University Press.

Chan, Joseph. 2014. *Confucian Perfectionism: A Political Philosophy for Modern Times*. Princeton, NJ: Princeton University Press.

Cline, Erin M. 2007. "Two Senses of Justice: Confucianism, Rawls, and Comparative Political Philosophy." *Dao* 6, no. 4: 361–381.

Confucius. 2013. *Analects*. Translated by Edward Slingerland. Indianapolis, IN: Hackett Publishing.

Hagen, Kurtis G. 2016. "Would Early Confucians Really Support Humanitarian Interventions?" *Philosophy East and West* 66, no. 3: 818–841.

Hui, Victoria Tin-bor. 2005. *War and State Formation in Ancient China and Early Modern Europe*. New York: Cambridge University Press.

Mencius. 2009. *Mencius*. Translated by Irene Bloom. New York: Columbia University Press.

Nye, Joseph. 1990. "Soft Power." *Foreign Policy* 80: 153–171.

Oneal, John R. and Russett, Bruce M. 1999. "The Kantian Peace: The Pacific Benefits of Democracy, Interdependence, and International Organizations, 1885–1992." *World Politics* 52, no. 1: 1–37.

Pettit, Philip. 2010. "A Republican Law of Peoples." *European Journal of Political Theory* 9, no. 1: 70–94.

Rawls, John. 1999. *The Law of Peoples*. Cambridge, MA: Harvard University Press.

Schwartz, Benjamin. 1968. "The Chinese Perception of Order, Past and Present." In *The Chinese World Order: Traditional China's Foreign Relations*, edited by John Fairbank, 276–288. Cambridge: Harvard University Press.

Tan, Sor-hoon. 2014. "The Concept of Yi in the Mencius and Problems of Distributive Justice." *Australasian Journal of Philosophy* 92, no. 3: 489–505.

Tang, Wenming. 2011. *Worry at Hand: Political Culture and the Future of China*. Shanghai: East China Normal University Press.

Wang, Huaiyu. 2009. "The Way of Heart: Mencius's Understanding of Justice." *Philosophy East and West* 59, no. 3: 317–363.

Xiao, Yang. 1997. "Trying to Do Justice to the Concept of Justice in Confucian Ethics." *Journal of Chinese Philosophy* 24, no. 4: 521–551.

Zhao, Tingyang. 2005. *The Tianxia System: An Introduction to a Philosophy of World Institution*. Nanjing: Jiangsu Education Press.

Zhao, Tingyang. 2016. *A Possible World of the All-under-Heaven System: The World Order in the Past and for the Future*. Beijing: CITIC Press Corporation.

9 Global justice without a center

Reappraisal of *tianxia* with non-domination

Jun-Hyeok Kwak

Introduction

Within the confines of Chinese political philosophy, "All-under-Heaven" (*tianxia* 天下) has been frequently regarded as an alternative to Eurocentric international relations (Li 2002; Carlson 2011; Zhang 2011; Wang 2017). This way of understanding the notion of *tianxia* is not limited to those scholars who wish to place China or a "Chinese-style IR (International Relations)" at the center of world politics. More and more Chinese intellectuals have written about *tianxia* as a way of overcoming world problems that have been situated in the very nature of the nation-state system since the Westphalian treaties.

On the one hand, Chinese scholars find in the traditional conceptions of *tianxia* another cosmopolitanism the backdrop of which does not relate to liberal democracy or Eurocentric universalism that conceives people everywhere as the same, providing that there are the universal norms and practices of "liberal" or "civilized" society. They do not deny the ethical imperative of cosmopolitanism in world politics. But they suggest the notion of *tianxia* which is interwoven with traditional Chinese concepts such as "nothing excluded" (*wuwai* 无外) and "benevolent governance" (*wangdao* 王道) as a paradigmatic alternative to liberal cosmopolitanism or Eurocentric universalism. At this juncture, the latter is chiefly perceived as an imperialistic dominance or a "failed" project (Zhao 2009; Yan 2011, 21–144; Gan 2012; Wu 2013; Wang 2017).

On the other hand, Chinese scholars redeploy the practices of *tianxia* in Chinese history as the very rationale for building up a "Chinese-style" peaceful coexistence as opposed to the post-Cold War world in which major powers compete to seize hegemony in world politics (Hua 2005; Han 2012). At first sight, such advocacy of a Chinese-style international order appears to be in opposition to the politics of hegemony in international relations, since it puts forward a "harmonious relationship" among states whose "diverse" and "plural" voices cannot be unified with a universal value. However, implicit in their emphasis on the Chinese tributary order in which China was placed at the center of a hierarchical empire while the neighboring countries were nothing but tributary states, they aspire to the revival of the Chinese empire in the post-Cold War world. By the same token, juxtaposed with the image of the Chinese empire for over two millennia, they attempt to recapitulate the vision of *tianxia* as the greatness of the Chinese empire that is strongly inscribed in the Chinese psyche as a benevolent empire ruling neighboring countries through concessions.

This chapter does not deal with the latter group of scholars whose main arguments consciously or unconsciously intend to embody a political culture that puts forward China as a global hegemon. Instead, it tackles the first group of scholars whose "Chinese-style" cosmopolitanism is espoused by the notion of *tianxia*. More specifically, this chapter is composed of three main parts. First, I examine the Chinese-style cosmopolitanism driven by the reinterpretation of *tianxia*. By doing so, I claim that it retains the very fallacy that can be found in the liberal cosmopolitanism that fails to provide us with a regulative principle through which culturally and politically different justifications for justice can be steered to a democratic and non-dominating deliberation between states. Second, analyzing the notions of *tianxia* in the periphery surrounding China, mostly in Korea, I explore a conception of *tianxia* in which all countries are placed on an equal footing without any center. Finally, I will suggest a model of reciprocal non-domination in which non-domination as a regulative principle can help better establish a discursive stance between states without a central hegemon.

Sino-centrism in Chinese-style cosmopolitanism

The Chinese-style cosmopolitanism in question has two general features. First, it opposes the nation-state system which is chiefly portrayed as a modern world system in which one or a group of superpowers pursue domination over weaker nation-states (Gan 2012, 105–107). At this juncture, the post-Cold War world under American hegemony is perceived as "essentially imperialistic in terms of *dominance*" (Zhao 2006, 6). In a similar vein, it has been maintained that the recent increase in globalization changes nothing in the modern world system which has been driven by the pursuit of power among nation-states but rather gives impetus to the enhancement of international conflicts in various spheres (Zhao 2011, 31–33). Such a reflection of international society is remarkably different from the currently dominating cosmopolitan accounts of a globalized world. As the contemporary liberal debates on global justice show (Valentini 2011, 1–68), liberal cosmopolitans give much weight to the increase in global interdependence. But the extent of global interdependence is severely downplayed in Chinese-style cosmopolitanism, and consequently a globalized world nowadays is regarded simply as another *failed world* (Zhao 2011, 12).

Second, "Chinese-style" cosmopolitanism seeks to find a universal system the normative foundations of which can be accepted universally as a set of regulative principles that steer or guide all states into a harmonious relationship. Interestingly, the advocates of Chinese-style cosmopolitans neither aim at nor pursue a borderless world community or a world government.

They instead take the nation-state system for granted and thereby suggest an alternative world system in which all states enjoy their independent sovereignty and exist harmoniously with each other. At the same time, they are confident in the probability that the traditional notion of *tianxia*, originating in Chinese philosophy 3,000 years ago, exhorts all states to pursue the common good of the world rather than their national interests. The notion of *tianxia*, at this juncture, is taken to signify a world institution embracing "all without exception" as well as a normative principle that regulates each state in the future. For instance, Zhao trusts that the world institution espoused by the notion of *tianxia* will benefit the people of all nations (Zhao 2009, 93–94). In a similar vein, Gan believes that a return to the principle of *wangdao* illuminated through the notion of *tianxia* will replace the order of *badao* (霸道), based on force, with that of a familyhood conceptualized through Confucian virtues such as "benevolence" and "harmony" (Gan 2012, 139–145).

At first glance, Chinese-style cosmopolitanism appears to be well prepared to avoid the accusation of "parochialism" that refers to a particular mode of Western cosmopolitanism the normative or value-laden principles of which are drawn exclusively from Western cultures. In particular, Chinese-style cosmopolitans do not assume that the notion of *tianxia* originating in Chinese contexts in particular needs to be imposed on all states universally. Rather they believe that the political ideals of *tianxia* will attract other states or peoples through their moral and political realization in any given country (Gan 2009; Wu 2013, 26–38). No one says explicitly that all peoples should be indoctrinated with its moral and political ideals. Borrowing the various conceptions of classical Chinese philosophy such as "things themselves" (*yi tianxia guan tianxia* 以天下观天下), "doing nothing" (*wuwei* 无为), and "great harmony" (*datong* 大同), they put forward the mode of "non-stance" that requires us to see the world order with a view "from others" or "from things" themselves (Zhao 2009, 42–48; Wu 2013, 335–338). The mere fact that the notion of *tianxia* emerged in Chinese contexts does not render it parochial.

Nevertheless, we can hardly deny that the Chinese-style of cosmopolitanism could be a parochial one. It is not because the world institution espoused through the notion of *tianxia* implicitly represents China as the center of civilization or as a new hegemon in world politics (Callahan 2008; Ge 2011, 91–131). It is because Chinese-style cosmopolitans do not provide us with an innate regulative principle with which we can guard ourselves against the cultural as well as political domination of one state over other states. Rather than criticizing the distinction between "civilized" (*hua* 华) and "uncivilized" (*yi* 夷) which was employed explicitly in justifying the tributary order in Chinese history, they espouse the world of *tianxia* as a hierarchical order in which barbarian states as well as tributary states should become enlightened through their competition with one another to resemble the superior state (Zhao 2009, 53–54; Gan 2012, 12–13). Then the transformation of the world into a family is suggested as the goal of getting the most appropriate relations between states.

> The notion of 'family' is thought to be the natural basis and strongest evidence of human love, harmony, mutual concern and obligations, a concentrated model of 'the very essence of humanity'.
>
> (Zhao 2009, 13)

As we can see above, the superiority of the notion of *tianxia* as a Chinese model of a world institution is insinuated between the lines. No one can deny that the underlying argument in the conception of family above is the Confucian formula of justifying a hierarchical order for moral cultivation. As a matter of fact, with several quotes from the Chinese Classics, Zhao calls attention to what has been canonized since Zhu Xi as "the road to *tianxia*" that starts from the cultivation of virtue in an individual person and ends up with that of the world (*tianxia*). Likewise, in his quote from *Daodejing* Chapter 54, what we need to reckon is not the acknowledgment of "diverse views" from different positions or "mutual love" across boundaries but the imperative of cultivating "virtue" (Zhao 2009, 9). At this juncture, the world order of *tianxia* construed as a "family" structure embracing all without exception is governed by or operated in a hierarchical order in which a superior state is expected to lead benevolently while others need to follow her voluntarily. Furthermore, there is nothing we can find in the notion of *tianxia* that can be applied to the weaker states to give them a voice against or resist the strongest state whose benevolent governance does not meet their general demands for reciprocal deliberation.

Zhao Tingyang recently proposed "compatible cosmopolitanism" (*jianrong pubian zhuyi* 兼容普遍主义) as a new Chinese-style cosmopolitanism (2013, 62–64, 2015, 20–21). According to him, Confucianism has developed a cosmopolitan ideal which embraces "a compatible multiverse united by universal relationship" (2013, 63). However, his new conception of cosmopolitanism is not new in the sense that the core principles of classical Chinese philosophy he used before are put forward again to conceptualize this new version of cosmopolitanism. Although "toleration of different forms of life for others" is suggested as one of the three basic principles, his "comparable" view is different from contemporary Berlinian pluralism in that there are irreconcilable values (Berlin 2013 [2000], 14–17). Rather, throughout his characterization of cosmopolitanism, harmony rather than conflict is taken for granted. In a similar vein, the priority of relationship over individuality differentiates his cosmopolitanism from contemporary Rawlsian cosmopolitanism with "reasonable pluralism" (Rawls 1993, 133–172, 1999, 11–23). In his cosmopolitanism, an overlapping consensus of "comparably" universal doctrines should be made, while a reasonably democratic deliberation between states is not necessarily given as a basic structure. For Zhao, *tianxia* deeply rooted in Chinese cultural and political experiences is for various reasons an alternative ideal to Western or Rawlsian "liberal" cosmopolitanism. Briefly, his comparable cosmopolitanism is nothing but a defense against the criticisms of his theory of *tianxia* for its Sino-centrism (Callahan 2008, 2013, 52–58).

What is still missing in Zhao's notion of *tianxia* is a democratic deliberation in which a "comparably" universal doctrine is composed by states. Certainly, he clearly detests imperial domination between states (Zhao 2015, 7–9), and he passionately envisions a combination of "human rights" in the Western tradition and "human obligations" in the Confucian principle of cooperative harmony (Zhao 2013, 65). However, he does not show how a cooperative relationship as well as its universal principles should be or can be constructed despite the asymmetrical power relations between states in the current global realm. Instead, he suggests a "Confucian relational justification" which is different from what he calls "the Western modern political justification" elaborated by him as "self-referential" and "democratic" (Zhao 2013, 61). At this juncture, it is worth considering a report about the Korean tribute mission.

> The Emperor of Ming should treat us as an equal person (*yishitongren* 一視同仁). And he shouldn't be suspicious and disdainful of us. But the Emperor treats our country pretty differently.
>
> (Requoted from Fuma 2015, 154, 640: *my translation*)

As we can see above, Huh Bong who led the tribute mission of Chosun to the Ming in 1574 recorded his disappointment in the "Confucian relational justification" which had been his moral and political compass before the mission. And, lamenting again and again over the Ming, he expressed his experience of Ming with the phrase, "nominally China (zhongguo 中国) but actually nothing but barbarian (*dazi* 達子: literally the Mongols)" (Fuma 2015, 151, 639). The global system of *tianxia* might have been able to evoke a voluntary obligation, while it couldn't be just permissively and admittedly without providing a deliberative stance in which each state could have equal access to justification. Shortly put, without a democratically discursive stance between states, a cooperative relationship or a Confucian relational justification can easily degenerate into domination. In other words, the proponents of Chinese-style cosmopolitanism might be able to vindicate the moral significance of the superior state with the notion of *tianxia*, but abiding by it would not suffice to render its governance democratically permissive or politically acceptable.

Reappraisal of *tianxia* from the periphery

As Zhao (2009, 27–28) elaborates, *tianxia* consists of three different but mutually interwoven conceptions. First, *tianxia* is a geographical term that refers to all under the heaven. In other words, it signifies the world as a geographical whole where all human beings can dwell. Second, it means "hearts of the people" (*minxin* 民心) that can be reflected through the minds of all living on the Earth. It is a psychological conception with which a transformation of enemies into friends through the notion of *tianxia* can be explained as moral or ethical assimilation. Third, it designates the ideal of the world system that could be realized through the notion of *tianxia*. It signifies a political ideal as well as a regulative principle with which we can evaluate our own system. Recently, he puts more moral principles into the notion of *tianxia* which embrace such a broad scope of global issues in the traditional Chinese sense that the Way of Heaven is the Way of Nature (2015, 19), such as "in accordance with nature" (*peitian* 配天: living within the limits given by Nature), "birthing birth" (*shengsheng* 生生: unceasing life), and "nothing excluded" (*wuwai* 无外).

However, as explained in the previous section, the notion of *tianxia* retains the persistently lasting conception that connotes a hierarchical system in which China is placed at the center of civilization. Combined with the concept of "*zhongguo*" (中国: central kingdom), *tianxia* frequently conveys that, for the world order, China is in fact the central state. In this Sino-centric order, neighboring states are classified as "barbarians," and thereby the employment of the word *tianxia* itself may be viewed as a strong self-consciousness of the political and cultural superiority of China over neighboring countries. Especially for the seventeenth- and eighteenth-century intellectuals in China's neighboring countries, such a Sino-centric view of *tianxia* was perceived as nothing but a political justification of China's illegitimate domination over the other states. Shocked by the emergence of the Manchuria-based Qing dynasty in 1644, Korean and Japanese Confucian scholars openly questioned the Sino-centric view of *tianxia* whose validity was severely damaged by the replacement of the Ming dynasty with the Manchurian Empire.

Some of them strove to place their own countries at the center of the world. For instance, Yamazaki Ansai (山崎闇斎 1619–1682), a Japanese neo-Confucian scholar, urged that one's own country would be more precious than anything else, and his disciple Asami Keisai (淺見絅齋 1652–1711) refuted the Sino-centric view of *tianxia* by conceptualizing Japan as the new center of the world (Nakai 1980). Similar features were found in the mentality of "little China" (*xiaogong hua* 小中华) which called the Qing dynasty a barbarian empire while rendering Korea as an alternative center. For proponents of the little China mentality, the highest duty was to respect highly the moral superiority of the Ming dynasty. And, needless to say, the denunciation of the Qing dynasty became a scholarly vogue among intellectuals in the late 17th century (Cho 1996; Park 2013, 229–366; Fuma 2015, 118–171). No substantial difference in the presupposition of a hierarchical system can be found between the Sino-centric view of *tianxia* in China and the "little Sino-centrism" in Japan and Korea.

In the meantime, there was a group of scholars in Korea who aimed to overcome both Sino-centrism and little Sino-centrism altogether. This group was called as *Silhak* (*shixue* 實學 practical learning) whose frequent encounters with Western disciplines of learning (*xixue* 西學) in the eighteenth century garnered an unprecedented interest in Korean history. Western astronomical science ushered in the re-evaluation of the Sino-centric view of *tianxia*, and subsequently the traditional notion of *tianxia* in which one state was placed at the center of the world started getting dismantled. For them, the little Sino-centrism that came to the fore in Japan and Korea after the emergence of the Manchuria-based Qing dynasty was not so very different from the Sino-centric view of *tianxia* that relegated all China's neighboring countries to the periphery.

Such an innovative view of *tianxia* was reflected most clearly in a booklet, *Dialogue on Mount Uisan* (醫山問答), which was written by a *Silhak* scholar, Hong Daeyong (洪大容 1731–1783). In particular, in substantiating the fallacies of Sino-centrism through the mouth of *Silong* (*shiweng* 實翁 practical old-man), Hong conceptualizes a new view of *tianxia*. First, he adduces that all countries are equal in *tianxia*.

> Seen from heaven (*tian* 天), how can there be any distinction between 'in' and 'out'? Thus China (*hua* 华) and barbarians (*yi* 夷) are all the same in the sense that each feels close to his own compatriots, each respects his own ruler, each defends his own country, and each finds comfort in his own customs.
>
> (Hong 2011, 148–149. *my translation*)

At first glance, the quote above appears to state something similar to what we have seen through the notions of *wuwai* and *datong* in Chinese-style cosmopolitanism. However, if we look carefully, we can see that *Silong* neither attempts to elaborate an ideal of *tianxia* nor aims to suggest the highest overall principle governing the world order. Rather he simply portrays a feature in which all, including China and her neighboring countries, dwell. In this feature, equality between countries, or at least an equal cause for justification between countries, is concretized as a condition through which the ideal of *tianxia* that all can be embraced is actualized.

Second, Hong goes further to suggest that in the order of *tianxia*, there is no center. Using his knowledge of Western astronomical science, *Silong* answers the question of whether the earth is the center of the universe.

> Of all the stars in the heaven, there is not one that is not a world unto itself. If we look from other heavenly stars, the Earth is nothing but another heavenly body. An unlimited number of worlds are spread out across the universe, and thereby saying that only the earth is the center of this is not reasonable.
>
> (Hong 2011, 61. *my translation*)

Based on scientific observation, Hong urges that any sort of centrism goes astray from the order of *tianxia*. At this juncture, the hierarchical order of *tianxia* promulgated with the distinction between China and barbarians is discarded, and any centrism that places one's country at the center is rejected. Rather, he maintains that all states, whether civilized or uncivilized, are identical to each other in their nature and thereby each state should be relativized as just one among many states existing in the order of *tianxia* (Hong 2011, 150).

Hong Daeyong's view of *tianxia* reveals what Chinese-style cosmopolitans miss in their interpretations of *tianxia*. First, they fail to suggest a set of conditions in which all states whose powers are asymmetrical can be embraced. Describing the order of *tianxia* as a historical experience, they instead depict the Chinese tributary order as a paradigmatic example for coming close to the ideal of *tianxia*. Second, they do not show us clearly how an effective discursive stance between states can be established in the first place. A deliberative stance and diverse voices among states are emphasized, but their visions of peaceful coexistence neglect the need for democratic deliberation. In fact, some of them do not regard democracy as an appropriate way of deliberation (Zhao 2009, 27). On the contrary, Hong portrays *tianxia* as a world order without a center in which all states enjoy equality at least in their basic claims to exist together with the others and seek for justice between them. In this portrayal, the view of *tianxia* itself constitutes a very condition under which a discursive stance between countries can be established.

Reciprocal non-domination

With respect to an equal access to justification between states, the recent criticisms of the neo-Roman republican theories of global justice are significantly meaningful.[1] In these internal and external criticisms, the neo-Roman republicans, Philip Pettit in particular, should have focused more on the question of "structural domination" and the problem of unequal "justificatory power" between states (Rigstad 2011; Forst 2013, 2015; Laborde and Ronzoni 2016). These partly indicate some of the criticisms provoked by Pettit's individualistic approach to sociopolitical relations or his reservation of freedom as emancipation (Markell 2008; Urbinati 2012). Rather, they penetrate deeply into the gist of all neo-Roman republican thought, that is, "the equal access to justification for non-domination." Actually, neo-Roman republicans are aware of the priority of justificatory power in actualizing non-domination across borders. For instance, Pettit maintains that liberty as non-domination is "a structural ideal that dictates a different content for different social or cultural contexts," and he also emphasizes that "the notion of un-dominated access is also likely to vary across social and cultural borders" (2015, 21–22). Yet, it is still not clear that reciprocal or intersubjective non-domination between states can be shaped through a normative appeal to freedom as non-domination. The upshot is that without entrenching a reciprocally non-dominating deliberative stance in the global relations between states, an appeal to the freedom of non-domination does not necessarily solve problems of asymmetrical power relations between states.

In this context, I will lay out the institution of democratic deliberation constituted by reciprocal non-domination as a regulative principle that prevents the practice of peaceful coexistence from leading to domination and thereby provides an institutional ground for non-dominating democratic deliberation among states. Here, reciprocal non-domination is not the first principle from which the rest of justice is derived but is rather a regulative principle that serves two different roles. First, it guides thinking in the ongoing process in which states as well as their citizens consider the requirements of global justice in the case of particular laws in specific contexts. Second, it shows the need for principles to fill out the content of the democratic process. Although I take seriously the suggestions of neo-Kantian republicanism with respect to "justificatory power," articulated by Rainer Forst (2007, 13–120, 2014, 17–91), my notion of reciprocal non-domination is based not on a transcendental right to justification but on the condition of "relational power" in which "subordination to a normative or political order that cannot be reasonably justified to each state" should be reconsidered in terms of non-domination.

First, a democratic deliberative stance with reciprocal non-domination between states focuses not on free choice but on non-dominating conditions under which the justification for freedom as non-domination is possible. If free choice is focused on, it is not in principle allowed to interfere with national self-determination by way of legal sanction or global humanitarian interference. This can generate the problem of the stronger: the stronger a state is in its relational power, the more freely it can enjoy wielding arbitrary power. If conditions are focused on, on the other hand, then legal sanctions or global interference concerning injustice becomes legitimate when the individual state in question hinders another state or states from making an adequate justification or when the state in question is under domination such that it cannot make a substantiated claim for justice. Even if democratic deliberation in the global realm is not enough to cope with a potentially dominating state, its actual practice rather than a moral appeal to non-domination will help better promote a "coalition" between states against domination. At this juncture, reciprocal non-domination may become an institutional ground which protects an individual state from being subjected to another's arbitrary will, legitimizes legal and institutional interference, and sets up the limits of such interference.

Second, democratic deliberation in the global realm should be aimed at transforming "passive" non-domination into "active" non-domination. The equal treatment that is ensured in democratic deliberation in the global realm is not enough. All states need to be guaranteed the least non-dominating status in order to have substantial political contestability against the arbitrary will of other states. Non-dominating status cannot be realized if a state is not free from the arbitrary domination of others or if there is an absence of sufficient power to check stronger states or international agencies. Thus, in the domestic arena, liberty as non-domination is to be guaranteed as a condition under which each individual can justify his or her desires. At the international level, this condition should be reciprocally recognized by all states in the international society. Here, reciprocal non-domination provides us with a coherent political and moral principle that is applicable to the process of negotiations between individuals, groups, and states. In circumstances in which conditions for reciprocal non-domination are not guaranteed, international cooperation is vulnerable to subordination or domination.

Third, cultural claims should be considered a serious matter of justification. In terms of reciprocal non-domination, a dominant culture or a potentially dominating claim in global society should be recognized as a "relational" power in which one's cultural justification may conflict with the basic requirements of non-domination. The ideal of reciprocal non-domination in this sense should be pursued collectively, so that what Pettit might call "co-exercisable" and "co-enjoyable" rules for justification can help better regulate culturally embedded and politically competing claims between states (Pettit 2014, 63–69). It is important to underscore non-dominating conditions such that any unilateral justification should not be permitted and connived at. Reciprocally non-dominating rules in the global deliberative stance do not have to be specific. But they should guard every state in global society against any possible situation in which any potentially dominating culture enjoys justification unilaterally. Given these "co-exercisable" and "co-enjoyable" requisites for cultural justification in the global realm, reciprocal non-domination may offer the best possible cultural complement to democratic deliberation in defense of mutual respect as well as interdependent cooperation between states across borders.

Conclusion

In this chapter, I have examined the Chinese-style cosmopolitanism driven by the current reinterpretation of *tianxia*, with a focus on its potential Sino-centrism, in order to present a deliberative stance in the global realm in which each state secures its power to justification for reciprocal non-domination. Specifically, I made three arguments. First, I maintained that the Chinese-style cosmopolitanism proposed as an alternative to Western or "liberal" cosmopolitanism is also beset by cultural parochialism into which "Chinese" cultural components are substantially smuggled. Second, exploring the conception of *tianxia* in which neither hierarchy nor a central state can be legitimate, I argued that without democratic deliberation between states, "Confucian relational justification" could easily degenerate into an illegitimate claim for domination. Third, reformulating the question of power with a co-exercisable and co-enjoyable access to justification for reciprocal non-domination, I proposed a model of democratic deliberation in the global realm which helps better secure a possible combination of social justice and global justice.

The neo-Roman republican theorists of global justice clearly feel uneasy about the problem of asymmetrical justificatory power between states in the global realm. This sheds lights on the current shift in neo-Roman republican theories of global justice. And it is quite clear to most neo-Roman republicans that there are diverse justifications for non-domination and thereby a democratic deliberative stance in the global realm should be set up in a non-dominating way. However, this unease with asymmetrical justificatory power does not direct them sufficiently to go beyond "passive" non-domination in that equal treatment of different political and cultural voices in global society is ensured in democratic deliberation. In this sense, I proposed the model of reciprocal non-domination that can help better regulate competing justifications for non-domination between states. The best way to overcome asymmetrical power relations between states is not to tone down the requirements of non-domination through a coalition of the weaker states but to enact a democratic deliberative stance between states. At this juncture, reciprocal non-domination as a regulative principle can replace power politics with non-dominating cooperation and thus form a ground for democratic deliberation on which various political and cultural calls for justice can be coordinated in a non-dominating way.

Note

This work was supported by the Humanities and Social Sciences Grant funded by the Ministry of Education in China (Grant Number: 17YJA720001).

1 Republican theorists have recently suggested that states rather than individuals should be placed at the center of creating and reforming global justice. This drift to a "state-based" rationale for global justice is not surprising in the sense that concerns over social justice within bounded societies or geopolitical territories lie at the center of republican thinking about civic responsibility and democratic rights. There is, however, a further concern in the recent shift to a state-based rationale for global justice in republicanism. That is the question of domination across borders. In particular, neo-Roman republicans whose theoretical backdrop is consistently one of the Roman republican traditions – in which freedom should be understood not simply as choice but as a social status or a legal condition that requires a secure independence from the arbitrary will of another (Pettit 1997, 21–27, Pettit 2014, xiii–xvii, 28–73; Skinner 1998, 81–83) – offer an incipient groundwork for a paradigm shift in the scholarly debate over global justice from distributive justice to freedom as non-domination (Bohman 2005, 2007; Ivison 2010; Laborde 2010; Pettit 2010, 2014, 150–187, 2016; Buckinx et al. 2015; Laborde and Ronzoni 2016; Lovett 2016). At this juncture, the standard republican accounts of global justice are not beset by the traditional republican distinction between civic responsibility toward compatriots and moral commitment to humanity across borders. By the same token, neo-Roman republicans may be seen as cosmopolitan in the sense that they are concerned with the problem of domination experienced by non-compatriots across borders. At the same time, their theories of global justice appear to be much more demanding than those of their liberal counterparts who place duty to compatriots before the global duty for assistance, such as John Rawls (1999), in the sense that they are concerned not only with decent domestic order but also with non-domination between states.

References

Berlin, Isaiah. 2013 [2000]. *Power of Ideas*. Edited by Henry Hardy. Princeton, NJ: Princeton University Press.

Bohman, James. 2005. "The Democratic Minimum: Is Democracy a Means to Global Justice?" *Ethics & International Affairs*. 19(1): 101–116.

———. 2007. *Democracy across Borders: From Demos to Demoi*. Cambridge: MIT Press.

Buckinx, Barbara, Jonathan Trejo-Mathys, and Timothy Waligore. 2015. *Domination and Global Justice: Conceptual, Historical, and Institutional Perspectives*. New York: Routledge.

Callahan, A. William. 2008. "Chinese Visions of World Order: Post-Hegemonic or a New Hegemony?" *International Studies Review*. 10(4): 749–761.

———. 2013. *China Dreams, 20 Visions of the Future*. New York: Oxford University Press.

Carlson, Allen. 2011. "Moving Beyond Sovereignty? A brief consideration of recent changes in China's approach to international order and the emergence of the tianxia concept." *Journal of Contemporary China*. 20(68): 89–102.

Cho, Youngrok [曺永祿]. 1996. "朝鮮의 小中華觀-明淸交替期 東亞三國의 天下觀의 變化를 中心으로." 『歷史學報』 149: 105–138.

Forst, Rainer. 2011. *The Right to Justification: Elements of a Constructivist Theory of Justice*. Translated by Jeffrey Flynn. New York: Columbia University Press.

———. 2013. "A Kantian Republican Conception of Justice as Nondomination." In *Republican Democracy: Liberty, Law and Politics*, edited by Adreas Niederberger and Philipp Schink. Edinburg: Edinburgh University Press, 154–168.

———. 2014. *Justification and Critique: Towards a Critical Theory of Politics*. Translated by Ciaran Cronin. Malden, MA: Polity.

———. 2015. "Transnational Justice and Non-domination: A Discourse – Theoretical Approach." In *Domination and Global Political Justice: Conceptual, Historical, and Institutional Perspectives*, edited by Barbara Buckinx, Jonathan Trejo-Mathys, and Timothy Waligore. New York: Routledge, 88–110.

Fuma, Susumu [夫馬進]. 2015. 『朝鮮燕行使と朝鮮通信使』. 名古屋: 名古屋大学 出版会.

Gan, Chunsong [干春松]. 2009. "王道与天下国家:从儒家王道政治重思天下国家观念." 纪念孔子诞辰 2560 周年国际学术研讨会暨国际儒联会员大会.

———. 2012. 『重回王道ー儒家与世界秩序』. 上海: 华东师范大学出版社.

Ge, Zhaoguang [葛兆光]. 2011. 『宅兹中国』. 北京: 中华书局.

Han, Yuhai [韩毓海]. 2012. 『天下: 包纳四夷的中国』. 北京: 九州出版社.

Hong, Daeyong [洪大容]. 2011. 『醫山問答』. 서울: 지식을만드는지식.

Hua, Shiping. 2005. "A Perfect World." *The Wilson Quarterly*. 29(4): 62–67.

Ivison, Duncan. 2010. "Republican Human Rights?" *European Journal of Political Theory*. 9(1): 31–47.

Laborde, Cécile. 2010. "Republicanism and Global Justice: A Sketch." *European Journal of Political Theory*. 9(1): 48–69.

Laborde, Cécile and Miriam Ronzoni. 2016. "What is a Free State? Republican Internationalism and Globalisation." *Political Studies*. 64(2): 292–296.

Li, Yangfan [李扬帆]. 2002. "天下_观念考." 『国际政治研究』 1: 105–114.

Lovett, Frank. 2016. "Should Republicans be Cosmopolitans?" *Global Justice: Theory Practice Rhetoric*. 9(1): 28–46.

Markell, Patchen. 2008. "The Insufficiency of Non-domination." *Political Theory*. 36(1): 9–36.

Nakai, Kate Wildman. 1980. "The Naturalization of Confucianism in Tokugawa Japan: The Problem of Sinocentrism." *Harvard Journal of Asiatic Studies*. 40(1): 157–199.

Park, Heebyung [박희병]. 2013. 『범애와 평등-홍대용의 사회사상』. 파주: 돌베게.
Pettit, Philip. 1997. *Republicanism*. New York: Oxford University Press.
———. 2010. "A Republican Law of Peoples." *European Journal of Political Theory*. 9(1): 70–94.
———. 2014. *Just Freedom*. New York: W. W. Norton & Company.
———. 2015. "Republicanism across Cultures." In *Republicanism in Northeast Asia*, edited by Jun-Hyeok Kwak and Leigh Jenco. London: Routledge, 15–38.
———. 2016. "The Globalized Republican Ideal." *Global Justice: Theory Practice Rhetoric*. 9(1): 48–68.
Rawls, John. 1993. *Political Liberalism*. New York: Columbia University Press.
———. 1999. *The Law of Peoples*. Cambridge, MA: Harvard University Press.
Rigstad, Mark. 2011. "Republicanism and Geopolitical Domination." *Journal of Political Power*. 4(2), 279–300.
Skinner, Quentin. 1998. *Liberty before Liberalism*. New York: Cambridge University Press.
Urbinati, Nadia. 2012. "Competing for Liberty: The Republican Critique of Democracy." *The American Political Science Review*. 106(3): 607–621.
Valentini, Laura. 2011. *Justice in a Globalized World: A Normative Framework*. New York: Oxford University Press.
Wang, Ban. 2017. "Introduction." In *Chinese Visions of World Order: Tianxia, Culture, and World Politics*, edited by Ban Wang. Durham, NC: Duke University Press, 1–22.
———. 2017. "The Moral Vision in Kang Youwei's Book of the Great Community." In *Chinese Visions of World Order: Tianxia, Culture, and World Politics*, edited by Ban Wang. Durham, NC: Duke University Press, 87–105.
Wu, Jiaxiang [吴稼祥]. 2013. 『公天下: 多中心治理与双主体法权』. 桂林: 广西师范大学出版社.
Yan, Xuetong. 2011. *Ancient Chinese Thought, Modern Chinese Power*. Edited by Daniel Bell and Sun Zhe & Translated by Edmund Ryden. Princeton, NJ: Princeton University Press.
Zhang, Feng [张锋]. 2011. "天下体系:一个中国式乌托邦中的世界秩序". 『复旦国际关系评论』. 1: 87–92.
Zhao, Tingyang [赵汀阳]. 2006. "A Political World Philosophy in terms of All-under-Heaven (Tian-xia)." *Diogenes*. 221: 5–18.
———. 2009. 『坏世界研究: 作为第一哲学的政治哲学』. 北京: 中国人民大学出版社.
———. 2011. 『天下体系: 世界制度哲学导论』. 北京: 中国人民大学出版社.
———. 2013. "All-under-Heaven and Methodological Relationism: An Old Story and New World Peace." In *Contemporary Chinese Political Thought: Debates and Perspectives*, edited by Fred Dallmayr and Zhao Tingyang. Lexington: Kentucky University Press, 46–66.
———. 2015. "天下秩序的未来性". 『探索与争鸣』. 1(11): 7–21.

10 A topography of Japanese socialism

Kōtoku Shūsui and global justice

Umemori Naoyuki

Introduction

The term "global justice" has a history covering a period of half a century. In the meantime, we have witnessed the transformations of its conceptualization several times. In the field of transatlantic political philosophy, the subject of global justice came to attract serious philosophical attention after 1968 when Vietnam War or nuclear deterrence provoked political dissent in the United States (Beitz 2019). Philosophical thought about justice in war was a major concern for the transatlantic political philosophers of the first global justice movement (GJM). Since then, justice in the war and justice in the world economy had been dominant topics in the political philosophy. However, after the end of Cold War, philosophical thought about global justice came to enter a new phase. Particularly, the protest against the World Trade Organization in Seattle in 1999 has been described as the beginning of a new age of GJM (Ness 2004).

What makes this movement distinct in comparison with traditional discussions on global justice? First, the major participants of this movement are not limited to the intellectuals in the United States and Western Europe. Rather, intellectuals and citizens outside of the Western world take a crucial role in the discussion. The establishment and the succeeding operation of the World Social Forum, whose purpose is to create a space for the meeting of all organizations, social movements, and individuals that have challenged neoliberal globalization, symbolizes it (Fisher and Ponniah 2015, 4–6). The first World Social Forum was held in Porto Alegre, Brazil, in 2001, then moved in 2004 to Mumbai, India, and returned to Porto Alegre in 2005, then went to Nairobi, Kenya, in 2007. In this newly created space, the historical experiences of the people outside of the West, notably Zapatista movements, came to catch attention from all over the world in terms of global justice (Della Porta 2005, 27).

Second, traditional binary opposition between "intellectuals" and "activists" became meaningless. For example, David Graeber, one of the most influential theorists of GJM, observed that a huge gulf between intellectuals and activists caused a "scandalous" situation in which what is referred to as the "anti-globalization" movement developed to "one that has in a mere two or three years managed to transform completely the sense of historical possibilities for millions across the planet" in a totally unexpected way after he participated in the movement in Seattle (Graeber 2002). Since then, philosophers have paid more serious attention to the significances and implications of the trajectory of the social movements outside the United States and West Europe. Also activists have explored the source of inspiration for their movements in various intellectual traditions on the global scale.

This resulted in a renewed interest in Marxist intellectual tradition among scholars of global justice (Wildel 2011). In the field of transatlantic political philosophy, liberalist thinkers such as John Rawls and Michael Waltzer have led discussions on global justice (Beitz 2019). However, since philosophers came to problematize the resistance against the neo-liberal hegemonic power in the GJM, the intellectual tradition of Marxism has revived as an important source of inspiration for conceptualizing global justice. Here, it is important to notice that traditional sectorial confrontations among leftist camps came to lose any significance. Since the end of the Cold War, which lead to the demise of the existing socialist states that had the authority to decide on the "true" Marxism, people have been more interested in exploring the sources of inspiration for conceptualizing and developing new types of social movements such as feminism or postcolonialism in different leftists' intellectual traditions (Postone 2003, 12–13). This leads to the renewed interest in examining the trajectory of transnational social movements inspired by various leftists' thoughts such as Marxism, anarchism, and socialism on the equal base from the perspective of global justice.

This chapter attempts to reinterpret the trajectory of social movements in Japan from the perspective of global justice. In contemporary discussions on global justice, theoretical contributions from East Asia have not been salient compared with the other regions such as Latin America or India. However, it does not necessarily mean that the philosophical considerations on global justice have not existed in this region (Murphy and Weber 2016). Rather, we can trace the rich philosophical traditions associated with global justice issues without using such terminology there. Among East Asian nations, Japan has unique historical experiences because it had kept receiving various oppressions from Western imperial powers as a non-Western nation in the periphery whereas it transformed itself to an Imperial Power inflicting political, economic, militaristic, and cultural oppressions on its neighboring areas (Peattie 1984). Therefore, Japanese intellectuals and activists were destined to take an ambiguous positionality: they conceptualized global-justice-related issues not only from victims' perspective but also from perpetrators' one. In the current globalized social conditions, the ambiguous positionality is no longer a unique condition for Japanese people. Rather, it has become a universal condition which any member of the global society must take it into account. This suggests that we can shed a new light on the theoretical discussions on global justice by tracing the genealogy of social movements in Japan.

In the following discussion, I analyze the thought of Kōtoku Shūsui (1871–1911) as an important origin of philosophical consideration on global justice in Japan. Kōtoku was recognized as an important founding father of the socialists' movement in Japan.[1] He made a debut as a public intellectual when he published his first book, *Imperialism: The Specter of the Twentieth Century* in 1901. Kōtoku was a founding member of Japan's first political organization based on socialism, the Social Democratic Party, which was also established in 1901. When he started publishing a newspaper called the *Heimin Shimbun* or *The Commoners' Newspaper* with Sakai Toshihiko (1871–1933) in 1903 with the aim of opposing the Russo-Japanese War, he was already known as the most influential leader of socialist movement in Japan. Kōtoku was also an important mediator to introduce the idea of socialism to China because contemporary Chinese intellectuals and activists translated his books and articles (Tierney 2018). However, in 1906, after coming back from San Francisco where he stayed for six months to escape the oppression by Japanese government, Kōtoku declared his conversion from socialism to anarchism. His conversion caused serious confusion among Japanese socialists and acted as a trigger for the High Treason Incident.[2] In 1910, Kōtoku was arrested on bogus charges as the leader of a conspiracy to assassinate the Emperor Meiji. He was executed as a protagonist of Japanese anarchism, along with eleven followers in 1911.

My argument is organized around the following three questions. What historical conditions encouraged him to tackle with the issue of justice on the global scale? How was Eastern traditional thoughts such as Confucianism intertwined with Western contemporary thoughts such as Marxism to produce his conception of global justice? How did Japan's ambiguous positionality between a victim and perpetrator of imperialism affect his theorization on global justice? In order to answer these questions, I attempt to focus on Kōtoku's first book, *Imperialism: The Specter of the Twentieth Century*. This text is one of the earliest book projects to analyze imperialism theoretically. We should remember that John Hobson's *Imperialism: A Study* was published one year later than Kōtoku's one and Vladimir Lenin's *Imperialism: the Highest Stage of Capitalism* appeared sixteen years later. In this text, Kōtoku analyzed how and why imperialism had developed and what misfortunes it brought on the world. By situating this text at the historical conjuncture of the development of capitalism and imperialism in East Asia, I hope I can show a complex and condensed nature of the beginnings of the considerations on global justice in Japan.

Early socialism: the West and the East

The term "global justice" has become increasingly popular in academy as well as journalism in recent decades. However, there have always been causes that have had global justice dimensions in human history. In Japan, the thoughts and activities of the "early socialists" are such examples. It was around 1890 when the ideas and policies called "socialism" were introduced into Japan from the West, notably the United States and Germany, and a group of people started to analyze and criticize various social problems such as political corruption and economic inequality on national and global levels (Katayama 1918; Crump 1983). They came to be mentioned as "early socialists" later by scholars in Japanese intellectual history.

In Western Marxist historiography, "early socialism" had been largely used as a synonym of "utopian" socialism (Engels and Aveling 1892). In the canonical narrative of Western Marxism, pre-Marxist socialists in the early nineteenth century, such as Saint-Simon, Fourier, and Owen, are criticized as "utopian" in order to emphasize the "scientific" nature of Marxism. In addition, orthodox socialist historiography tends to marginalize the historical role of anarchism by emphasizing Marx's successful campaign to expel Bakunin from the International Working Men's Association in 1872. In this way, orthodox Marxists have understood their own history as a process of chronological development from the utopian form, through a separation from anarchism, to the stage of "scientific" socialism.

However, the recent development of the GJM has sparked a renewed interest in the history of various international leftist movements. At this juncture, the developmental historiography of traditional Marxism has been challenged from various aspects. For example, Ernesto Laclau and Chantal Mouffe developed a political theory of post-Marxism by shedding new light on such thinkers as Eduard Bernstein and Georges Sorel, who had been marginalized in canonical Marxist intellectual history (Laclau and Mouffe 2001). Also, David Graeber, one of the most influential theorists and participants in the contemporary GJM, praises the theoretical and practical tradition of anarchism for showing the historical significance of recent eruptions of strong resistance against the existing world order (Graeber 2002). Here, the legitimacy of orthodox Marxist historiography was problematized through reinterpreting non-orthodox Marxists and/or non-Marxist socialists, including anarchists as important inspirational sources for the contemporary social movement.

In contrast, in East Asia, few attempts have been made to analyze the theoretical and practical connections between contemporary GJMs and the tradition of social movements there. Generally speaking, socialists under the Cold War structure had strong tendencies to understand their own history through the canonical developmental scheme of Western Marxism. A Japanese intellectual historian once called this characteristic of early socialism in Japan a "nebulous atmosphere" (Matsuzawa 1973). In the traditional Marxist historiography, the "nebulous" nature of early socialism had been largely dismissed as a manifestation of the backwardness of contemporary Japanese Marxism. In the following discussion, I argue that this "nebulous" nature of early socialism is a key moment that allows us to shed new light on the nature and development of capitalism and its countermovements in East Asia.

Traditional Marxism has theorized the history of capitalism as a sequential development of historical stages. Here, we can remember how orthodox historical materialism presupposed that all societies develop from feudalism to capitalism through the stage of bourgeois revolution. We can also situate Lenin's analysis of imperialism as the "highest stage of capitalism" in this theoretical tradition. However, historical experiences in East Asia indicate that these developmental schemes are only applicable to the history of Western Europe completely, where capitalism developed gradually and organically in comparison with the other areas. In the periphery such as the late nineteenth century in East Asia, capitalism developed quite differently. Here, capitalism was imported and promoted in a much more condensed way by such agents as colonial or developmental states. Scholars have theorized this historical experience as "late development" and found a common characteristic of late developing capitalist societies in the coexistence of different temporalities (Harootunian 2015). In East Asia, just as in other peripheral areas, highly capitalized social spaces coexisted alongside traditional communities persisting in their lifestyles and values. In this way, the development of capitalism was experienced in East Asia as a disjuncture of different temporaries, not as a smooth transition from feudal to modern. Uneven development is an integral part of capitalist modernity, which is particularly salient in the periphery (Harvey 2005).

This consideration sheds new light on the "nebulous" nature of Japanese early socialism. While traditional Marxism has interpreted it as a manifestation of the premature nature of Japanese socialism, I claim that it is a truthful representation of contemporary Japanese society, which is characterized by uneven development and the coexistence of different temporalities (Harootunian 2000). While early socialism was conceptualized in traditional historiography as a premature stage, people in East Asia encountered "utopian" socialism, anarchism, and "scientific" Marxism simultaneously in the age of early socialism. In contrast to the chronological understanding of Western socialism, I characterize this perspective as "topographical" by emphasizing the coexistence of heterogeneous time and space.

Socialism in Japan was born as a reaction to a new form of social interdependence produced by capitalism. In the early 1900s, several important books on socialism were published, including Abe Isoo's *Shakai Mondai Kaishaku Hō* (How to Solve the Social Problem) (1901), Kōtoku Shūsui's *Shakaishugi Shinzui* (The Quintessence of Socialism) (1903), and Katayama Sen's *Waga Shakaishugi* (My Socialism) (1903). Abe and Katayama spent substantial time in the United States and encountered socialism there. They accepted industrial development as an evolutionary process and regarded the fundamental problem of capitalism as the unequal distribution of the wealth (Abe 1901; Katayama 1903). As the fundamental "remedy" for capitalism, they proposed public ownership of the means of production. Because they introduced many examples of public ownership of businesses such as trams (streetcars), gas, and water that they had seen implemented in cities in

America and Germany, their proposals were called "municipal socialism." Abe and Katayama conceptualized socialism as a rational and scientific system of distribution that could overcome the anarchy of capitalism. For this purpose, they promoted the social movement for universal suffrage as the most important method to realize socialist government.

However, it is important to notice that Kemuyama Sentarō's *Kinsei Museifushugi* (Modern Anarchism) was published in 1902 – almost simultaneously with these classics of Japanese socialism. Kemuyama's book was the first systematic attempt to introduce the theory and practice of anarchism to Japanese readers (Kemuyama 1902). His book contrasts with the socialist classics mentioned above in several important aspects. First, while Abe introduced the Social Democratic Party in Germany as a model for Japanese socialism, Kemuyama focused on the history of nihilist movement in Russia. Second, while Abe and Katayama described the city as the crucial site for realizing socialism, Kemuyama perceived the frustration of Russian peasants, who desire for equal distribution of land as a fundamental cause of the revolutionary movement. Third, while socialists such as Abe and Katayama rejected the violence of the Russian nihilists, Kemuyama characterized their violence as a reaction to the oppression of the Tsarist government.

In his preface, Kemuyama made it clear that his own position was anti-anarchist. He regarded anarchism as a disease of society and wrote his book to prevent the spread of anarchism. However, as a talented positivistic historian, he succeeded in describing the history of Russian nihilist movement from the assassination of Alexander II in 1881 up to the beginning of the 20th century in great detail. In the first half of his book, he introduced the thought and activities of Russian revolutionaries such as Vera Zasulich. In the latter half of his book, he attempted a comparative analysis of anarchist movement in different nations. He found that "excessive autocracy" in Russia and the "corruption of politics and decadence in spirit" in Italy and Spain provided a fertile ground for anarchism. On the contrary, the growth of anarchism in Germany was prevented by the rise of the Social Democratic Party; and in England, by the "pragmatic social customs" and "elegance of the nobility." Ironically enough, his descriptions of Russian autocracy and the nihilists' movement against it produced a number of their sympathizers in Japan.

In traditional Marxist historiography, the coexistence of anarchism and socialism was evaluated as a manifestation of the lack of a "scientific" understanding of capitalism, as exemplified by Marxism (Hoston 1986). However, I argue that the coexistence of anarchism and socialism was rather a correct representation of the contemporary Japanese capitalism. On the one hand, with the success of rapid industrialization between Sino-Japanese War and Russo-Japanese War, Japanese society came to share similar social problems with advanced Western nations. On the other hand, Meiji Japan shared many aspects with contemporary Russia. Autocratic government, strong bureaucracy, emperor worship, the rapid influx of modern Western political thoughts, and the survival of rural communities were such examples. While the socialism introduced by Abe and Katayama was more "futuristic," the anarchism introduced by Kemuyama was more "actual" to contemporary Japanese society. In Meiji Japan, capitalistic social interdependence and traditional communal customs became intertwined and interacted as an effect of late development and colonial modernity. In the traditional historiography of Japanese socialism, researchers have argued over whether anarchism or socialism was more legitimate. However, I claim that the coexistence of both ideologies was crucial because anarchism and socialism shed light on different aspects of contemporary Japanese society, which was characterized by uneven development and the coexistence of different temporalities.

Capitalism as lived experience and reactions by Japanese intellectuals

When Japan embarked on the project of modernization, as mentioned above, in the late nineteenth century, Western Europe and the United States had already reached a high level of capitalist development. Japan encountered capitalism as a fully developed system without groping for it by itself. In this context, many Japanese intellectuals perceived capitalism not as a historical stage of social evolution but as an alien form of social domination imported from the outside. In other words, Japanese intellectuals tended to conceptualize capitalism more spatially than chronologically. We can find one such example in Fukuzawa Yukichi's comparison of Western and Japanese civilizations. Although he did not use the term capitalism, his analysis of Western civilization focused on the specificities of social interdependence that characterized contemporary Western capitalism.

In *An Outline of a Theory of Civilization* (1875), Fukuzawa conceptualized the essence of Western civilization as the particular social attitude which had been cultivated in the condition of competition and communication and explained its function as follows. "The only requirement of civilization is that one use one's natural endowments of body and mind to the fullest extent" (Fukuzawa, Dillworth, and Hurst 1970, 24). Then, he analyzed how Japanese social structure had hindered the development of civilization in Japan (Fukuzawa, Dillworth, and Hurst 1970, 209):

> The millions of Japanese at the time were closed up inside millions of individual boxes. They were separated from one another by walls with little room to move around. The four-level class structure of samurai, farmers, artisans, and merchants froze human relationships along prescribed lines.

In this way, he recognized the universal value of Western civilization. However, it is important to note that he also showed an ambiguous attitude to

Western civilization in a different context. For example, in the opening to his 1885 newspaper editorial "Good-bye Asia," Fukuzawa explained the essence of Western civilization as follows (Fukuzawa 1996):

> Transportation has become so convenient these days that once the wind of Western civilization blows to the East, every blade of grass and every tree in the East follow what the Western wind brings. Ancient Westerners and present-day Westerners are from the same stock but are quite different from one another now. The ancient ones moved slowly, but their contemporary counterparts move vivaciously at a fast pace. This is possible because present-day Westerners take advantage of the means of transportation available to them. For those of us who live in the Orient, unless we want to prevent the coming of Western civilization with a firm resolve, it is best that we cast our lot with them. If one observes carefully what is going on in today's world, one knows the futility of trying to prevent the onslaught of Western civilization. Why not float with them in the same ocean of civilization, sail the same waves, and enjoy the fruits and endeavors of civilization? The movement of a civilization is like the spread of measles.

Interestingly, Fukuzawa compared Western "civilization" with the pandemic of "measles," positing it as the system that infected people and transformed their individual constitution. Despite their diverse cultural backgrounds and sense of values, the people who were "infected" by civilization metamorphosed into the agents who were equipped with the spirit to use their "natural endowments of body and mind to the fullest extent." In the opening of the age of global transportation, this particular spirit spread by infecting and transforming all the other people who came to be involved in the system of global competition and communication. This is the secret of expansion of Western civilization that Fukuzawa discovered.

In this context, Nakae Chōmin's diagnosis of contemporary Japan is also instructive. In his *A Discourse by Three Drunkards on Government* (1887), Nakae explained how the Japanese experience of late development lead to the coexistence of contradicting ideologies (Nakae 1984, 103):

> Any nation deciding to climb the path of civilization behind other nations must completely change its earlier culture, character, customs, and feelings. It is thus natural that two opposing groups will emerge within its population: the lovers of nostalgia and the lovers of novelty. For the nostalgic, all the new culture, character, customs, and feelings seem shallow and exaggerated. They think that their eyes are soiled by looking at the new things and their ears dirtied with the new sounds. They feel dizzy and nauseated by any mention of the new.

According to Nakae, the simultaneous production of "the lovers of nostalgia and the lovers of novelty" becomes destiny for any late developing nation. Nakae's classification resembles Partha Chatterjee's categorization of nationalism which he induced from the Indian case. In his discussion on the development of Indian nationalism, Chatterjee explains the paradigmatic form of the development of nationalist thought as the following three stages (Chatterjee 1986, 50–51). First, "moment of departure," the awareness and acceptance of an essential cultural difference between East and West arrived. Then, "moment of maneuver," which is characterized as a tension between the thematic (the modern) and the problematic (the national), two conflicting lines of progressives who emphasize the modern and conservatives who emphasize the national, became salient. Finally, the "moment of arrival" was achieved, where people came to recognize that the forces of modernity within the Eastern society can be allowed to fully develop by replacing the colonial state with a national state. While most intellectual historians, including Chatterjee, consider the confrontation between the modern and tradition as a period of transition, I rather claim that the coexistence and confrontation of both camps should be analyzed as an enduring marker of modernity in periphery, which was characterized by the uncoordinated coexistence of different temporalities within it.

Kōtoku Shūsui as a pioneer of global justice theory

It was this historical conjuncture in which Kōtoku crystallized the idea of "global justice" from the "nebulous" intellectual atmosphere of Japanese early socialism. We can observe how "traditional" senses of morality and "modern" Western thoughts were intertwined to produce a new sense of global morality in Kōtoku's intellectual development. Here, I would like to revisit Nakae Chōmin's *A Discourse by Three Drunkards on Government* which contains the discussion on the relationship between justice and war. As Kōtoku was a disciple of Nakae, he must have been familiar with his mentor's analysis.

Nakae's text was constructed as a hypothetical debate between "the Gentleman," a spokesman for democracy and progress, and "the Champion," an exponent of militarism and samurai values. When the Gentleman said, "Democracy is necessary for abolishing war, promoting peace, and making all the nations on earth one family," the Champion asked, "what if some vicious nation should take advantage of our disarmament and send its troops to attack us?" Then, the Gentleman replied (Nakae 1984, 91):

> If there were indeed such a vicious nation, we would have no choice but to find our own countermeasures. It is my hope that without calling up a single soldier or producing a single bullet, we would calmly state, 'We have never committed any incivility against you … We do not want you to disturb our country. Please go home immediately.' If the invaders would refuse to listen, loading their rifles and taking aim, we would simply cry in a loud voice, 'How uncivil and inhuman you are!' We would then be shot to death. I have no special remedy.

The Gentleman's ideological stance overlapped with the position of the early socialists who opposed the Russo-Japanese War. When Abe Isoo, one of the representative early socialists, was asked what the Japanese should do if a nation would invade them on the eve of Russo-Japanese War, he replied, "if Peace is to be at one with the ideal of humanity, we should advocate peace and accept the destiny to be ruined by our enemy" (Unknown 1903). Scholars have recognized the influences of anti-war movements by his contemporary Christian sects such as Quakers in this message. Later, some intellectuals came to recognize the origins of the renunciation of war in the current Japanese Constitution in it (Takano 1970). In any case, the Gentleman's declaration of anti-war philosophy has been considered as a product of "modern" and "Western" morality that was alien from traditional moral values.

In 1901, Kōtoku published his first book, *Imperialism: The Specter of the Twentieth Century*. I claim that this is one of the earliest calls for global justice by a Japanese intellectual based on traditional morality. Kōtoku's position was unique in comparison with the other early socialists. He was the only non-Christian member among the founders of Social Democratic Party in 1901. Although he shared the anti-war idea with the other members, his ideas were colored by traditional values more than the other members'. Rather, his anti-war thought was a unique amalgam of modern Western theories and traditional Eastern morals.

In *Imperialism*, Kōtoku characterized imperialism as a policy woven from the wrap of "patriotism" and the woof of "militarism," and criticized it as follows (Tierney 2018, 143, 202):

> The construction of a so-called empire is not based on any real necessity but simply on the free reign of greed, it confers no benefits but results in disaster, it is not an expansion of the nation's people but an expansion of a small minority's vanity and love of fame, it does not develop trade but only stimulates speculation, it does not encourage production but only pillage, it does not signify the implanting of civilization overseas but rather the destruction of other civilizations. Can this be the aim of a truly civilized society? Is this the real objective of national governance?

In the conclusion of the book, Kōtoku insists that scientific socialism is the only remedy for the pathology of imperialism (Tierney 2018, 206):

> But what are the projects and plans that will bring a remedy to our current crisis? There is only one solution. We must launch a great cleansing of the state and society, or, in other words, start a revolutionary movement worldwide in scope. Let us transform the few nations of the present time into a vast number, free the nation from the iron grip of the army and navy and transfer it to the peasants, workers, and merchants, reform our societies where an aristocracy rules autocratically into one where the common people rule themselves, change our economy,

> now monopolized by capitalists, to one in which the workers own all in common. The spirit of justice and humanity will overwhelm narrow chauvinism, scientific socialism will destroy barbaric militarism, and cosmopolitanism and universal fraternity make it possible to uproot and eliminate predatory imperialism.

Kōtoku's position resembles the claim of the Gentleman of Western Learning in Nakae's text or Abe Isoo's anti-war policy. On the one hand, his text is filled with up-to-date information on the development of imperialism from foreign media. For example, he opened up this discussion of patriotism to quote the following latest news (Tierney 2018, 142):

> England battles with South Africa, the United States invades the Philippines, Germany seizes the region of Jiaozhou, Russia annexes Manchuria, France conquers Fashoda, and Italy makes war on Abyssinia. These are the most striking manifestations of imperialism in recent years.

On the other hand, if we read Kōtoku's text closely, we notice how much he was influenced by traditional moral values. In this text, when Kōtoku attempts to explain why patriotism should be criticized, he often relies on traditional Chinese texts such as *Mencius*. For example, he explains the existence of philanthropic human instinct by quoting a famous passage from *Mencius*, one of the most important Chinese classics (Tierney 2018, 143):

> I agree with Mencius that any human being would, without hesitation, rush to rescue a child about to fall into a well. If patriotism were nothing more than the natural empathy that motivated this generous act, and if it were an emotion filled with the spirit of charity and love, then it would be a beautiful and glorious thing. I would have nothing more to say on the topic. On second thought, however, a human being moved by such selfless love and charity does not pause to think whether the child is a family member or a close relative. When he rescues the child from danger, he does not even ask himself whether the child is his own or belongs to another. For the same reason, righteous and benevolent men in every nation in the world pray that the people of the Transvaal will win their freedom and that the people of the Philippines will gain their independence.

This paragraph is quite interesting to show that Confucius morality motivated Kōtoku to participate in the global movement of anti-imperialism in a particular way. When he discusses about the issue of justice, he did not make any distinction between the East and the West or his own nation and the other nations. In his thought, spatial distance lost any significance. The loss of physical sense of distance is a unique epistemological feature of Kōtoku's *Imperialism*. We encounter the same feature many times in his text. For example, in another part of his text, Kōtoku praises Émile Zola, the French novelist and critic known for his anti-war and anti-imperialist essays and for his courage to stand up for Alfred Dreyfus, the French army officer charged with espionage (Tierney 2018, 177–178):

> Mencius writes: 'I refuse to yield even when millions oppose me if to yield is to betray my conscience.' Why is it that one never encounters such a courageous spirit, epitomized by the man of letters Zola, among the splendid and imposing soldiers of the army?

Here, Kōtoku praised a deed by French novelist as a true manifestation of Confucian morality. In this regard, we cannot categorize his anti-imperialist thought as an import from the West. Rather, Kōtoku developed his anti-imperialist ideas by unconditionally applying traditional moral teachings such as those of Mencius to the contemporary global issues.

Telegraphic imagination of anti-imperialists' network

How did this particular epistemology come to exist? In this context, it is instructive to remember that Kōtoku started his career as a journalist by translating foreign news delivered to Japan through the global telegraph network. When he was hired by a newspaper publishing company, Jiyū Shinbunsha (The Free Press) in 1893, he was assigned the task of translating telegraphic dispatches from foreign news agencies (Tierney 2018, 23). Here, it is important to notice that he started his career in the age of the revolution in communications and transportation. Samuel Morse (1791–1872) discovered the possibility of the telegraph just before the Opium War broke out, and a network of submarine cables crossed all the oceans and larger seas in 1870s (Wenzlhuemer 2015; Müller 2016). The Atlantic was first broached in 1858, and a secure operational cable was established in 1866. Japan was linked to the rest of the world by a submarine telegraph cable in 1871. Initially it connected Nagasaki and Vladivostok. The network was extended to Tokyo in 1873. This made it possible for people in the capital to send and receive messages all over the world. Subsequently, the telegraph network extended rapidly all over Japan. The network between major cities was completed in the 1880s, then extended to local cities in 1890. A cable was laid across the Pacific in 1902, finally encircling the world. Kōtoku was a member of the first generation who could appreciate the fruits of this revolutionary transformation of communication technologies in East Asia.

Scholars agree that the role of such communication technologies is pivotal for the development of European imperialism (Headrick 1981). Because of the development of communication technologies, it became possible for the center to know what was going on at its peripheries more clearly. Duncan Bell argued how the establishment of the infrastructure of dense global communications made it possible for people to imagine a politically integrated Angloworld (Bell 2007). However, Kōtoku's case shows another possibility which was realized by the establishment of global communication network. It gave Kōtoku an opportunity to imagine the creation of the global network of anti-imperialists. The revolutionary transformation in communication technologies offered not only more refined ways of colonial expansion for Western Powers, but also an imagination for organizing a global social movement against them for intellectuals in the periphery (Anderson 2005).

Kōtoku's anti-imperialism was the first cry for global justice from Japan. Ben Middleton, in his pioneering work, attempts to situate Kōtoku's *Imperialism* as a node in an international network of Radical opposition to imperialism (Middleton 1999). Middleton focuses on the four figures who appeared in the following section of the preface of *Imperialism* (Tierney 2018, 137):

> The theories of imperialism set forth in this work were first developed in insightful analyses by Western intellectuals. I have taken up the most progressive theses propounded by renowned thinkers who hold to the highest ideals, such as Tolstoy, Zola, John Morley, Bebel, and Bryant.

In his article, Middleton introduced the careers and the political backgrounds of those five figures (Middleton 1999). Leo Tolstoy (1828–1920) was a Russian novelist whose commitment to pacifism was widely known. Emile Zola (1840–1902) was a French novelist who condemned imperialism and war as a "contagion," a "madness," and "a folly which threatens the destruction of Europe in a frightful, general massacre." John Morley (1838–1923) was known as a leader in the English Liberal Party who strongly advocated anti-imperialist policies along the lines of development and investment at home rather than speculation and conquest abroad of the liberal party in England. August Bebel (1840–1913) was known as the venerated leader of the German Social Democratic Party and the leading authority of the Second International. He had an experience of imprisonment for opposing the annexation of Alsace-Lorraine during the Franco-Prussian War. William Jennings Bryan (1860–1926) was a leader of the Democratic Party in the United States and nominated as US Democratic Party presidential candidate in 1896, 1900, and 1908. Although he was known as a staunch believer in a virtuous white American civilization, he protested the continued maintenance of the standing army and the prospect of the usurpation of Spain's colonies after the treaty with Spain was signed.

Middleton also pointed out that John Mackinnon Robertson's critique against the British imperialist trajectory, *Patriotism and Empire* (1899), formed the template around which Kōtoku crafted his *Imperialism*, yet there is no mention of his name anywhere in that text. By revealing how Kōtoku appropriated and reinterpreted the ideas of those authors, Middleton shows skillfully how Kōtoku succeeded in producing an imagination of anti-imperialist global network despite obvious variations in terms of their cultural backgrounds and political orientations. Interestingly enough, those authors, except Bebel, were not usually recognized as socialists; therefore, Middleton names the position of those authors as Radical Liberals (Middleton 1999). If so, what Kōtoku performed in his *Imperialism* was to reinterpret the various arguments of anti-imperialism prepared by Radical Liberals in the metropole of Empire from the perspective of a socialist in East Asia to create a new discursive space. By doing so, he attempted to participate in the imaginative global network of anti-imperialism as a non-Western activist.

Philosophy of violence

Kōtoku was not satisfied with introducing Western ideas of anti-imperialism as a theorist. He also attempted to participate in the global struggle against imperialism as an activist. Because of the positionality as an activist in the periphery, he gradually changed his own policy from socialist to anarchist. In 1903, the eve of the outbreak of Russo-Japanese War, Kōtoku and his friend Sakai Toshihiko established a socialist organization and started publishing a socialist magazine titled *Heimin Shimbun* in order to prevent the war and advocate the cause of socialism. Initially, this project got a success: the initial issue of *Heimin Shimbun* recorded the sales of more than 6,000 copies. However, the War began in 1904, and the government strengthened the oppression toward socialists. *Heimin Shimbun* was strictly censored and their public meetings were banned many times. The Home Ministry reinforced legal actions particular after the publication of the translation of *Communist Manifesto* on *Heimin Shimbun* on November 13, 1904. Kōtoku himself was sentenced to prison on charges of violating the press laws. Kōtoku and the other members decided to discontinue *Heimin Shimbun* in January, 1905. Kōtoku entered prison in March, 1905 (Tierney 2016, 96–99).

After Kōtoku was released from jail, he went to San Francisco and stayed there for eight months in 1905–1906. His stay in the United States had a crucial significance for the history of Japanese socialism as well as for his personal life. Immediately after he came back to Japan, he declared his conversion from socialism to anarchism. In the article published in February 1907, he declared that the universal suffrage movement would never lead to the real socialist revolution. He insisted that only direct action and general strike could realize it (Kōtoku 1975). Generally speaking, his declaration has been evaluated negatively because it caused serious confusions and sectorial confrontations in still premature Japanese social movement (Hoston 1986, 22). However, if we interpret Kōtoku's conversion from socialism to anarchism from the perspective on the global scale, we can notice this declaration was Kōtoku's strong desire to reimagine the global network of the social movement from the perspective of periphery.

How could America be a source of anarchism for Japanese intellectuals at that time? Unlike the cases of most Japanese intellectuals who hoped for studying in established universities on the east coast, Kōtoku stayed in the community of immigrants in San Francisco. Kōtoku himself was quite conscious of the implication of his choice: He wrote in a letter from San Francisco as follows: "I have not known the middle or upper class of America yet, I do not want to know it either" (Kōtoku 1907). A group photo taken on that occasion showed what kind of people he interacted with during his stay; most of them are immigrants and refugees from Japan and Russia. He also express his own idea to create "a troop concentration" for Japanese social movement in the United States, where "the oppressed comrades were able to escape from oppression just as Russian revolutionaries made Swiss their own base ground" (Kōtoku 1907). Through the experiences of living together with the people who left their nations behind, Kōtoku discovered the possibility of people living without the state. He was already familiar with some of the works of anarchists such as Kropotokin, but it was in San Francisco that he came to understand the possibility of anarchism from the bottom of his heart.

It was not coincident that Chinese revolutionaries in Tokyo were attracted by Kōtoku's thought. After the Russo-Japanese War, seven to ten thousand Chinese students were sent to Japan by Qing government and enrolled in Japanese schools and universities for the purpose of learning modernization. However, some of them became radicalized and attempted to have a connection with Japanese socialists. In addition to those students, some prominent opponents of the Qing dynasty, including Sun Yat-sen who organized "Tongmenghui" or the Chinese United League in Tokyo in 1905, gathered in Tokyo. From 1906, younger Chinese revolutionaries in Tokyo attempted to develop close contacts with Kōtoku and his colleagues including Ōsugi Sakae (1885–1923), the most earnest young supporter of Kōtoku's anarchism. Shortly after Kōtoku returned to Japan in 1906, Zhang Ji (1882–1947), one of the most active members of Chinese anarchists in Tokyo at that time, came to visit Kōtoku's place with his colleagues (Saga 1996, 76–77). They participated in the lecture series organized by Kōtoku and his colleagues regularly. For example, when Kōtoku gave a lecture for the Socialist Study Group on the theme of anarchism on August 31, 1907, ninety people including those Chinese students attended. His lecture was translated and published in *Tianyi*, a pioneering Chinese anarchist journal (Saga 1996, 121–136).

The interactions between Chinese and Japanese revolutionaries produced an interesting transnational organization, Ashū Washinkai or the Asian Solidarity Association. It was organized in Tokyo by intellectuals including Ōsugi Sakae and Sakai Toshihiko from Japan and Zhang Binglin (1869–1936), Zhang Ji, and Liu Shipei (1884–1919) from China. Later, participants from the Philippines, India and Vietnam also joined (Saga 1996, 136–144). The statutes (*kiyaku*) of the association were written by Zhang Binglin in classical Chinese. In this document, the author explains the causes for establishing the association as follows (Tierney 2018, 119–120):

> For the past century, Europeans have advanced toward the East and the Asian continent has weakened. Asia has not only lost political

> influence and military power, but its different peoples have become servile, arts and letters have declined, and people only think of their narrow selfish interests [...]. [The Asian Solidarity Association will] oppose imperialism and protect our peoples. In the future, we will expel the foreign invaders, win independence, and stand together like the trees of the forest. The countries of the East and South will join forces, support one another, and form a union strong as a bundle of reeds. We will form a confederation of many different ethnic groups and recover the friendship that used to bind us in the past but from which we have grown estranged.

Kōtoku could not be involved directly in this association because of his health condition, but he wrote about his strong expectation of the alliance of Asian revolutionaries as follows (Tierney 2018, 121):

> Among Filipinos, Vietnamese, and Koreans there are many revolutionaries with firm convictions and knowledge. Their movements do not go beyond demands for national independence and ethnic unification and they have not acquired much visible influence. However, if the different revolutionary parties of Asia start to look beyond differences of race or nation they will form a grand confederation under the banner of socialism and one-worldism. The East Asia of the twentieth century will be the land of revolution.

Between global theorist and anti-colonial activist

It is important to note that going "beyond demands for national independence" does not necessarily mean giving up nationalism entirely. This is clearly reflected in Kōtoku's sympathy toward An Jung-geun, a Korean patriot who assassinated Ito Hirobumi, the first Japanese Resident-General of Korea, in October 1909. An was tried by a district court administered by the governor-general of the Kwantung Leased Territory in Port Arthur, because the incident occurred under the purview of the South Manchurian Railway Company. After interrogation by Japanese prosecutors there, An was executed on March 26, 1910.

It was in June of 1910 that Kōtoku was arrested on the charge of his involvement in a plot to assassinate the Meiji Emperor. Eventually, twenty-four people were accused of violating article 73 of the 1908 Japanese criminal code, an article known as the High Treason Statute. On January 18, 1911, the Japanese Court of Cassation imposed death sentences on all twenty-four defendants, then the Meiji emperor commuted twelve of the death sentences to terms of life imprisonment in order to show his benevolence for his subjects. Now most historians agreed that the incident was the plot concocted by the government to eradicate the socialist/anarchist movement from Japan. On January 24, Kōtoku was hanged with other convicts.

It is a quite interesting episode that when Kōtoku was arrested, he kept a postcard printed by Japanese anarchists in the United States in honor of An Jung-geun, where he penned the following Chinese-style poem for celebrating him (Tierney 2018, 125–126):

> By throwing away your life, you took the path of righteousness.
> By sacrificing yourself, you embodied benevolence with your one action.
> By your action, An, you make the heavens and earth shake.

His sympathy with this Korean patriot is quite interesting if we remember that he fiercely attacked patriotism as the main engine to promote imperialism in his first book. We can also contrast this episode with an article published in *Heimin Shimbun*, "*Keiai naru Chōsen*" (A Message to Dear Korean People) on June 19, 1904 (Kinoshita 1904). This article appeared anonymously but now is known as the work by Kinoshita Naoe, who was a quite influential Christian socialist and also Kōtoku's close friend then. In this article, Kinoshita asked "how we should rescue Korea"; then he himself replied that the denial of "the conception of nationhood (*Kokkateki Kannen*)" was the only answer. According to his argument, a person can perform an important duty to advocate "the gospel of peace" only after he discards "vanity" as the sense of nationhood. He continues that Koreans are most suitable people for performing this mission because they experienced invasion by the strong states many times and they understood deeply how killing and attacking people was meaningless and immoral. He concludes, "this is the only way to make name of Korea splendid among nations."

Kōtoku originally believed that the path to the world without war would be opened only after all people in the world equally discard their conception of nationhood. However, this position was too idealistic for Korean intellectuals in the situation in which the Empire of Japan was preparing the colonization of their own nation. Through the interactions with the immigrant activists in the United States and the Asian revolutionaries in Tokyo, Kōtoku came to understand the limitations of the absolute pacifism, the original policy of the Japanese socialists including himself. He attempted to overcome it by recognizing the effectiveness of the use of violence under the particular condition, which he attempted to theorize under the concept of "direct action." Then Kōtoku was able to share the same horizon with Chinese revolutionaries and Korean patriots as an activist of anti-imperialism in the periphery.

Conclusion

Kōtoku's anti-imperialism, the first cry for global justice from Japan, was not simply prepared by advanced Western schools of thought such as socialism or Marxism. Nor was it simply a manifestation of traditional morality such as Confucianism. Rather, I argue that it was a product of historical conjuncture which was conditioned by two elements. The first one was the uneven development which brought about the coexistence of different temporalities. Uneven development was a universal condition of capitalist development itself, but it was particularly salient in the periphery such as Japan at that time. The second one was the technological development in communication and transportation which caused the time-space compression in epistemology on the global scale. On these two conditions, it became possible for Kōtoku to fuse modern Western thoughts such as socialism and traditional Asian morality such as Confucianism together into a new consideration on global justice and apply it to the entire planet. In this way, he became a pioneer who imagined and attempted to organize a global network of anti-imperialism.

However, more importantly, Kōtoku transformed his policies and positionality as he came to understand the realties in East Asia. Originally, Kōtoku attempted to participate in the global network prepared by Western Radical Liberals. Later, he was more interested in arranging an alliance with revolutionary activists from Asia against Western imperialism. In this juncture, he came to reinterpret the role of violence and recognize the effective use of violence for the purpose of resistance and revolution. He expresses this policy and positionality as "anarchism," but it was not a readymade ideology imported from Western countries. Rather, it was a position he attained by experiencing the time-space compression brought about by communication and transportation technologies and desiring to live the world as a global activist in East Asia.

Once Benedict Anderson characterized the revolution in communications and transportation in the last third of the nineteenth century as "the age of early globalization" (Anderson 2005). Now we are experiencing the next wave of globalization, which is characterized by the revolution in internet communications, and observing the eruptions of various GJMs. This is why we should rescue Kōtoku and the other early socialists from oblivion and re-examine their ideas as part of the history of the present.

Notes

1 As for Kōtoku's biographical information, see Tierney (2018) and Notehelfer (1971). Tierney's book also contains the full translation of Kōtoku's *Imperialism: The specter of the twentieth century*. When I quote from this text, I use Tierney's translation.

2 As for my own analysis of this incident, see (Umemori 2013).

References

Abe, Isoo. 1901. *Shakai Mondai Kaishaku Hō*. Tokyo: Tokyo Senmongakko Shuppanbu.

Anderson, Benedict. 2005. *Under Three Flags: Anarchism and the Anti-Colonial Imagination*. London: Verso.

Beitz, Charles R. 2019. "Fifty Years of Global Justice: Five Theses." *Fudan Journal of the Humanities and Social Sciences* 12 (2): 177–192.

Bell, Duncan. 2007. *The Idea of Greater Britain: Empire and the Future of World Order, 1860–1900.* Princeton, NJ: Princeton University Press.

Chatterjee, Partha. 1986. *Nationalist Thought and the Colonial World: A Derivative Discourse.* London: Zed Books.

Crump, John. 1983. *The Origins of Socialist Thought in Japan.* New York: Palgrave Macmillan.

Della Porta, D. 2005. *The Social Bases of the Global Justive Movement. Some Theoretical reflections and Empirical Evidence from the First European Social Forum.* New York: UNRISD/UN Publications.

Engels, Friedrich, and Edward Bibbins Aveling. 1892. *Socialism, Utopian and Scientific.* New York: Swan Sonnenschein & Co, Charles Scribner's Sons.

Fisher, William, and Thomas Ponniah. 2015. *Another World Is Possible.* Edited by William Fisher and Thomas Ponniah. London: Zed Books.

Fukuzawa, Yukichi. 1996. "Good-Bye Asia." In *Japan – A Documentary History,* edited by David Lu, 351–353. Armonk, NY: M. E. Sharpe.

Fukuzawa, Yukichi, David A. Dillworth, and G. Cameron Hurst. 1970. *An Outline of a Theory of Civilization.* Tokyo: Sophia University.

Graeber, David. 2002. "The New Anarchists." *New Left Review* 13 (1): 61–73.

Harootunian, Harry D. 2000. *Overcome by Modernity: History, Culture, and Community in Interwar Japan.* Princeton, NJ: Princeton University Press.

———. 2015. *Marx after Marx : History and Time in the Expansion of Capitalism.* New York: Columbia University Press.

Harvey, David. 2005. *A Brief History of Neoliberalism.* Oxford: Oxford University Press.

Headrick, Daniel. 1981. *The Tools of Empire: Technology and European Imperialism in the Nineteenth Century.* New York: Oxford University Press.

Hoston, Germaine A. 1986. *Marxism and the Crisis of Development in Prewar Japan.* Princeton, NJ: Princeton Unversity Press.

Katayama, Sen. 1903. *Waga Shakaishugi.* Tokyo: Shakaishugi Toshobu.

———. 1918. *The Labor Movement in Japan.* Chicago, IL: C. H. Kerr & Company.

Kemuyama, Sentaro. 1902. *Kinsei Museihushugi.* Tokyo: Tokyo Senmongakko Shuppanbu.

Kinoshita, Naoe. 1904. "Keiai Naru Chōsen." *Heimin Shimbun*, 1904.

Kōtoku, Shūsui. 1907. "Sōkō Yori." *Hikari* 1 (5): 6.

———. 1975. "Yoga Shisō No Henka." In *Kōtoku Shūsui Shu*, edited by Masamichi Asukai, 291–295. Tokyo: Chikuma Shobo.

Laclau, Ernesto, and Chantal Mouffe. 2001. *Hegemony and Socialist Strategy: Towards a Radical Democratic Politics.* London: Verso.

Matsuzawa, Hiroaki. 1973. *Nihon Shihonshugi No Shiso.* Tokyo: Chikuma Shobo.

Middleton, Benjamin. 1999. "Kōtoku Shūsui to Teikokushugi Heno Kongenteki Hihan." *Shokisyakaisyugi Kenkyu* 12: 134–193.

Müller, Simone. 2016. *Writing the World: The Social and Cultural Creation of Global Telegraph Networks.* New York: Columbia University Press.

Murphy, Tim, and Ralph Weber. 2016. "Ideas of Justice and Reconstructions of Confucian Justice." *Asian Philosophy* 26 (2): 99–118.

Nakae, Chōmin. 1984. *A Discourse by Three Drunkards on Government.* New York: Weatherhill.

Ness, Immanuel. 2004. "Global Justice Movement: Introduction." In *Encyclopedia of American Social Movements*, edited by Immanuel Ness, 1454–1502. London: Routledge.

Notehelfer, Frederick George. 1971. *Kōtoku Shūsui, Portrait of a Japanese Radical.* Cambridge: Cambridge University Press.

Peattie, Mark R. 1984. "Introduction." In *The Japanese Colonial Empire, 1895–1945*, edited by Ramon H. Myers and Mark R. Peattie, 3–52. Princeton, NJ: Princeton Umiversity Press.

Postone, Moishe. 2003. *Time, Labor, and Social Domination: A Reinterpretation of Marx's Critical Theory.* Cambridge: Cambridge University Press.

Saga, Takashi. 1996. *Kindai Chugoku no Kakumeigenso.* Tokyo: Kenbunshuppan.

Takano, Zenichi. 1970. *Abe Isoo: Nihon Shakaishugi No Chichi.* Tokyo: Abe Isoo Kankokai.

Tierney, Robert Thomas. 2018. *Monster of the Twentieth Century: Kōtoku Shūsui and Japan's First Anti-Imperialist Movement.* Oakland: University of California Press.

Umemori, Naoyuki. 2013. "The Historical Contexts of the High Treason Incident: Governemtality and Colonialism." In *BT-Japan and the High Treason Incident*, edited by Masako Gavin and Benjamin Middleton, 52–63. New York: Routledge.

Unknown. 1903. "Hisenron Enzetsukai No Ki." *Heimin Shimbun*, November 15, 1903.

Wenzlhuemer, Roland. 2015. *Connecting the Nineteenth-Century World.* Cambridge: Cambridge University Press.

Wildel, Lawrence. 2011. "Marx, Morality, and the Global Justice Debate." *Global Discourse* 2 (1): 24–38.

Index